THEOLOGICAL REFLECTION AND EDUCATION FOR MINISTRY

A major and continuing problem for theological education and the practice of Christian ministry is how to best achieve a genuine integration between theory and practice, theology and experience. The key claim of this book is that theological reflection, beginning with experience, is a method of integration and that pastoral supervision is a vehicle for theological reflection. In establishing this claim, John Paver demonstrates that the model and method have potential to be a catalyst for reform within theological colleges and seminaries. Three different theological reflection models are developed and critiqued in this book, and their capacity to be developed in particular contexts is explored. This book does not stop at ministry, cultural and personal integration, but is bold enough to make recommendations for structural integration within the theological institution.

Explorations in Practical, Pastoral and Empirical Theology

Series Editors: Leslie J. Francis, University of Wales, Bangor, UK
and Jeff Astley, Director of the North of England
Institute for Christian Education, UK

Theological reflection on the church's practice is now recognised as a significant element in theological studies in the academy and seminary. Ashgate's new series in practical, pastoral and empirical theology seeks to foster this resurgence of interest and encourage new developments in practical and applied aspects of theology world-wide. This timely series draws together a wide range of disciplinary approaches and empirical studies to embrace contemporary developments including: the expansion of research in empirical theology, psychological theology, ministry studies, public theology, Christian education and faith development; key issues of contemporary society such as health, ethics and the environment; and more traditional areas of concern such as pastoral care and counselling.

Other titles in the series include:

A Reader on Preaching
Making Connections
Edited by David Day, Jeff Astley and Leslie J. Francis
0 7546 5003 0 (Hbk); 0 7546 5009 X (Pbk)

Evangelicals Etcetera
Conflict and Conviction in the Church of England's Parties
Kelvin Randall
0 7546 5215 7 (Hbk)

Engaging with Contemporary Culture
Christianity, Theology and the Concrete Church
Martyn Percy
0 7546 3259 8 (Hbk)

Renewing Pastoral Practice
Trinitarian Perspectives on Pastoral Care and Counselling
Neil Pembroke
0 7546 5565 2 (Hbk)

Theological Reflection and Education for Ministry

The Search for Integration in Theology

JOHN E. PAVER
Uniting Church Theological College, Parkville, Victoria, Australia

ASHGATE

Published by
Ashgate Publishing Limited
Gower House
Croft Road
Aldershot
Hampshire GU11 3HR
England

Ashgate Publishing Company
Suite 420
101 Cherry Street
Burlington, VT 05401-4405
USA

Ashgate website: http://www.ashgate.com

British Library Cataloguing in Publication Data
Paver, John E
  Theological reflection and education for ministry : the search for integration in theology. –
  (Explorations in practical, pastoral and empirical theology)
  1. Pastoral theology – Field work 2. Religious education – Philosophy
  I. Title
  253'.01

Library of Congress Cataloging-in-Publication Data
Paver, John E., 1938–
  Theological reflection and education for ministry : the search for integration in theology /
  John E. Paver.
      p. cm. – (Explorations in practical, pastoral, and empirical theology)
  Includes bibliographical references and index.
  ISBN-13: 978-0-7546-5754-5 (hardcover : alk. paper)
  1. Pastoral theology – Field work. 2. Pastoral theology – Field work – Supervision.
  3. Theology – Methodology. I. Title.

  BV4164.5.P38 2007
  230.071'1–dc22

2006021156

ISBN-13: 978-0-7546-5754-5
ISBN-10: 0-7546-5754-X

Printed and bound in Great Britain by MPG Books Ltd. Bodmin, Cornwall.

To those teachers who have informed and influenced me in the art, science and theology of pastoral care and field education:

Roy A. Bradley
Graeme M. Griffin
Bruce D. Rumbold
Herbert Anderson
L. Douglas Fullerton
Harold Pidwell
Kenneth H. Pohly
David W. Sharrard

To Marlene who has taught me the importance of social analysis and the meaning of a spiritual life based on lived experience.

Contents

List of Figures

List of Tables

Foreword

I was born in 1936 while my father was a pastoral intern in his third year of theological education when field work (as it was then known) was not part of the standard divinity degree curriculum. The school he attended, Augustana Theological Seminary in Rock Island, Illinois (USA), was among the first seminaries to require a year of pastoral internship as part of theological education for ministry. My own experience of internship from that same school twenty-five years later demonstrated that pastoral supervision had not yet been established as an integral dimension of theological education. Contextual or field education was still tacked on to real theological study in the classroom. Although teaching the practices of ministry is now a regular part of the curriculum, I would conclude from my own work in seminaries over the last four decades that pastoral supervision still struggles to find its identity as part of theological education.

From its early years, field or contextual education has either been marginalized or regarded as derivative in teaching theology. Until recently, the practices of ministry were thought of primarily as applied theological theory. What was learned from reflection on the practice of ministry was of little consequence for understanding theology. The advent of supervised clinical pastoral education professionalized the practice of supervision but it did not settle questions about theological identity. And, despite several recent efforts to put contextual education at the center of the theological enterprise, it is still thought of largely in terms of skill development for ministry and not as theological work.

In this book, John Paver has taken up this challenge without flinching by making theological reflection the central work of pastoral supervision. Paver critically evaluates notions of field education that emphasize skill development or the application of theology to pastoral practice and instead promotes pastoral supervision as the locus of pastoral theology and therefore a theological discipline. The aim of the book is to strengthen contextual learning by enhancing the centrality of theological reflection in pastoral supervision. This bold claim for theological reflection at the heart of the supervisory relationship in contextual education is the unique contribution of this book.

In one of my favorite *Peanuts* cartoons, Linus, Lucy, and Charlie Brown are lying on their backs in the grass on what seems like a fine summer's day. Lucy makes a remark that if you use your imagination you can see all sorts of things in the clouds. 'Yes,' says Linus, 'I see the forces of good and evil lined up in full battle array on the day of Armageddon. And over there I see Dante being led by Beatrice into the heights of heaven.' 'And what do you see, Charlie Brown?' Lucy asks. Somewhat hesitantly, Charlie Brown says: 'I was going to say I saw a ducky and a horsey, but I think I've changed my mind.' John Paver presents a method of theological reflection that allows freedom to reflect on personal and pastoral experiences in radical, imaginative ways while at the same time keeping the focus on our response to God's call to participate in God's redemptive work. Sorting out between duckies and horsies on the one hand and the battle of Armageddon on the other is the critical work of theological reflection.

You will discover that John Paver does not shy away from big themes. Integration is one. Paver understands that the fragmentation of disciplines has made theological education less than whole, thereby diminishing the possibility of forming candidates with integrity for ministry. The major gap is between theory and practice. Paver understands integration in theological education as the harmony of personal, professional and faith elements of life. Theological reflection is the way to achieve that integration and pastoral supervision is the vehicle for facilitating theological reflection. Self-deception or theological dishonesty is another major theme. Because theology is born out of reflection on experience, there is no room for dishonesty about oneself. John Paver's radical honesty about his own experience makes this book both compelling reading and a challenging model for theological reflection.

The approach to theological reflection in this book presumes the larger framework of practical theology in which tradition, culture and experience all interact on a level playing field. Because the experience of God is relational and attentive to just action, theology is communal and oriented toward justice. Paver finds support for his emphasis on experience and justice in the feminist theology of the Mud Flower Collective. The aim of theological reflection is a decision of faith that may lead to action, further reflection or a changed perception. In the end, however, theological reflection leads to the transformation of the soul.

Pastoral supervision has as its final aim the formation of candidates for pastoral ministry who embody integrity and authenticity. The way to integrity is through an acknowledgment of vulnerability. Pastoral identity is enhanced when we offer our vulnerability to others through a ministry of authentic presence. As he reflects on his own struggle to live with and beyond cancer, John Paver models what he writes about in the book: self-deception, the enemy of authenticity, is overcome through relentless reflection on personal experience and ministerial practice. If you read this book from the beginning with the awareness that it was written by someone aware of his finitude and comfortable with his vulnerability, you will discover a rich treasure of insights and durable hope for ministry in hard times.

Herbert Anderson
Easter Monday, 2006
Berkeley, California

Acknowledgements

There have been many people who have contributed to the development of this book but I must name a few. My colleagues at Theological College have not only supported me emotionally and spiritually, but also provided me with a grant to undertake some preliminary editing of the manuscript. I am grateful to Sandra Goldbloom Zurbo who undertook this task. I am especially thankful to Peter Matheson for his ongoing support of this project, not the least for his support for theological field education. I could not have written Chapter 4 without the consent of the students who allowed me to use their materials for case studies: Alan Lockwood, Fiona Garrigan, Janet Turpie-Johnstone, Paul Teusner and Madeleine Barlow.

It has been a delight to work with Sarah Lloyd, Anne Keirby, Ann Newell and Emily Ebdon from Ashgate Publishing Limited, who have supported and critiqued my work.

There have been many authors whose work has enriched this book and I wish to cite but a few: James and Evelyn Whitehead, Stephen Bevans, Charles Wood, David Kelsey, Joe Holland, Peter Henriot, S.J. and Kenneth Pohly.

I have appreciated the dedicated contribution of Beverley Freeman in the initial typing of the manuscript. Heather Cameron's advice, wisdom and expertise in the formatting of the manuscript in the final stages of the book has been invaluable.

I am particularly thankful to Herbert Anderson for his willingness to write a foreword to this book. Herbert has been an influential person in my professional life in the area of pastoral theology and he is one amongst others to whom I dedicate this book.

Roy Bradley who was my first supervisor in clinical pastoral education formed my understanding of pastoral supervision. I could not have completed this manuscript without the early supervision of Bruce Rumbold who prodded and critiqued me and continues to offer invaluable support.

Pastoral care and field education was at its zenith in the 1980s and 90s and the teachers who influenced me during this period were my colleagues Graeme Griffin, who is a true pastoral theologian, Bruce Rumbold, David Sharrard (Lexington Theological Seminary, USA), who made pastoral care come alive during my doctoral studies, and Harold Pidwell who gave theological field education creditability at an ecumenical level. I also thank Doug Fullerton who pioneered the modern field education movement in Australia. In writing this book I recognize those people who have been instrumental in the formation of my life.

I am indebted to Gerald Beaumont; artist, priest and bishop for the painting depicted on the front cover. Gerald expressed his enthusiasm and gratitude, at the conclusion of his clinical pastoral education experience at Peter MacCallum Cancer Centre in 1981 in this unique and spontaneous way.

On a personal note I could not have completed this project without the ongoing support of a number of close friends and family and to them I am most grateful.

I give thanks to the special woman in my life – my wife Marlene, to whom I am ever thankful and to whom I dedicate this book.

John Paver
June 2006

List of Abbreviations

ANZATFE   Australian and New Zealand Association for Theological Field Education
The main purpose of this national body for theological field education is to arrange field education conferences in the various states of Australia and New Zealand.

ASPEA   Association for Supervised Pastoral Education in Australia
The Victorian (State) body of Clinical Pastoral Education in Australia. The purpose of this body is to train and accredit CPE supervisors, programs, centres and develop conferences.

CPE   Clinical Pastoral Education
A world wide pastoral care and education movement, mainly centred in hospitals where personal, pastoral and professional identity is emphasized. This movement has a fine history in developing models of supervision and a belief that pastoral supervision is at the heart of integrating theory, theology and practice.

MCD   Melbourne College of Divinity
The accrediting body for a number of theological colleges in Melbourne, Australia. Recently it has developed a number of new post-graduate theological programs. It is the oldest theological accrediting body in Australia and is respected for the quality of its standards and theological rigor.

SFE   Supervised Field Education
Another name for field education.

SUMP   Supervised Urban Ministry Program
A program with similar principles to CPE but with more emphasis on social analysis and urban ministry.

TFE   Theological Field Education
Another name for field education.

TRG   Task Review Group
A group established by the Uniting Church in Australia to review ministerial education at a national UCA level.

TRS   Theological Reflection Seminar
A seminar within Theological Field Education. The aim of this seminar is for students to review a number of theological reflection models with the ultimate aim of developing their own models of theological reflection.

UCA   Uniting Church in Australia

UCTC   Uniting Church Theological College (formerly Theological Hall), Melbourne, Australia.

UFT   United Faculty of Theology
A pioneering ecumenical venture (Jesuits, Anglican and Uniting Church) established in 1969 with an emphasis on theological education and research. The UFT offers teaching at all levels: undergraduate, graduate and postgraduate programs of the Melbourne College of Divinity.

VATFE   Victorian Association for Theological Field Education
The state association for theological field education whose main purpose is to accredit programs and develop models and methods of pastoral supervision and theological reflection.

Introduction

This book is titled *Theological Reflection and Education for Ministry*. My interest in the topic was stimulated at a theological education conference held in Bowral, New South Wales, Australia in June 1995, when I presented a paper on theological reflection and its contribution to theological education. The responses to my presentation led me to believe there were seeds for ongoing research. The following is an account of this research, supported by the sound principles in the practice of ministry.

Integrating theory with practice

The contemporary blurring of boundaries between modern academic disciplines in universities, the growing emphasis on vocational training and the accompanying debates about curricula have also affected theological schools. It is now generally recognized that the curricula structure of the modern era, which are based on theologian Friedrich Schleiermacher's division, separates theory from practice, privileging rational and universal ways of knowing at the expense of other forms of knowledge.

Calls for reform of the curriculum have come from students, churches and at least some members of the academy. The focus of most proposals for reform is upon the gap between theory and practice; in recent decades various proposals to bridge this gap have been put forward.

The first attempts introduced field placements to the curriculum. While these acquainted students with some skills for ministry they also tended to reinforce the division between theory and practice as there was no intentional link between field experience and the academic curriculum. The next major step was to introduce programs centred on theological reflection upon practice. In contrast with placements alone, these programs were intentional about connecting current academic learning with the practice of ministry through the relationships established between placement and theological school and reflection groups in the school. Their emphasis was firstly upon theological reflection as primary tools for integrating theory and practice in students' experience. However, an understanding of what constituted 'theological reflection' as practised in theological schools left a lot to be desired. It was soon realized that theological reflection and integration required skilled supervision, both in the theological school and in placements. Thus field education programs, soon renamed SFE programs or TFE programs, became (and remain) a standard tool for bridging the gap between theory, taught by the theological school, and practice, carried out in ministry placements in a variety of contexts. Clearly, reliance upon TFE as an integrative tool falls a considerable distance short of reforming the curriculum. It is, however, possible that TFE may be developed in ways that catalyse reform. This is the focus of this book.

Personal, professional, and theological interest in integration

My interest in integration has been a key issue for me – personally and professionally – over many years. I am a product of the CPE movement in which the action–reflection methodology of learning gives a high priority to experience and values pastoral supervision. It was through this learning process, which demands and tests integration, that my personal and professional life was turned upside down. I was one of those people whose life was fragmented due to a dichotomy of knowledge and experience. During the early years of my ministry as chaplain and educator at the Peter MacCallum Cancer Institute in Melbourne, Australia, people who had been diagnosed with cancer exposed the incongruity of the personal, professional and faith dimensions of my life. For two years my life was shattered to the extent that I became deeply depressed as a result of my work there. It was only as I addressed these painful discrepancies between what I believed and what I was experiencing that healing began to occur. The meeting of this challenge transformed my life as I began to strive to live authentically. The living of an authentic life is a continuing challenge and should not be interpreted in moralistic terms, but seen as a genuine attempt to live an integrated life. My reaction to fragmentation in individual and community life is acute. It was during these early years of ferment that my personal, professional and pastoral identity was formed. These were years of critical reflection.

It became apparent to me during these years of turmoil at the Peter MacCallum Cancer Institute and in my CPE experience that there was a deficiency in my theological understanding of human and spiritual events. In 1982, I was granted fifteen months (without pay) to commence my Doctorate of Ministry (DMin) degree at Lexington Theological Seminary, Kentucky, USA; the doctorate was awarded in 1985. The methodology of the professional degree allowed my personal and ministry experience to interact with biblical studies, systematic theology, cultural studies and pastoral theology. The significance of the DMin degree gave me respect for both knowledge and experience and provided me with a new understanding of the word 'integration'. As a result of this study and experience I felt that all the elements of my life - personal, professional and faith – were in harmony. My whole being was affected during this time of study and reflection, which also provided a renewed passion for my ministry.

The last twelve years of my ministry have been committed to theological education: Professor of Ministry and Director of Field Education, Lexington Theological Seminary, Lexington, Kentucky; Director of Ministry Studies (Master of Ministry degree), MCD, Melbourne, Australia; Professor of Ministry and Director of Field Education, UCTC – formerly known as the Theological Hall – Melbourne, Australia. In each position I was appointed because of my professional competence rather than my academic ability. My experience in pastoral ministry, CPE, pastoral supervision and theological reflection and the value of my DMin degree were all key factors in my appointments. Therefore, I bring to this study a different approach to the debate on theological education as most of what has been written on this subject has come from an academic perspective. While this different approach will be highlighted in this study it will not take away from my central belief that theory and practice must critically have a dialogue with and inform each other in order that theological education becomes a unified rather than a fragmented enterprise.

Theological reflection and pastoral supervision

While I contend that pastoral supervision is a theological discipline, for the purpose of this book the emphasis is on theological reflection as a method of integration and pastoral supervision as a vehicle for facilitating theological reflection. These two claims are placed in the context of TFE and theological education, especially in relationship to the curriculum at UCTC. My heart is in pastoral supervision as I have witnessed its capacity to provide new life. My venture into theological education in recent years has deepened my understanding of pastoral supervision. My interest in theological reflection grew initially in my DMin studies and then developed as I took on the responsibility of Director of Field Education. It continues to be refined through my initiative in developing the TRS (see Chapter 4) and is being developed further through the writing of this book.

The problem

Pastoral supervision and theological reflection have been a crucial part of TFE programs and an accepted part of the theological curriculum for a great number of years. While pastoral supervision has been accepted as having value, it has not been fully understood and therefore not been fully accepted or integrated into the ethos of the theological education enterprise. Nor have many academicians adequately understood theological reflection. While most would claim they undertake theological reflection, the reality is that most do not, at least not as I understand its meaning. Not all the responsibility can rest at the feet of the classical disciplines, as theological field educators have made little impact on the theological education debate. Indeed, while there has been much creative ferment within theological education in North America and, to a lesser extent, in Australia in the last fifteen years, the role of field education has received scant attention. It is my belief that field education has not been sufficiently integrated into the theological system and, as a result, its potential is largely unrealized. I do not make this statement lightly, as it is not my intention to criticize the wonderful and creative ministries exercised by field educators in the USA and certainly not those in Australia. Without their contribution field education would not have the status it enjoys today. But it is the opinion of some field educators that field education is at the crossroads and needs to redefine its goals and purpose within theological education if it is going to make a viable contribution. Pastoral theologian James Whitehead and Evelyn Whitehead, a developmental psychologist, believe that the fundamental problem for theological education is the fragmentation of two theologies: one academic and one derived from practice.[1] This problem is commonly stated in theological circles as the theory-to-practice debate. It certainly has been a crucial issue in the theological education debate over the last few years. This issue will be highlighted in the Chapter 1 in a review of the literature of the debate.

The theory-to-practice debate is certainly not a new issue for field education. In 1969 the North American Association for TFE addressed questions of the adequacy of models of supervision and the vagueness of the meaning of 'theological reflection' in the context of theological education.[2] In Melbourne, in 1982, Director of Field Education Douglas Fullerton wrote and spoke at the JTC with enthusiasm about the impact of a three level theological reflection model on the supervisors and students.[3] In a 1995 survey, taken at the 23rd Biennial Meeting of the Association for TFE held in Minneapolis, the greatest concern among theological field directors, although expressed in a variety of ways, continued to be 'to assist students to integrate academic and ministry perspectives'.[4] In a paper delivered to the 1997 Conference for the ANZATFE, pastoral theologian John Chalmers made a plea that: '[O]n the cusp of a new millennium, we Field Educators must embrace theological reflection as the very heart of the supervisory relationship.'[5] And, more recently, a study surveying attitudes of field directors in Australia and New Zealand identified integration as the primary purpose and goal of their work.[6]

It appears that no matter how much attention has been given by field directors to supervision and theological reflection their value as an integrating factor within theological education continues to be questioned. There is no doubt that the issue is

---

[1]   James D. and Evelyn E. Whitehead 1995, Method in Ministry: Theological Reflection and Christian Ministry, Kansas City, MO: Sheed and Ward.

[2]   James W. Bergland 1969, 'Field education as the locus for theological reflection', Theological Education, Vol. V, No. 4, 341.

[3]   Douglas Fullerton 1982 'Three level theological reflection model', unpublished paper presented to the Jesuit Theological College, Melbourne.

[4]   Donald Beisswenger 1996, 'Field education and the theological education debates,' Theological Education, Vol. 33, No. 1 (1996), 49–58.

[5]   John Chalmers 1997, "Deep structures": reforming supervision on the cusp of a new millennium', unpublished paper presented at ANZATFE Conference, Banyo, Queensland.

[6]   John E. Paver 1999, 'Field education and its contribution to theological education', paper presented to a seminar conducted by the Victorian Association for TFE, November. In this survey participants generally gave expression to this integration as bridging the gap between theological perspectives and ministerial perspectives. However, they wanted the integration to be more inclusive and holistic. As a result, there is an emphasis in integration that includes personhood, spirituality and ministerial skills. This book will place emphasis on this more inclusive understanding of integration.

important, but the questions in my mind are why does it keep coming up and why is field education still on the edge of the main body of theological education? Particular focus will be placed on these questions through a consideration of the place of pastoral supervision and theological reflection in the TFE program at UCTC.

The challenge

This book will not be an evaluation of the place of field education within the theological enterprise as such, but will focus specifically on a semester unit of TFE termed the TRS. Ministry candidates within UCTC are required to complete two placements and a TRS during the period of their ordinand course. One year of TFE placement is usually equivalent to a year's study in any other discipline. Normally, the placements are taken in the second and third years, with the TRS being taken in the second or third year. Candidates are required to do one placement in a parish setting. Candidates often select CPE or the SUMP as one of their placements. Pastoral supervision is a key element in the TFE program and the field education supervisors undertake a year's training, as a rule concurrently, during the student's placement. In addition to the one-to-one supervision, candidates are required to participate in a lay consultative group whose responsibility is to oversee the student's placement from a layperson's perspective. The evaluation process involves the student, the pastoral supervisor and the lay consultative group. While the two placements are not part of the degree studies, students must be graded satisfactorily in order to be ordained. Students also must pass the TRS unit within the degree structure in order to be ordained. While the principles of supervision and theological reflection are present in the one-to-one pastoral supervision of the student, they take on a different dynamic when placed in a communal setting and are part of the theological education curriculum.

The published literature would suggest that it would be naive of me to postulate that this enquiry is an original one, nor would it be collegial to suggest that a great amount of research and work has not gone into the effectiveness of theological reflection within the theological enterprise.[7] However, there is little evidence, from documentation at least, of the value of pastoral supervision and theological reflection to the main body of knowledge in the theological curriculum in the Melbourne theological schools and, more specifically, in the UFT in Parkville.

A review and evaluation of the TRS within the UCTC will, first, test my argument that theological reflection and pastoral supervision are integrating factors and do in fact enable students to do theology themselves; second, and perhaps

---

[7]   While this book focuses on theological reflection and pastoral supervision within field education, the Practical Theology Department in the UFT has, for twenty years, taught a method of theological reflection as part of the unit Theology of Pastoral Care. Most of the students take this subject in the final year of their degree, when they have usually completed CPE and Field Education. It could be argued that the subject comes in the wrong place in the educational process.

cautiously, show that this model and method has the potential to be a catalyst for the reform of the curriculum within UCTC. There is the danger that too much can be claimed for pastoral supervision and theological reflection as an integrative force in theological education. Self-deception is subtle and can be revealed by claiming too much or too little. It is hoped that this research will provide a realistic assessment of the value of pastoral supervision and theological reflection within the theological institution.

Organization of the book

Chapter 1 sets the scene for the theological education debate, which includes a brief history of the origin of the theory and practice division within theological education. The chapter includes a response to this fragmentation by TFE, some members of the academy and the church.

Chapter 2 proposes theological reflection as a method of integration in theological education. There is a general discussion of the theory and purpose of theological reflection within theological education. Three different models of theological reflection are reviewed, adapted, and evaluated for their contribution to integration within theological education.

Chapter 3 discusses the place of pastoral supervision as a vehicle for facilitating theological reflection. It discusses the characteristics of pastoral supervision and develops an educational and supervisory model, which facilitates theological reflection. In particular, the chapter will address pastoral supervision's contribution to the vocational training goals of the UCA.

Chapter 4 proposes an integrated approach to theological education through the TRS. In so doing it tests the claims I have made above for theological reflection and pastoral supervision. This chapter outlines the history, structure, and theory of the TRS and illustrates its integrative influence, not only for theory and practice, but also for the whole of a student's life.

Chapter 5 examines attempts within a particular theological college of the UCA to implement the vision, educational philosophy and theology of a task group set up by the church's General Assembly to review theological education. Key proposals of the task group's report are identified and the way in which this institution faced the challenges of implementing the spirit of the report's recommendations is examined. The author also offers his own recommendations for effective structural integration within the theological enterprise.

The conclusion reflects on the strengths and limitations of the seminar model for theological education and discusses areas for further research. While it reflects disappointment at the difficulties of implementation at the local level, it asserts strongly that an integrative theological reflection model is essential for any theological curriculum. The conclusion also contains recommendations regarding the integrative character of TFE in theological education and the need for continuing research and action.

Chapter 1

Setting the scene

The focus in this book is upon pastoral supervision and theological reflection in Theological Field Education. It needs to be noted, however, that TFE was proposed as a solution to the problems experienced in theological education. To understand TFE we need to first understand the context from which it emerges and the situation it seeks to redress. The problem is the separation of theory and practice in theological education.

This chapter will discuss the influence of theologian Friedrich Schleiermacher whose scheme institutionalized the theory–practice division in modern theological education. It will then review the attempts of TFE and the theological academies to provide more effective methods of integration. Finally, there will be some discussion on the *Report of the Task Group to Review Ministerial Education in the UCA*. The implications of this report for the curriculum and TFE at UCTC will be discussed in later chapters.

The influence of Schleiermacher on the formation of theological education

Friedrich Schleiermacher (1768–1834) is regarded as being responsible for the definitive categorization of theological studies in the modern academy. He is the theologian from whom several significant trends in recent pastoral and practical theology can be traced. Schleiermacher set about to produce a rationale for his understanding of theological studies with the publication in 1811 of his theological treatise, *A Brief Outline on the Study of Theology*,[1] which was an attempt to re-establish *Wissenschaft* or – disciplined critical research – on the one hand and professional education for ministers on the other. Because the University of Berlin was deliberately designed as a research university it was questionable whether a theological faculty had any place in it.

This question was to be answered by the appointment of Wilhelm von Humboldt as head of the cultural and educational affairs section in the Prussian government, which commissioned a three-person committee to help him draft provisional statutes for the new University of Berlin. Schleiermacher, who was one of these three, wrote the founding document. The Berlin model for theological education can be said to be Schleiermacher's important legacy to theological

---

[1]   Friedrich Schleiermacher 1966, *Brief Outline on the Study of Theology* (trans. W. Farrer), Richmond, VA: John Knox Press. Terrence N. Tice has prepared a new translation.

education, but even he had to make a case for including theology at this new research university. Research and teaching students how to do research were the overarching goals of the university; its secondary goal was to be enquiry that aimed to master the truth, whatever subjects were studied. The only degree this university would award was the doctorate, the research degree. The desire to develop theological education in this newly founded University of Berlin played itself out in the decision to include, in 1810, a Faculty of Theology.

However, including theology in a research university could be seen as a betrayal of the educational revolution that the research university represented. Schleiermacher had to answer these objections if theology was to have a place so he added another pole by advocating that theological education should constitute professional education. His argument was partly sociological and partly philosophical–theological. Schleiermacher's sociological argument was that every human society has sets of practices dealing with bodily, health, social order and religious needs. These are socially necessary for the wellbeing of society as a whole and each of these requires properly trained leadership. Schleiermacher's philosophical–theological argument proposed that religions such as Christianity do not rest on principles, but on a kind of intuition or insightful experience, which can be the subject of philosophical enquiry. Hence, Christian theology can be a subject of *Wissenschaft* enquiry without threat or compromise to Christianity's integrity or the integrity of the university. Schleiermacher advocated three levels of enquiry.

Historical theology

The first round of enquiry is the attempt to describe the condition of the faith community in the past and the present. Its outcome will be an account of what the Christian religion has shown itself to be throughout its history. In this account, which is evaluative and constructive, the church of the past is evaluated in the light of its faithfulness to its Christian identity. Thus, Biblical studies, church history and systematic theology come under the heading of 'historical theology'. The community of faith was primary for Schleiermacher, serving as a critical point of reference for the truth claims and the relevance of the scholarly study of theology.

Philosophical theology

The second round of enquiry seeks to develop criteria to address the question: What is essentially Christian? To answer this question the results of the historical study of Christianity are subjected to a philosophical analysis to determine the essence of Christianity.

Practical theology

The third round of enquiry is practical theology. It attempts to delineate the means by which the faith community may preserve its integrity as the present gives way to the future. Its purpose is to determine the normative rules for carrying out the tasks of a specifically Christian ministry. It is a 'theoretical undertaking rather than an action oriented function'. Theologian Stone and Church Historian Duke define it as 'the serious thinking that reviews, evaluates, and orders activities so that Christian practice never loses sight of or strays from its properly Christian aims'.[2] Theologian David Kelsey says the third round of enquiry 'brings the description of theology in the research university back from research to "professional" education'.[3]

Schleiermacher believed that previous treatments of practical theology were too narrowly focused on preaching the word and administering the sacraments. While Schleiermacher focused on the ordained ministry his response to this narrow focus was not merely to construct a clerical paradigm: his practical theology was more interested in theological formation than who was responsible for the application of practical hints and helps. The study of theology is not to be constructed on the basis of whatever is playing in the parish at the moment, but on a theological analysis of the purpose of theological activity in the church. The purpose is to 'ensure the Christian faithfulness of the ministry of the church'.[4] Schleiermacher called for accountability, not to the actual practice of ministry, but to a theology that called for Christian faithfulness.

It was Schleiermacher's intention that each aspect of this threefold pattern of enquiry should be in equal partnership with the other. He believed that each contributes to the overall task of theological education and that together they form an 'organic unity'. In fact, in the 1811 edition of *Brief Outline*, he drew upon the image of an organic being, a tree, in order to depict the relationship between the three disciplines:

1. Philosophy – the root
2. Historical – the trunk
3. Practical – the crown[5]

Pastoral Theologian Graham says:

> He argued for the essential unity of theory and practice, by stating that the practical should be given preferential status in assessing the authenticity and validity of the truth-claims of theological discourse. Thus it is the congregational reality that serves as the validating norm for Christian theology, and not simply abstract or ideal philosophical principles.[6]

---

[2] James O. Duke and Howard Stone 1988, *Christian Caring: Selections from practical theology*, Philadelphia: Fortress Press, p. 22.

[3] David H. Kelsey 1993, *Between Athens and Berlin*, Grand Rapids: William B. Eerdmans, pp. 17–18.

[4] Duke and Stone, *Christian Caring*, p. 21.

[5] Schleiermacher, *Brief Outline*, pp. 96–7.

[6] Elaine L. Graham 1996, *Transforming Practice*, London: Mowbray, p. 60.

This was Schleiermacher's intention for practical theology, but in reality what emerged was the subordination of practical theology to the other two patterns of theological enquiry. Duke and Stone point out that:

> Reference to this image [of an organic being, the tree] was dropped from the revised edition of 1830. Schleiermacher, it seems, feared that readers would mistakenly believe that he intended to subordinate philosophical and historical theology to practical theology, when his true intention was to emphasize the equality of all three.[7]

Whether it was Schleiermacher's intention or not it was the beginning of some incongruity towards the stated unity, interconnection, and equality of all three disciplines. In fact, Schleiermacher himself makes some compromising statements. Again, Duke and Stone write that:

> He argues that practical theology draws, and so depends, upon the interplay of philosophical and historical theology without itself exerting a direct influence on that interplay. He points out that practical theology tries to produce 'rules', whereas the other fields deal in knowledge.[8]

The evidence is clear that although Schleiermacher emphasized the integrated nature of theological studies and the serious contribution of practical theology to the academy, he regarded it as intellectually inert. And so:

> ... for 150 years after Schleiermacher, his legacy dominated: as a discipline in the service of Christian ministry, the focus of practical theology was more or less exclusively upon the activities of the ordained pastor.[9]

Schleiermacher categorized practical theology as applied theology, where pastoral ministry is the outworking rather than the source of theological understanding.

The other legacy that has endured is a debate concerning the place of practical theology within the theological curriculum. This development by Schleiermacher and others meant that practical theology became divorced from the new movements in systematic theology and biblical studies. Practical theology has to assume some responsibility for this situation as it has a history of detachment from systematic and biblical theology and attachment to psychology, which has often resulted in what some would term an 'identity crisis'. In this case it was detachment from historical and systematic theology resulting in practical theology being understood as applied theology.

---

[7]   Duke and Stone, *Christian Caring,* p. 22.
[8]   Ibid, p. 23.
[9]   Graham, *Transforming Practice,* p. 61.

The early formation of practical theology

The beginnings of practical theology (*Praktische Theologie*) lie in the establishment of ministerial training in German universities in the mid eighteenth century. A rationalization of theological education took place and from this a recognized syllabus or curriculum emerged. This occurred primarily through the publication of the *Theological Encyclopaedia* that sought to categorize theological texts according to their major emphases, pertaining either to matters of dogma and belief or to practice and conduct. Thus, the boundary between theoretical and applied knowledge in theology was established with the study of Scripture, doctrine, and church history in one category and the practical disciplines of ministry in the other.[10]

Practical theology was grouped under the following sub disciplines: homiletics (preaching), poimenics (pastoral care or the 'cure of souls'), liturgics (public worship), jurisprudence (church government and discipline) and catechetics (education, usually of children). In principle, it was understood that these activities were not only the prerogative of the clerical or priestly office, but also characteristic of the life and work of the whole church. However, in practice, theologian Edward Farley argues, these areas of church practice became the domain of the clergy.[11] By the first quarter of the nineteenth century the term 'practical theology' was being used to denote the various functions of ministry, while 'pastoral theology' indicated the specific tasks of the classical definition, which were the 'four pastoral functions of healing, sustaining, guiding, and reconciling'.[12] The future of practical theology in the theological enterprise was also being shaped through other nineteenth-century textbooks on practical theology. Alastair Campbell, a pastoral theologian writing on this era, says that 'The subject was sub-divided into various branches related to the different functions of the ministry: homiletics, liturgics, catechetics, poimenics and occasionally halieutics ('man fishing') and works of charity'.[13] As the textbooks multiplied in the latter part of the nineteenth century the concern with the teaching of techniques became all-important. Seward Hiltner, a prominent pastoral theologian, states his concerns about this development in a brief historical sketch of the recent history of the subject:

> The notion of 'hints and helps', implying the right to dispense with structural and theoretical considerations, to set aside scholarship in this area, and to appeal to the more degraded forms of practicalism, helped to drive most systematic books out of this field by the turn of the century.[14]

---

[10] Graham, *Transforming Practice*, p. 58.

[11] Edward Farley 1987, 'Interpreting situations: An enquiry into the nature of practical theology', in L. S. Mudge and J. N. Poling (eds), *Formation and Reflection: The promise of practical theology*, Philadelphia: Fortress Press, pp. 2–5.

[12] W. A. Clebsch and C. R. Jaekle 1964, *Pastoral Care in Historical Perspective*, Englewood Cliffs, NJ: Prentice Hall, pp. 32–66.

[13] Alastair V. Campbell 1990, 'The nature of practical theology', in Duncan B. Forrester (ed.), *Theology and Practice*, London: Epworth Press, p. 11.

[14] Seward Hiltner 1958, *Preface to Pastoral Theology*, Nashville: Abingdon Press, p. 48.

This breakdown in the equality of Schleiermacher's three aspects had negative implications and an enduring legacy for the future of practical theology within theological education.

- The relationship between practical theology and historical and systematic theology was seen as a deductive one, with practical theology being understood as applied theology. Alastair Campbell says:

  > Such a relationship, however, is not satisfactory for either side. On the one hand it removes the independent status of practical theology, making it into a subsection of dogmatics, while on the other hand it opens systematic theologians to charges of irrelevance and inapplicability from practical theologians.[15]

- The question of whether practical theology was an art or a science remained unanswered. Whether practical theology has a body of knowledge (that is, a theology) or whether it is a discipline that offers hints and helps remains an issue for some.
- Perhaps the most discussed legacy of recent times was the total identification of the discipline with church-directed functions of ministry. The church was seen in Schleiermacher's terms as the fellowship of the pious, which meant that practical theology was wholly identified with the world of the religiously minded. In this view the centre of attention was on the clergyman (in those times) and his ministry to the people within the church. The world outside became a secondary concern. Spiritual maintenance was the key and practical theology provided the guidance that guaranteed the perfection of the church. Further, if the purpose of theology was to serve the congregation, Schleiermacher failed to articulate any critical criterion by which the nature and mission of the church itself might be assessed.
- While practical theology has been cast aside by some in the role of applied theology and the practical, and has often been portrayed as prostituting its theological rigour for the cheap grace of the social sciences, it has never abandoned its search for a distinctive disciplinary identity because it is 'aware that the relationship between the *theory* of Christian tradition and theology could not be severed from the *practice* of enacted ministry and care'.[16] While practical theology has at times made the mistake of allowing the social sciences to form rather than inform theology, it has done so in good faith. Its action has been to clarify an understanding of the Gospel and to engage the world. Practical theology has not been afraid to take risks in a changing world for the sake of the Gospel.

I have noted the dichotomy between theory and practice and the subordination of practical theology to historical and systematic theology and outlined its far-reaching implications for how theology is taught in our theological schools today.

---

[15] Campbell, *Theology and Practice*, p. 12.
[16] Graham, *Transforming Practice*, p. 57.

The remainder of this chapter will focus on the responses from TFE, the academies for theological education in USA, and, in the case of my own constituency, the UCA.

Responses from theological field education to the theory-praxis debate

Field education in the USA

In 1935 the American Association of Theological Schools appointed its first committee of supervised training, but the 1936 standards document did not mention field work (as it was then known) as required for the standard divinity degree curriculum. However, pressures to place some kind of field-based learning in the curricula of seminaries and divinity schools continued to gain momentum. Professors of several disciplines with administrative expertise were enlisted to develop field education programs. This led to the development of a new discipline and the eventual creation of the Association for TFE. Theological Field Educator Jackson summarizes this particular stage of history by indicating that many colleges and seminaries had begun to require ministry under the supervision of an experienced minister as degree requirements as early as the mid 1950s. Professors directed the work in a variety of disciplines. Repeating the history of previous groups, the emphasis was first in field work before shifting the emphasis to field education.[17] In the churches, candidate ministers were placed in parish positions and challenged to learn, but progress was often slow due to the limited availability of trained supervisors. This resistance by seminary administrators to field-based learning was largely overcome by the impact of Charles Feilding's (1966) essay, 'Education for Ministry'.[18] This paper, in emphasizing the educational potential of supervised field experience, was a watershed in that Feilding distinguished 'field education' from other activities, variously called 'field employment' and 'field service'.

In his essay Feilding provided the clearest articulation of the educational value of field work and also signalled the need for a stronger theoretical base to underpin the educational philosophy. 'Education for Ministry' contributed to the already ongoing consultations that field education was having with the American Association for Theological Schools. Through Feilding's essay and the influence of the field education consultations the theological education community gained a greater understanding of the value of field-based education. Feilding stated unequivocally that, as a consequence of the study, the most important and immediate task for seminaries was to direct their concerted efforts towards a professional model of theological education, of which field education could be an important component.

---

[17] William T. Pyle and Mary Alice Seals (eds) 1995, *Experiencing Ministry Supervision* , Nashville: Broadman & Holman Publishers, p. 7.

[18] Charles R. Feilding 1966, 'Education for ministry', *Theological Education,* Vol. 111, No.1, 47.

The search for a supervisory method

The 1969 field education consultation marked not only the last meeting of the 1960s, but also the first time that one topic, namely, supervision, had permeated every session. Particular attention will be paid to this consultation as it marked the beginning of a distinctive search for supervisory models and methods in theological education; it also represented an ongoing search for an identity within the theological education enterprise.

Thomas Klink, a veteran of the clinical training movement, contributed a chapter on supervision in the same volume as Feilding's 'Education for Ministry' essay, in which he defined supervision from the CPE perspective. Klink's definition of supervision became the focus for his presentation at the 1969 field education consultation. Klink pointed out that much confusion existed because some supervisors were not clear about their role. He cited CPE as having a precise and focused goal by 'its almost unvarying insistence upon reserving supervision as the proper term for designating processes around the goal of practice as a professional'. Klink challenged the field education directors to recognize that their role of identifying at times as teacher and at other times as supervisor led inevitably to tension. His criticism of seminary 'peer groups' was stinging. He felt that these 'field work seminars' may communicate knowledge, but unless attention was paid to the formation of the group as colleagues in the process, the experience essential for any place of supervision would be missed. Klink concluded his presentation with a reminder to the directors that their understanding of supervision was limited and encouraged them to examine the exciting possibilities found in the CPE model. While Klink was critical of many aspects of the role of supervision in field education he saw its possibilities when he said:

> It is a field of action; it is a style of work; it is a mode of change; it is a device for growth and progress, which has many possibilities. And the recognition of the variety of possibilities of place, of organization, of goal, of style, the recognition of these and the making of advised decisions within them constitutes, I think, the intelligent [*sic*] promise of the utilization of the field of supervision in theological education.[19]

Of course there was a reaction to his critical comments. The most constructive of them came from Earl Dahlstrom, whose extensive experience in field education enabled him to place things in their proper perspective through his good-humoured approach. Dahlstrom's advice to peers was that they had to take a long view of field education. However, what he said about old patterns of supervision and the temptation to limit them to one model of supervision only was the key to developing models of supervision for the field education context. It is significant to note that his words flag the possible departure from the CPE model of supervision to a philosophy that would 'set up standards of supervision that work whether or

---

[19]   Thomas W. Klink 1969, 'Supervision from a clinical/pastoral care perspective' *Report of the Proceedings of the Tenth Biennial Consultation on Field Education,* Berkeley, 15–18 January, 25.

not they measure up to the particular standards of supervision used by other disciplines'.[20]

The 1969 consultation marked the beginning of the search for supervisory models for a practice-based field education program and supervision became an agenda item for all following consultations. The question arose: What model of supervision is most appropriate for practice-based education? The only model that makes sense is the one that grows out of the opportunities and limits that the particular theological college situation represents. The goals of the field education programs at particular theological colleges will have a significant influence on the model of supervision used.

In 1975 Jesse Ziegler, Executive Secretary of American Association for Theological Schools, raised the key supervisory issue for theological education.

Ziegler asked the question:

How can the study of Scripture, theology, church history, sociology, psychology, and other disciplines bearing some relation to religious faith and institutions prepare one for the practice of ministry? How can abstract ideas be translated into the concrete realities of ministering to people in their joys and in their troubles?[21]

The response to these questions created another set of questions. What is the role of field education in fostering theological enquiry within theological education? What is the role of supervision in the above endeavour? If the 1969 consultation was a breakthrough and the beginning of a search for quality supervision models, the 1975 consultation marked the first serious effort to locate the field educator's position in theological education. The 1975 consultation suggested that supervision and theological enquiry were closely linked. That is, supervision was a vehicle for promoting theological enquiry.

The Whiteheads were the first to recognize and develop a systematic approach in field education to the connection between supervision and theological reflection. They pointed out that 'one's model of theological reflection will profoundly influence how one goes about doing this theological reflection' and that this will 'have consequences for supervision'.[22] They identified three models, which are summarized as follows:

---

[20] See Maureen Egan 1987, 'The history of the Association for Theological Field Education and its contribution to theological education in the United States', PhD (candidate), St Louis: St Louis University, 164.

[21] Jesse H. Ziegler 1975, Editorial, *Theological Education*, Vol. 11, 262–3.

[22] James D. Whitehead and Evelyn E. Whitehead, 1975, 'Educational models in theological education', *Theological Education*, Vol XI. No. 4, 273. This summary format from the Whitehead paper is credited to Maureen Egan 1987, 'The history of the Association for Theological Field Education and its contribution to theological education in the United States', 240-241.

1. Field education as the application of theology in the practice of ministry

   Basic educational assumption

   Theological education occurs in the academic setting of classroom and library, in biblical, historical and philosophical study.

   Placement

   A site that will enable students to apply theology learnt in classroom on a practical level; any additional learning in placement is not theological but practical.

   Role specification

   Student's role becomes that of administrator, communicator of tradition, a non-theologian and, at times, a functionary.

   Supervision

   Supervisor helps student apply appropriate theological answers to questions arising in ministerial practice.

   Theological reflection

   Becomes one-directional; student tries to interpret pastoral experience in light of tradition. Because tradition must be mastered student becomes convinced of inability to reflect and relies on professional theologian for direction.[23]

2. Field education as the acquisition and development of ministerial skills

   Basic educational assumption

   Theology is learnt in the academic setting, but expertise in extra-theological knowledge and skills is very important.

   Placement

   A site that offers extracurricular skills that will prepare students for pastoral roles.

   Role specification

   Student's role becomes that of counsellor, leader of worship, community organizer;

---

[23]   Ibid., 272–4.

student often experiences self as an inadequate theologian and inadequate counsellor because differences between minister's role and that of counsellor are unclear.

Supervision

Supervisor tries to ensure that student acquires particular pastoral skills.

Theological Reflection

Very little occurs because student's time in field education is spent learning another discipline, for example, counselling, without exploration of theological implications.[24]

3. Field education as the locus of pastoral theology

Basic educational assumption

Field education and the academic theological disciplines both contribute to the theological objectives of education for ministry; the contemporary experience of the believing community is a valid source of data for theological insight.

Placement

A learning site, not just for practical skills, but also for the acquisition of theological skills.

Role specification

The student identifies as pastoral theologian through experience in the TRS of relating Christian tradition to ministerial experience and vice versa.

Supervision

Supervisor and student collaborate in examining how theology comes together in particular settings.

Theological reflection

Two-directional; student learns habit of critical reflection, a method of allowing experience to question theological tradition and tradition to confront experience so that pastoral decisions will be theologically informed and personally owned.[25]

---

[24]   Ibid., 274–6.
[25]   Ibid., 276–7.

This was a groundbreaking paper for the future of field education as the themes of supervision and theological reflection were prominent among field educators at future consultations. This material became part of *Method in Ministry*, a publication by the Whiteheads that was to be a guide for future models and methods for theological reflection in TFE.[26] Before exploring the relationship between supervision and theological reflection, which, for the purposes of this study is the integration of theology with the practice of ministry, I wish to visit a little of the history of field education in Australia.

Field education in Australia

William H. Ives's DMin is a very impressive and seminal work on field education in Australian colleges.[27] In this study he produces findings from a survey conducted in December 1977, which highlights the similarities and differences in field education in Australia and USA.[28] The following chart highlights these similarities and differences.

---

[26]   James D. Whitehead and Evelyn E. Whitehead, 1995, *Method in Ministry*: *Theological Reflection on Christian Ministry*, Kansas City, MO: Sheed and Ward.

[27]   See William Ives 1979, 'Field educational and ministerial training in Australia: An analysis and a proposal', DMin, San Francisco: San Francisco Seminary.

[28]   Ibid., 194.

Table 1.1 Similarities and differences in field education in Australia and the USA

Aspect of Program	USA	Australia
Placements	Great variety available, especially agencies and institutions.	Limited variety of institutions and agencies.
Finance	Placements important to derive student income.	Placements less important for providing finance in most denominations.
Supervision	Acknowledged as key role. Training of supervisors and regular student–supervisor sessions the norm.	Acknowledged as a key role. Training of supervisors and regular student–supervisor sessions accepted as important, but need considerable development.
Educational objectives	Clearly defined as part of most programs. Concept of professionalism readily accepted and rated high.	Not clearly defined. Concept of ministry as a profession not universally accepted. Pragmatic rather than professional approach.
Lay participation	Not strongly indicated in literature.	Little apparent involvement of laity.
Integration	Process under development.	Acknowledged as important and practiced by one-third to one-half of colleges/seminaries
College initiative and control	Important and normal procedure.	Important and normal procedure.
Directors of field education	Full-time appointments the norm.	Rare and mainly part-time where appointed at all. Most people responsible have other areas of prime concern.
Reports	Regular, important and normal procedure.	Reports required by most, but follow-up lacking.
Evaluation	Normally an ongoing procedure. Credit given for satisfactory progress.	An area for development. Most require field education for graduation.
Experience in ministry	Appears somewhat limited except internships.	Broad in parish, less in specialist ministries. Internships being developed.
General	Field education well developed.	Developing in a positive manner with advantage of USA experience. Some individual programs compare well with those in the USA.

It is apparent from the table that many Australian field education programs have come a long way in the last twenty plus years. There is a greater variety of placements, the quality of training of supervisors has improved, lay participation has increased, evaluation procedures have been refined and more full-time field education directors are being appointed. There is no mention of the term 'theological reflection' in the table, however, that process could have been included in the meaning of the word 'integration'. Field education needs to undertake more research in the area of educational objectives, an issue that will be addressed in Chapter 3.

The Uniting Church and the Anglican Diocese of Melbourne undertook much of the development of field education in Melbourne. There were a number of reasons why field education developed in the UCTC, not the least being the appointment of a full-time Field Education Director, Professor D. L. Fullerton, who was director from 1976–83. Dr S. Ames was Director of Field Education for the Anglican Diocese of Melbourne during these field education developments. Fullerton developed structures and standards for field education that resulted in field education becoming part of ordination studies. An indication of interest in the development of this program was the inclusion of UCTCs *Field Education Manual* in a publication on field education written by Dr George I. Hunter, Director of Field Education, Episcopal Divinity School, Massachusetts.[29] In Melbourne, Ames and Fullerton have been at the forefront of developing the theological dimension in TFE. In 1989 they conducted a seminar entitled 'Doing Theology in the Parish – Three levels of Theological Reflection'.[30]

The training of supervisors and members of lay evaluation groups became a priority for this program. Added to this was the ecumenical cooperation in the training of supervisors from the Uniting and Anglican churches. Overseas visits from Dr George Hunter (1980), Dr D. McCarty, Director of Field Education and Professor of Ministry, Golden Gate Theological Seminary, San Francisco, (1983), and Dr Tjaard Hommes, Director, Institute of Advanced Pastoral Studies, Yogyakarta, Indonesia, (1983), had an influence on the hierarchy of the churches and field education programs.

These visitors conducted field education seminars and spoke on a number of occasions at which people became enthused for the potential of field education in theological education. It is apparent that most attempts to integrate theology and the practice of ministry were through the traditional field education procedures of covenanting, goal setting, feedback from supervisors and lay consultative groups and evaluation.

Dr I. Williams succeeded Dr Fullerton as Director of Field Education in 1984 and held that position until 1993. Dr Williams was instrumental in a policy review and changes to field education. He also placed more emphasis on the issues of

---

[29] George I. Hunter 1982, *Supervision and Education – Formation for Ministry*, Cambridge: Mass., pp. 113–34.

[30] Stephen Ames and Douglas Fullerton, 'Doing theology in the parish – three levels of theological reflection', outline of a paper presented at a seminar held in 1989 at Otira College, Melbourne.

social justice within the program. During his tenure as Director of Field Education both faculty and students encouraged him to develop a program of community theological reflection. It was left to me as the incoming Director of Field Education, appointed in 1994, to implement this program. I did so in the form of a theological seminar entitled 'Theological Reflection on Pastoral Care', a Bachelor of Theology unit within the UFT, Melbourne.

Field education has, for some time, enjoyed an important place within the formation program at UCTC. However, this is beginning to change with new appointees to faculty who have a different emphasis on formation.

At the state level in Australia the newly created VATFE is attempting to develop models and methods for pastoral supervision and theological reflection as a means of bridging the division between theory and practice.[31] While VATFE recognizes the contribution of CPE to theological education, the new standards for supervision envisage a different model of supervisory training and accreditation. VATFE has been recognized by the MCD as a professional body that advises on accreditation for any units or subjects in TFE (this only applies to those associated teaching institutions within the MCD) submitted for inclusion into the degree of Bachelor of Theology curriculum structure. The significance of this new association is its potential to influence and educate theological schools.

While VATFE does not compulsorily require that member institutions be formally accredited (indeed, it does not have the authority to compel them, nor the desire), some institutions have invited the Association to accredit or review their programs. Further, the development of supervisory standards in programs is a requirement of the Victorian Higher Education Advisory Committee in Melbourne, Australia, which regards supervision as a discipline. In many ways these accrediting bodies are further advanced in their thinking about the value of supervision than some of our theological institutions. Accreditation panels across Australia are increasingly looking for external benchmarks and training of supervisors in courses related to TFE or supervised ministry. The acceptance of such courses for degree purposes is encouraging, but the process will put increasing onus on us – VATFE and associates – to provide rigorous training and demonstrable benchmarking to ensure best practice. At this point VATFE provides one of those benchmarks. We are called on to provide benchmarks for pastoral supervision, however, we need to continue developing our accreditation processes.

I am aware that this truncated history of field education in Australia has been narrowed to Melbourne and, in particular, to the development of field education in the Uniting and Anglican churches. I am also aware that there is much creative thinking in the area of pastoral supervision and theological reflection among some of my colleagues in VATFE and the ANZATFE.

---

[31] Paver 1999, 'The birth of a professional association', *Ministry, Society and Theology*, Vol. 13, No.2, 76–89. The Victorian Association for TFE was established in October 1996. After a considerable number of meetings and consultations, including between theological colleges, the association has recommended standards for programs and supervision.

In the last two decades there has been a body of literature published that has endeavoured to address this issue of fragmentation within theological education. Much of the literature cited here has been initiated by individual faculty in overseas theological schools and therefore is scholarly in approach, with the exception of the Assembly's *Task Group Report* into the future of theological education in the UCA, which was initiated by the church.

Dr Barbara Wheeler, president of the Auburn Theological Seminary in New York, and theologian Dr Edward Farley have pointed out that the debate in recent years has moved from orthodoxy (that is, the theological orthodoxy of those who will be permitted to teach and the matter of practical application and technique) to theological grounds about how theological schools should define their mission. This is another way of asking the question: 'What is theological about theological education?' A number of writers argue that the current schemes of disciplinary organization and the concept of disciplines have undermined the theological character of theological education.[32] It is my intention to review the responses to the theological education debate at the conclusion of the chapter.

Responses from the academy

The Mud Flower Collective makes a radical critique of the structure of theological education. They are extremely critical of the discipline structure as it excludes women's experience and is anchored in the hegemony of white, male and Western history and experience.[33] *God's Fierce Whimsy* is the written record of seven feminists' commitment 'to make incarnate both the fierce and the whimsical character of that which is born in every shared effort to teach and learn with minds set on justice'.[34] They make it clear in their publication that women's experience is itself no one thing, but rather pluralized by race, ethnicity and class, and that theological schooling's inadequacy to promote genuine pluralism correlates with its reliance on universalizing. The standard way to do theology:

> is to assess the nature and character of universals, to sweep with broad strokes the particularities of personal and specific events; to bypass the nitty-gritty pains and problems, whims and fantasies, of the common folk in an effort to direct us away from ourselves toward that which cannot be known in human experience.[35]

According to the Collective the key to correcting this inadequacy and moving towards a genuine pluralism lies in making it properly theological. And the way to do theology is to do it in a manner 'that it is foundationally oriented toward justice

---

[32]   Barbara G. Wheeler and Edward Farley (eds) 1991, *Shifting Boundaries: Contextual approaches to the structure of theological education*, Louisville: Westminster/John Knox Press, pp. 8–9.

[33]   The Mud Flower Collective 1985, *God's Fierce Whimsy*, New York: Pilgrim Press.

[34]   Ibid., introductory comments to the book.

[35]   Ibid., p. 64.

and that is relational in character. To do theology ourselves we must begin with our experience of ourselves in relation'.[36] This must be done in a collaboration, which includes a diversity of cultures, in accountability to very particular people, such as black and Hispanic women and those white women who are struggling against racial, sexual, and economic injustice. The Collective is committed to transforming theological education so that their needs and interests 'are realized as basic to the methods and content of the enterprise' by 'beginning with our own lives-in-relation. We believe that this is where all research, teaching and learning should begin'.[37] To do this concretely in theology is to begin with the stories of the people engaged in this collaborative and mutual enterprise.[38]

This process quickly exhibits ways in which those lives have been victimized by injustice. Beginning with people's stories, it keeps the focus on relationality and on justice as concrete as possible. Kelsey says there are three theological assumptions about God in this process:

1. God is known as God is experienced
2. God is experienced in a diversity of relationships – as present or as absent in relationships with a mother or a father, as positive or negative, with people who are ethnically or radically 'Other'
3. God is experienced when the focus is on relationality and on justice as concrete as possible.[39]

Certainly, the concreteness advocated for theological reflection dictates a different set of criteria of adequacy for doing theology. Its primary values include 'perceptiveness, insight, depth and breadth of critical illumination, and respect for the diversity of experiences of people in different social locations'.[40] For the Mud Flower Collective 'theology is critical self-reflection on the narrative of persons' lives that attends to the concrete particularity of different persons' experiences of God and to the ways in which those same lives have been victimized by injustice'.[41]

A primary target of criticism has been the assumption that theological education is best conceived as the preparation of clergy for their tasks. One response to these issues is the endeavour to discern the shape and direction for actual structural change. Theologians Charles Wood and Edward Farley argue that the pattern of theological education should be determined and unified by the structure and movement of theology itself, not, as is now the case, by the paradigm of functional specialities that clergy are expected to perform. Wood and Farley define theology broadly, not as a discipline identified by subject matter, but as a series or collection of studies unified by its goal.

---

[36]   Ibid., p. 104.
[37]   Ibid., p. 23.
[38]   Ibid., p. 134–207.
[39]   Kelsey, *Between Athens and Berlin*, pp. 139–40.
[40]   The Mud Flower Collective, *God's Fierce Whimsy*, p. 150.
[41]   Kelsey, *Between Athens and Berlin*, p. 151.

First, it is generally agreed that Farley initiated the current debate around theological education with the publication of his book, *Theologia: The Fragmentation and Unity of Theological Education*,[42] and its sequel *The Fragility of Knowledge*.[43] An understanding of the terms '*theologia*' and 'the fragility of knowledge' is clarified when he writes that '[k]nowledge, therefore, is fragile, since it is more a responsive activity than a precious possession'.[44] Knowledge, then, is something to be possessed, which resides in and becomes part of a person. Farley uses the terms 'disposition' or *habitus*, not only to describe the location of this knowledge, but also to describe the aim of theological education. Further, he uses the term '*theologia* rather than *theology* in order to underline that it is a kind of wisdom and not, as *theology* tends to suggest, a body of information and theory about God'.[45] This kind of wisdom is rooted in and develops in situations of faith where, for Farley, 'faith describes the way in which the human being lives in and toward God and the world under the impact of redemption'.[46] And so, according to Farley, *theologia* is a personal wisdom, a way of being human, not information or theory about a way of being human. However, *theologia* requires a disciplined reflection in order to achieve this purpose and this comes through the modes of theological reflection, theological understanding and theological knowledge.

1. The first mode is described as theological reflection, in which reflection is on the believer and his or her understanding of the life of faith in the world.[47]
2. The second mode describes theological understanding, in which this understanding is the situation of leadership in the church, ordained or not, with a focus on the redemptive community. The aim of this mode is to elicit the believer's understanding and action.[48]
3. The third mode of understanding is theological knowledge, which Farley classifies as enquiry and scholarship. The social context of this mode 'is usually, but not necessarily, the school'; the task is the uncovering of truth in orderly, disciplined and systematic ways. *Theologia* is evoked by faith's understanding to be faithful in the situation. In every mode, as faith's pre-reflective insightfulness is brought to reflective insightfulness, *theologia* is wisdom and understanding, but only in the mode of enquiry and scholarship is it knowledge. This mode does not replace or exclude the other two modes:

   … [t]he leader of the church as believer will pursue the reflective life of a believer, and the development of that reflective life will surely be part of the education of the leader

---

[42]   Edward Farley 1983, *Theologia: The fragmentation and unity of theological education*, Philadelphia: Fortress Press.

[43]   Edward Farley 1988, *The Fragility of Knowledge: Theological education in the church and the university*, Philadelphia: Fortress Press.

[44]   Ibid., p. 3.

[45]   Kelsey, *Between Athens and Berlin*, p. 102.

[46]   Farley, *Theologia*, p. 156.

[47]   Ibid., p. 157.

[48]   Ibid., p. 158.

of the church. In addition, the leader of a church may, because of particular situations of leadership, also pursue the third mode of enquiry and scholarship.[49]

Farley outlines a complicated structure of theological education curricula, and he is certain that the hermeneutical mode of *theologia* 'can no longer be restricted to the interpretation of texts'.[50]

However, what is significant in Farley's understanding of *theologia* is that this *habitus* can occur outside the structure of a theological college curriculum. Therefore, *theologia* is the province of all people, not just for those who choose to prepare for a professional ministry in a theological college or seminary. If theology is a kind of wisdom that is available to all people as they engage their faith at the level of private or public life, then this gives people a new understanding of the meaning of theology.

By way of contrast theologian Charles Wood's Christian theology is 'a critical enquiry into the validity of Christian witness'.[51] Wood defines theology as an activity constituted by a type of enquiry.[52] This activity has objective and subjective elements to it. It is 'objective' because the objective of theological enquiry is to validate truth claims for the purposes of professional church leadership. It is 'subjective' in the sense that one participates in this activity and appropriates the claims for oneself that come from the theological enquiry. In this sense this theological enquiry engages the whole person. Wood speaks of this activity as a process of 'transformation'.[53] However, this process will not occur through a paradigm which tends to perpetuate the dichotomy between academic and practical disciplines and therefore fragments the 'whole' person who engages it.[54] While he recognizes that the present disciplinary structure fragments theological education, he nonetheless proposes an alternative scheme, lest theological enquiry, for lack of disciplinary housing, become unstable and vulnerable through the ancillary disciplines on which it relies.[55] And so he introduces three dimensions, which he names as Historical Theology, Philosophical Theology and Practical Theology, whose purpose is in a sense judgemental, for they constitute a critical enquiry into the validity of Christian witness.[56] These three dimensions are in a reciprocal relationship with each other.[57]

Now, what helps to illumine the reciprocal interdependence of the three dimensions of theological enquiry? Wood proposes that the distinction is vision

---

[49] Ibid., p. 159.

[50] Farley, *The Fragility of Knowledge*, p. 133.

[51] Charles Wood 2002, *Vision and Discernment: An orientation in theological study*, Eugene, Oregon: Wipf and Stock Publishers, p. 21. Previously published by Scholars Press, 1985.

[52] Wood, *Vision and Discernment*, p. 34.

[53] Ibid., p. 59.

[54] Ibid., pp. 63–5.

[55] Ibid., pp. 57–9.

[56] Wood, *Vision and Discernment*, pp. 41–55.

[57] Ibid., p. 67.

and discernment in each of its three dimensions.[58] He draws on these visual metaphors from the Greek poet Archilocus – '[t]he fox knows many things, but the hedgehog knows one big thing' – to explain what he means.[59] Jackson Carroll, Professor Emeritus of Religion and Society, explains that 'The hedgehog is a metaphor for the capacity to develop a coherent vision of things; the fox represents the capacity to see the concrete thing in all its capacity.'[60] The purpose of these two moments is to bring some unity and validity to the 'Christian witness as a whole'.[61]

Wood is aware that there are inbuilt dangers if theology remains at the level of vision. The dangers are ideological distortion, universalization and the temptation to gloss over the ambiguity and tragedy of life.[62] For an adequate vision of the unity of Christian witness we need an interplay between vision of that witness, which draws on all three types of resources – historical, philosophical and practical – and, in each dimension, discernment.

Wood is insistent that the character of theological enquiry cannot be explained by using the theory–practice argument for 'it is discernment and not "practice", which is the proper counterpoint to theory or vision in this respect ... *Both* vision and discernment are informed by, and in turn inform, practice'.[63]

This theological enquiry is further complicated by Wood when he adds systematic theology and moral theology to the historical, philosophical and practical theology dimensions of critical enquiry. Systematic theology is concerned about the unity of the three dimensions of critical enquiry. It brings these three dimensions into conversation in the service of its own integrative task.[64]

The other theological dimension is moral theology, the defining interest of which is the 'validity of Christian witness concerning human conduct', personal and communal, individual and institutional.[65] Wood is concerned that these two disciplines are not seen as brokers between theory and practice, but as an enquiry are defined by an interest in the integration and unity of these three reciprocally interrelated dimensions of theological enquiry.

The outcome of this process, which is called 'theological enquiry', has a normal and educational value. Its normal use is to assist in making decisions for the practice of ministry as 'Christians ordinarily engage in theological reflection for the sake of their own Christian practice'.[66] The aim of its educational value is to make sound theological judgements, where judgement 'informs practice by equipping the practitioner not with ready-made deliberative judgements but rather

---

[58]   Ibid., p. 69.

[59]   Ibid., p. 68.

[60]   Jackson W. Carroll 1991, *As One With Authority*, Louisville: Westminster/John Knox Press, p. 124.

[61]   Wood, *Vision and Discernment*, p. 69.

[62]   Ibid., p. 72.

[63]   Ibid.

[64]   Ibid., p. 53.

[65]   Ibid., p. 54.

[66]   Ibid., p. 80.

with the capacity to make them'.[67] It is not the mere possession of a theology that is the measure of a theological education; it is rather one's ability to form, revise and employ theological judgements so that vision and discernment are exhibited in practice.

While Wood and Farley have, as noted above, many objections to the theory-to-practice model, Joseph Hough, president of the Union Theological Seminary, New York, and process theologian John Cobb fault it for not providing an adequate description of the complex ways that thinking and action are related to each other.[68] Hough and Cobb identify a different starting point for the structure of studies with the focus on the retention of the preparation of church leadership as the explicit goal of theological education. They propose a change in image and definition of professional leadership from a functionalist one to a more complex model that they call '[t]he Practical Christian Thinker'.[69] Their understanding of the word 'professional' is a dynamic rather than a functional concept. Borrowing from the insights of a dynamic management model they propose a church leadership model that they consider to be the work of the practical theologian. What makes leadership church leadership is that it is the work of the practical theologian. A practical theologian is the combination of a 'practical Christian thinker' and a 'reflective practitioner'.[70] Hough and Cobb propose that practical thinkers are pathfinders and visionaries and reflective practitioners are implementers and problem solvers for the church. In addition to engaging in practical thinking they participate in reflective practice. It is at this point that Hough and Cobb reject the concept of church leadership as a movement from theory to practice. Their alternative model is based on Donald Schön's understanding of reflective practice, which leads them to assert that 'practical Christian thinkers reflect not only about practice. They also reflect in practice'.[71] Neither the practical Christian thinker nor the reflective practitioner can be subsumed in the other. Together, in my s view, they contain the best image for a professional church – the practical theologian:

---

[67] Ibid.

[68] Joseph C. Hough Jnr. and John B. Cobb Jnr. 1985, *Christian Identity and Theological Education*, Chico: Scholars Press.

[69] Hough and Cobb, *Christian Identity*, p. 81.

[70] Ibid., p. 90.

[71] Ibid., p. 85. Their understanding of reflective practice is derived from the work of Donald A. Schön, *The Reflective Practitioner*, Basic Books, 1983, pp. 308–9. Hough and Cobb contend that research is an activity of practitioners and 'it is triggered by features of the practice situation, undertaken on the spot, and immediately linked to action. There is no question of an "exchange" between research and practice or the "implementation" of research results, when the frame or theory testing experiments of the practitioner at the same time transform the practice situation. Here the exchange between research and practice is immediate, and reflection-in-action is its own implementation.'

Practical theology is not one function along with others. It is a mode of reflection that continuously re-evaluates the use and time and energy in and by the church in light of what the church truly is. A shift of roles or functions would not affect its appropriateness.[72]

This model of reflection departs from the professional paradigm where professionals see themselves as experts having a theoretical knowledge that their parishioners or clients do not. This model acknowledges that:

[r]eflective practitioners, on the other hand, work with those they serve. They offer insights and knowledge gained mainly through experience in similar situations. They share this and come to decisions in collaboration with those who seek their help.[73]

Their proposed curriculum is based on their model and includes 'The Heritage that Shapes Our Identity', 'The Global Context of Our Lives', 'Issues for Practical Christian Thinking' and 'Professional Preparation for Pastoral Ministry'.[74] The Hough and Cobb proposal ejects training in the functions of ministry from the theological curriculum. They assert that reflective practice should be carried out under ecclesiastical supervision in the actual settings of practice. They argue that the experience based teaching as focused in field education in theological schools has been unsuccessful for a number of reasons, but in particular, because of the lack of quality supervision and the lack of interest and understanding from full time faculty.[75]

Finally, I present the recommendations from the *Report of the Task Group to Review Ministerial Education within the UCA*.[76] Unlike the other proposals or enquiries into theological education this one was initiated by the church rather than by any one individual.

First, it should be noted that the report is not a report into theological education as such, but a report into ministerial education. The clear message from this report is that theological education must be shaped to meet the context and goals for mission and ministry.

The report affirms seven goals for ministerial education. In the view of the Task Group the Uniting Church seeks to form ministers who:

---

[72]   Ibid., p. 92.
[73]   Ibid., pp. 87–8.
[74]   Ibid., pp. 129–30.
[75]   Ibid., p. 119.
[76]   *Report of the Task Group to Review Ministerial Education in the UCA*. The final draft of this review was presented to the Eighth Assembly of the UCA held in July 1997. With some minor amendments the report was accepted by the Assembly, which has the overall national responsibility for theological education. This responsibility is delegated to its constituted body, the Ministerial Education Commission. This body is compromised of delegates representing theological colleges in the various states of Australia and includes Nungalinya College, which provides theological education for Aboriginal and Torres Strait Islander candidates for ministry.

1. Have a deep faith in Jesus Christ, are committed to growth in their own faith and to a spirituality that will sustain their lives;
2. Have a critical understanding of the nature of ministry and mission and an appreciation of the importance of the conscious commitment to and participation in the task of mission though worship, witness and service;
3. Have a critical knowledge of the Christian tradition and are able to help the church shape its future in the light of that tradition;
4. Are equipped to help the church discover its identity and lead the church in mission within a rapidly changing and diverse cultural and social context;
5. Have skills for the practice of day-to-day ministry and the quality of being and awareness that gives integrity to the exercise of such skills;
6. Are able to engage the tasks of ministry with critical imagination, courage, theological judgement and self-reflection;
7. Exercise this ministry within the ministry of the whole people of God.

Further, it is important to acknowledge that these goals will be exercised in a context that recognizes that:

• Australia is a nation facing rapid change
• the rights of Aboriginal and Islander people
• our context is also multicultural
• educational philosophy is changing
• the ethos of the UCA is changing.

The significance of the report is that it places these general goals within the national and local context, which includes particular concerns for ministry, race, gender, multiculturalism and the particularity of denominational goals.

In order to incorporate these goals and essential principles for ministerial education the report proposes a framework that sees ministry as part of lifelong ministry, lifelong learning. The report suggests a four-stage process:

A period of discernment

During the period of discernment people will explore their call to ministry. This will be open to any person who wishes to reflect on a particular ministry (word, deacon and youth worker). The curriculum during this process could involve core study, field education, elective modules and mentoring. A candidating process may follow this if a person's call leads them towards ministry.

The core theological curriculum

The core theological education is a period of study and field education necessary for ministry. Its focus is the exploration of the sound understanding of ministry and the knowledge that underpins ministry experience. This is to be integrated in an interactive process with field experience so as to develop skills and wisdom for ministry. The core areas of study would include Bible and theology, historical and liturgical studies, development of the capacity for critical reflection and an awareness of cultural realities. The model is emphatic that the core disciplines must not stand alone, but engage in an ongoing conversation with culture, experience, tradition, the church and Scripture. During this period there will be a concentration on three aspects in formation for ministry, which include spiritual, vocational and personal formation.

Licensed year

A licensed year offers a supervised experience of ministry with many aspects of accountability and responsibility at a greater level than that of the Core Program field education component. There is a requirement that 25 per cent of time focus on continuing study, the remainder being on the exercise of ministry. If appropriate, ordination will occur after this licensed year.

Lifelong continuing education

Long-term ministry depends on continuing the learning process developed in the core program and the licensed year. Therefore, continuing education needs to be built into the ongoing program of all those in specified ministries.[77]

Theological education in this model does not focus on research as its aim is to produce ministers as leaders who will promote a vision for ministry and mission for the whole church, which includes lay people. Mission is the central activity of this model and is described as an 'outward directed, reconciling and gathering (activity) raising new communities in unlikely places, engaged with injustice, oppression, poverty, discrimination and violence'. The church is called to be committed to the following of Christ in costly love for the world.

I have outlined the response of TFE to the division of theory and practice together with ways in which it has sought to develop models of theological reflection and pastoral supervision as a means of combating this division. An extension of this response will be found in the following chapters. In this chapter I have also presented five models of theological education that attempt to address the issues of fragmentation and integration. There are a number of themes that appear in these proposals.

The common theme in the first four proposals centres on a particular understanding of theology. For example, the Mudflower Collective theology is critical reflection on personal experience. Farley believes that theology is critical reflection on the meaning of faith, while Wood advocates theology as activity constituted by a type of enquiry; Hough and Cobb interpret theology as reflection

---

[77]   Church of England Working Party 2003, *Formation for Ministry within a Learning Church*, Summary of the report, pp.1-20. In a period where many seminaries are undertaking curriculum reviews the Church of England in UK has undertaken a review of their formation for ministry program. There are some similarities with the UCA report. The full report can be found on the Church of England website: www.cofe.anglican.org.

on the 'Christian story'. Each proposal offers a way to bridge the gap between theory and practice.

There are a number of elements in the proposals that have validity for the restructure of theological education. I don't believe, however, that any one proposal could be recommended because each proposal reflects differing contexts and goals. I am encouraged by the assertion of some writers who believe that the process of preparation for ministry is not one of function, but the development of the 'disposition of the soul' (Farley), or a 'disposition to some critical activity' (Wood). The aim of this disposition is to integrate the cognitive, effective and behavioural components of the practice of ministry. I identify with this stance because I believe it to be of primary importance to formation. Unless this primary aim is recognized as valid in our theological colleges then we will continue to perpetuate the theory–practice dichotomy.

Therefore, in this regard, perhaps the most encouraging contribution comes from Charles Wood who advocates mutuality and reciprocity between the various theological conversation partners in the theological education enterprise. The use of the metaphor 'vision' highlights the need for each conversation partner not only to have an understanding of the vision of other disciplines, but also to incorporate that vision. In order that the vision does not become distorted or vulnerable to idolatry, critical insight (discernment) is necessary.

I align myself with the Mud Flower Collective's radical understanding of theology in that it proposes particularity, relationality, plurality and justice as bases for understanding theology. The Collective believes that, unless the above issues are addressed, there can be no unity or integration within theological education. I do have some concern about the absence of an external accountability. It is obvious that each member of the group is accountable to each other, but there appears to be no external critique of the individual biases each person brings to the group. Farley is correct when he says that the 'total Christian mythos' (sustained reflection on religious and theological language) must be present in our discussions, or else we become vulnerable to idolatry or ideological distortions.

The Uniting Church report advocates a ministry contextual model in which leaders will be prepared for a new understanding of church. The influences that have guided this report do not come from the sources from which I have quoted, but from input received from churches (Canada, the USA and the UK), UCA constituencies, the Church Life Survey and resources from the World Council of Churches, as is apparent in the report's emphasis on 'ministerial formation' and mission and evangelism. There is no obvious evidence that the overseas literature used in the UCA report was influenced or shaped by the academic debate. There is no specific discussion on TFE and its potential to be an integrating agent. The report affirms personal, spiritual and pastoral integration, but provides no rationale as to how these might be achieved. It is less tolerant of the *Wissenschaft* model and encourages a professional model of theological education. While the report is critical of applied knowledge and encourages an integrated approach, which includes interdisciplinary teaching and ongoing conversations with culture, experience and the tradition, it once again lacks any discussion of a methodology for how this might occur. The report is less definite about its understanding of what it means to be theological and is not theologically driven. I will show in chapter 5 how its lack of theological understanding has been an impediment in curriculum discussions at UCTC. The report has a particular view of what it means to be 'formed' as an ordained minister within the UCA.

Perhaps the Hough and Cobb model is similar to what the UCA report is advocating. For Hough and Cobb the aim of theological education is professional preparation for church leadership. This occurs when the theological school trains the student to be a practical theologian, which involves them in not only reflecting about practice, but also reflecting in practice. Hough and Cobb believe that one of the tasks of the theological school is to devise a curriculum that will begin to assist them in an understanding of what it means to be a reflective practitioner. It surprises me, therefore, that they propose to eject field education from the curriculum and make it the responsibility of the church. Removing field education from the curriculum indicates that Hough and Cobb fail to understand the integrative capacity of TFE. Either that or they have decided that integration is impossible within the theological schools and so have decided to locate it in the parish. Whatever their position, they have failed to provide a clear rationale or viable method.

It is my understanding that few of these proposals have been tested within a teaching theological community.[78] One exception is the Mud Flower Collective, which identifies itself as five Christian feminists who developed their model in a particular theological community. They describe some of this process thus:

> Together, we have told stories, read books, and analyzed what has been happening among us as well as elsewhere in theological education. We have laughed and we have cried more than we had anticipated in our collective effort to learn and to write an honest, constructive essay on Christian feminism and theological education.[79]

This is a good place to begin in tackling the issue of fragmentation in theological education.

---

[78]   The Division of the faculty departments of Perkins School of Theology suggest the schema developed by Charles Wood in his book is present in the curriculum of his theological school. I am not in a position to say whether his propositions have been tested nor are the concepts of vision and discernment alive and well in his institution. See www.smu.edu/theology/

[79]   The Mud Flower Collective, *God's Fierce Whimsy*, ix.

Chapter 2

Theological reflection as a method of integration

Chapter 1 highlighted the fragmentation in theological education and various responses to the problem. With the exception of the study commissioned by the UCA into theological education, which I refer to again in Chapter 5, all the responses came from theological faculties. In this Chapter, I will reflect on the meaning of integration within the context of theological reflection as a method of integration in theological education.

An understanding of integration

My understanding of the word 'integration' is bringing the parts together to make something complete in order to unify or unite. Integration is related to 'wholeness and comes from the base word, whole, meaning completeness, not divided up; containing all its elements or parts; that which is not broken, damaged or injured; in sound health'.[1] Wholeness describes the state of one's being, the quality of a person's life. By integrating or bringing together all the parts one becomes whole. In this context; 'Wholeness defines the state of the student and the goal for theological education that would have all the parts of the student's life to come together within a whole, healthy person.'[2]

The forging of whole, healthy people has been the challenge and the struggle of theological education for decades. There is recognition that integration of the curriculum in theological education is a complex, challenging and frustrating task. It appears that students are cut into slices, then, it is left up to them to bring those slices together to make a whole. While students have some personal responsibility to integrate the parts of their theological education, the task is made more difficult when the theological institutions themselves create and cultivate the parts rather than the whole.

How does one integrate academic learning and the practice of ministry? Further, how do we develop the ministry formation (personal identity, pastoral

---

[1]   Carla Adele Stengel 1999, 'Pastoral supervision in theological reflection: The role of the ministry reflection report and supervisory conversation in ministry', DMin, Dayton: United Theological Seminary, 47.

[2]   Ibid.

care, pastoral and professional leadership) and theological reflection of our students in a way that is neither oppressive nor competitive? I believe that field education with an emphasis on theological reflection and pastoral supervision does contribute to the formative processes of theological students in an integrated way. The aim of theological reflection and pastoral supervision is integration. A recent study confirmed the high priority of integration among TFE directors within Australia and New Zealand regarding '[c]hanges anticipated in Field Education in the next decade'. Thirty-four per cent of respondents indicated their first priority was '*To assist students to integrate academic knowledge with personhood, life in the spirit, and professional skills* [emphasis in the original]' Twenty-three per cent of respondents indicated that '*to assist students to integrate academic study with ministry*' was their second choice.[3] Survey participants generally gave expression to this integration as bridging the gap between academic perspectives and ministerial perspectives. However, they wished the integration to be more inclusive and holistic. Therefore, the emphasis in integration includes personhood, spirituality and ministerial skills. The emphasis is more than knowledge; it includes matters of wisdom and the heart too. This chapter will seek to highlight theological reflection and its contribution to integration within theological education by bringing together some of those slices of the student's formation that contribute to the whole.

Concern for integration

The concern for integration is most clearly expressed in field education. Field education was renamed TFE because of the desire of those who wanted to bridge the gap between theory and practice. Despite this, both CPE and TFE have been slow in fostering theological enquiry. Both methods have developed supervisory models that fostered personal, professional and pastoral identity, but the theologizing function has received less attention than other functions. This could be partly due to the fact that some field education directors and supervisors have not always been trained to facilitate theological reflection. At the back of the training failure may be inadequate models of field education. James and Evelyn Whitehead point out that 'one's model of field education will profoundly influence how one goes about doing this theological reflection' and that this will 'have consequences for supervision'.[4] These differing conceptions of field education and pastoral education reveal very different standpoints. If left unarticulated these underlying assumptions can lead to unfulfilled expectations and confusion among supervisors and students and, indeed, can undermine the particular field education program. The implications for this incongruence in purpose, structure and process in field education programs will be discussed in the history of pastoral supervision in Chapter 3.

---

[3]   Paver 1983, 'Field education and its contribution to theological education', 25 November.

[4]   Whitehead and Whitehead 1975, 'Educational models', *Theological Education*, 11, Summer 1975, 273.

The remainder of this chapter will advocate dialogue and critical reflection as the preferred mode of communication in theological reflection. It will discuss the priority of experience in theological reflection, the place of the case study reflection mode in theological reflection and make some general comments on the purpose of theological reflection. Further, this chapter will seek to define an understanding of models and methods of theological reflection and, finally, present three models and their purpose as a means of illustrating their integrative aims and contribution to the formation of students.

The priority of experience in theological reflection

Theological reflection begins with concrete lived experience, involving the past and the present. The lived experience of one's life is shaped by personal and community relationships, religious tradition, culture, politics, work, leisure time and all the multiplicity of feelings and thoughts that go to make the very fabric of a human being. Experience is an essential source of wisdom, for it is here we find God's presence and Spirit – not only in moments of tragedy and crisis, joy and exaltation, but also in the sometimes mundane routine of daily life. It is this experience that we bring to theological reflection.

Our theology begins not with a proposition, but with experience. Experience plays a significant role in theological reflection. Pastoral supervision begins with lived experience – begins with the context. It can begin elsewhere (tradition, Scriptures, social sciences), but we have placed a priority on experience as the beginning point for pastoral supervision and theological reflection and, indeed, as the basis for developing our theology. This starting point has traditionally placed us at odds with the methodologies of systematic theologians and other disciplines within the theological enterprise. However, in saying this there is little literature of depth in pastoral supervision and theological reflection available on the nature of experience. It is in this area that we need to pay further attention. David Kolb, a philosopher, has assisted us in understanding experience relating to learning styles.[5] The Melbourne Institute for Experiential and Creative Arts Therapy in Australia is deepening our understanding of the creative nature of experience. The Rev Dr Colin Hunter is in the forefront of researching lived experience of the students and developing its relationship with field education.[6] Pastoral theologian Robert Kinast's book, *What Are They Saying About Theological Reflection ?*,[7] is a welcome addition to a number of books published on the subject of theological reflection over the last few years. Kinast identifies five styles of theological

---

[5]   David A. Kolb 1984, *Experiential Learning: Experience as a Source of Learning and Development.* Englewood Cliffs, NJ: Prentice Hall.

[6]   Colin James Hunter 2002, 'An enquiry into the experience of making a presentation to the GradDip, MA training group', thesis in partial fulfilment of the Master of Arts (Supervision), Melbourne: Melbourne Institute for Experiential and Creative Arts Therapy.

[7]   Robert L. Kinast 2000, *What Are They Saying About Theological Reflection?*, Mahwah, NJ: Paulist Press.

reflection: ministerial, spiritual wisdom, feminist, enculturation and practical. 'Style' is a wise choice of word here as its use is intended to highlight the interplay of substance and style (form and content). Kinast concedes that great strides have been made in an attempt to heal the rupture between feeling–thought and theory–practice, but very little attention has been given to the separation of style and substance. He says this is in part because thought does not pay enough attention to an understanding of experience. He deepens our understanding of experience by highlighting the different types of experience in each style of theological reflection. Proponents of theological reflection and pastoral supervision are usually content to let experience stand for what happens in the life of the individual or community. While this may give the impression that theological reflection is not intellectually sophisticated, it actually means that any experience can be reflected upon theologically.

Obviously, some experiences are more suitable than are others. Part of the task of theological reflection is to help people choose experiences wisely. It is this experience that we bring to theological reflection. For me the appeal to human experience is based on the assumption that it is not a spiritual void waiting to be filled with meaning from the outside. 'Either it already contains theological meaning or it has analogous elements that can be used to fashion a real (rather than a nominal or hypothetical) connection to the sources of Christian faith.'[8] I am of the opinion that human experience by itself already contains theological meaning, but it also can have connection to the sources of the Christian faith. I am less than convinced by the stretch of imagination used by some when they seek to impose a theological model on anything and everything human. In doing so it takes out the human face of God and therefore the incarnation is placed at risk.

I have been writing about experience in theological reflection and pastoral supervision as it alludes to the individual and corporate experiences *we bring* to theological reflection. These experiences have the potential to inform and shape our theological reflection. An understanding of experience in this argument is not fully based on what we bring, but how open we are to new and often unexpected experiences that enter our lives and have the potential to change and transform us. Usually, these experiences occur at the intersection of knowledge and belief. These unexpected experiences have been identified as 'critical moments' or 'convictional moments'; they are discussed and elaborated on in Chapter 3. This understanding of experience does not deny other interpretations of experience, but when one is open to these unexpected experiences and one is willing to place them in the context of tradition and culture, a deeper understanding of God can occur. This understanding of experience requires further elaboration.

The experience I wish to highlight is not only that experience when one participates in or encounters some reality, but also includes new knowledge discovered as a result of reflecting upon the reality of the experience. Experience without insight is only experience and may have a neutral or negative impact upon the participant involved in the experience. As will be indicated later, theological reflection advocates action, change and transformation and, for this to occur,

---

[8]　Ibid., p. 65

insight is required by the participant. Philosopher H. G. Gadamer has argued that, in its pure sense, experience is always new. Only through being surprised can we really acquire new experiences. For an experience to be truly an experience, according to Gadamer, it must run counter to our expectations.[9] Thus, insight is more than just knowledge of a given situation; it involves liberation from something that deceives us and holds us captive. In experience there is a rupturing of expectations – something happens or we discover something that we did not expect and our familiar world of understanding is put in question. For Gadamer 'experience is a process of disillusionment and disinvesture that leaves us standing before the world without the protection of familiar concepts'.[10] Experience, therefore, entails a certain negativity in which our plans and expectations break down, our purposes and desires are defeated.

It is a painful process that teaches us the limitations and finitude of all our arrangements and expectations. The breakdown of expectation, however, is also a breakthrough to a new type of openness, a type of emancipation or release from some prior certainty or settled self-understanding. The experienced person, paradoxically, is someone who is open to new experience, because that person is better disposed to expect the unexpected.[11] In this understanding of experience control is wrested from the participant as it is not so much we who raise questions, rather, questions arise and present themselves to us and in so doing enable new and liberating insights to occur. Theologian Terry Veling says:

> The same holds true in our conversation with tradition. The wandering question always has priority over the settled answer. Knowing that we do not know is to live within the openness of a question, of the still undetermined possibilities of both the situation and the tradition we find ourselves in. In this clearing something new emerges and takes shape that did not exist before.[12]

The enemy of this understanding of experience is not ambiguity or ambivalence, but certitude. Pastoral theologian Herbert Anderson reflects some of this understanding of theological reflection when he writes:

> In order to engage fully in the process of theological reflection we need to be able to be surprised, be willing to respect the ideas of others as valid, regard every conclusion as provisional, and set aside cherished conclusions for the sake of community. Courage, curiosity, imagination, and humility are hallmarks of the practical Christian thinker.[13]

---

[9]   Brian H. Childs 1990, 'Experience–Enlightenment', in Rodney J. Hunter (ed.), *Dictionary of Pastoral Care and Counselling*, p. 389.

[10]   Gerald Bruns 1992, *Hermeneutics Ancient and Modern*, New Haven: Yale University Press, p. 155. Cited in Terry A. Veling, *Living in the Margins*, New York: Crossroad, 1996, p. 41.

[11]   Hans-Georg Gadamer 1989, *Truth and Method* (2nd rev. edn) (trans. Joel Weinsheimer and Donald Marshall), New York: Crossroad, pp. 355–7. Cited in Terry A. Veling, *Living in the Margins*, p. 42.

[12]   Ibid., p. 43.

[13]   Herbert Anderson 1984, 'Forming a pastoral habitus: A rich tapestry with many threads', *Journal of Supervision and Training in Ministry*, 15, 238.

This understanding of experience has religious implications. New experience may challenge our expectations and illusions of being in full control of our lives. Experience confronts us with our human finitude. Anton Boisen, founder of the CPE movement, pointed this out when he described acute psychotic experience as a religious crisis. In psychosis the apparatus for predicting the future, explaining everyday life and describing self-identity fails. The struggle to regain balance in this eruptive situation is a religious one and, I believe, a revelatory experience. The Whiteheads affirm this stance in indicating that 'Revelation – God's self-disclosure, which surprises us, overturns our certitudes and transcends our best imaginings – is registered in experience'.[14] The Whiteheads affirm the place and validity of experience and its interaction with the sacred story by saying that:

> Bringing God's revelation into experience's intimate embrace does not diminish Scripture's holiness or compromise God's transcendence, rather it opens us more fully to the meaning of the incarnation. The religious authority of experience is rooted in a recognition of God's continuing, disturbing presence among us.[15]

While I agree with their affirmation of experience and the revelatory nature of experience I do not believe we 'bring' God's revelation into our theological reflection so much as we are open to God's revelation.

This approach to experience can be illustrated in my own life. The experience of my cancer surprised me, disrupted my life, challenged my identity, but unknowingly, unconsciously, through my experience as chaplain to a Cancer Clinic fifteen years prior to my diagnosis, I had developed an openness to many painful experiences that had confronted me, experiences that were, in the end, liberating. It was through this openness to many painful experiences that I developed a new understanding of self, my faith and of others. My present enlightened experience continues to create many new surprises in my continued understanding of self, God and other people.

I am aware of the dangers of giving precedence to experience in theological reflection. Experience must be tested and scrutinized by the tradition and the culture. As tradition and culture in theological reflection are critiqued for their ability to create new life, so too, in order to test its genuineness, integrity and lasting witness, is experience under the microscope. History can vouch for the pain and destruction when experience remains untested. The experiences that we all bring are unique and varied. Theology has been criticized for its neglect of women's experience, inattention to the diversity of cultural mores and the ongoing priority it gives privileged groups. It is hoped that the models presented for theological reflection will not only be representative, but will also be true to the many experiences of people who call for recognition.

---

[14]　James D. Whitehead and Evelyn E Whitehead 1995, *Method in Ministry – Theological Reflection and Christian Ministry*, Kansas City: Sheed and Ward, p. 45.
[15]　Ibid.

Conversation as the preferred mode of communication in theological reflection

The preferred mode of communication in theological reflection came out of a response to the complexity and remoteness of the classical models of theology and the inability of the field education discipline to develop models and methods for theological reflection. In response to this 'stuckness' the Whiteheads developed the conversational model. They point out that: 'Through much of the twentieth century, theologians have described theological method as a correlation of Christian faith and contemporary experience … to some people, correlation suggests that the interaction of faith and culture proceed on a coolly rational plane.'[16] By contrast, they propose the 'livelier metaphor of conversation' because 'when we gather to reflect on the vital implications of our faith, something more robust and less controllable than a "correlation" occurs'.[17] While I believe correlation to be an important discernment function for theological reflection it takes on new meaning when the image of theological reflection as correlation is replaced by the livelier metaphor of conversation: '*Conversation*, with its possibilities for interruption, disagreement and surprise, seems a more adequate image.'[18] Pastoral theologian Mary C. Boys endorses the metaphor of conversation when she issues a challenge to teaching faculty to adopt 'engaged pedagogues' who are grounded in dialogue and critical reflection. She says; 'Teaching that is more than mere transmission of knowledge involves entering into unfamiliar worlds – not only of texts that present radically different perspectives, but also of hearts and minds and of those whom we meet in the classroom.'[19] I have summarized some of her comments on dialogue and the art of conversation as they contain important insights concerning theological reflection.

1. In conversation one has partners, not adversaries
   Dialogue, though it does not preclude debate, resolves more around conversation than argument. Argument, however important to analytic clarity, is not everything. It does not necessarily lead to wisdom (which is an important ingredient for theological reflection). Debaters too often listen only in order to refute; they are contestants. In conversation, conversely, 'one listens to people, not just utterances. Here one comes close to people, to what they know, desire, imagine and can barely say – and a person who simply listens can be profoundly connected and filled with living force'.[20] Bernard Lonergan says a good rule about conversation is to 'be attentive, be intelligent, be responsible, be loving, and if necessary, change'.[21]

---

[16] Ibid., p. 4.

[17] Ibid., pp. 4–18. I am aware of the extraordinary contribution of Paul Tillich, and David Tracy and a number of other contributors to the understanding of theological reflection, but I have chosen for this book a different methodology and approach to theological reflection.

[18] Ibid., p. 4.

[19] Mary C. Boys 1999, 'Engaged pedagogy – dialogue and critical reflection', *Teaching Theology and Religion*, 2, 130.

[20] Ibid.

[21] See Bernard Lonergan, *Method in Theology* New York: Seabury, 1972. p. 321.

2. The sharing of ignorance should not be confused with conversation

 The art of conversation requires preparation and a 'journey towards [finding your] voice'. Participants will have difficulty finding their voice if teachers are convinced of the rightness of their own judgements and believe that conversation is beneath them. 'Conversation requires cultivating spiritual values such as humility, faith and self-denial, and includes a willingness to listen to what angers people.' [22] Conversation depends on attentive listening, regard for the other, recognition that each of us knows more than we can say and a willingness to restrain oneself in order to hear others.

3. Conversations permit us to bridge the gap between our world and another's, and blur some of the boundaries of power

 We need conversation partners so we can hear how we sound to others.

4. Lively conversations depend on students speaking in their own voice

 We need to draw others out in a way that respects their experience, and encourages them to speak authentically. Helping students to find their own voice is no easy matter, especially when they carry scars from previous educational experiences. These scars may be even more tender when students are not from the dominant culture.

5. To facilitate conversation, one needs to be comfortable with silences

 The art of conversation requires us to know when to be silent and when to speak. The art of conversation depends in large part on what Thomas Green calls a 'hermeneutics of affection',[23] a willingness to listen to the lives and loves of others.

6. Dialogue is not a mere method, it is a way of life

 Dialogue calls for attentiveness to the emotions, virtues and skills that nurture relationship. Emotional authenticity is required. Those involved in dialogue need to work on creating and maintaining bonds of mutual concern, trust, respect, appreciation and affection.

7. Conversation requires conversational partners.

 This may seem obvious, but for theological reflection purposes it is important. Therefore, from this extensive understanding of theological reflection as conversation I highlight in this book the communal aspect of theological reflection and the ingredients which make theological reflection critical enquiry.

8. Conversation must allow for difference and otherness

 While New Testament scholar Dorothy Lee and theologian David Tracy direct their remarks to the reading of the text, the principles they espouse are important for any conversation. Dorothy Lee believes and affirms that the reader has a vitally important 'role to play in discerning meaning and embracing the transformation that the text evokes'.[24] Lee says that meaning emerges in the interaction between text and reader who is drawn into the

---

[22] Boys 1999, 'Engaged pedagogy – dialogue and critical reflection', 130.

[23] Ibid., p. 131.

[24] Dorothy Lee 2002, *Flesh and Glory: Symbolism, Gender and Theology in the Gospel of John*, New York: The Crossroad Publishing Company, p. 235.

drama of the narrative and 'becomes a conversation partner in the dialogue that the text itself creates and shapes. Only by appreciating the active participation of the reader is transformation possible'.[25] David Tracy is more specific as to how the transformative process occurs when he says: 'In conversation we find ourselves, in losing ourselves in the questioning provoked by the text.'[26] And this questioning 'must allow for difference and otherness'.[27] In this sense conversation occurs only when we risk ourselves by allowing the questions of the text, however initially different, other, or even strange to our present experience; it is only then that the possibility of a similarity-in-difference can occur.[28] It is in these realms of possibilities that 'moments of recognition' can occur'.[29]

The purpose of theological reflection

Anglican parish priest Brett Morgan provides a focus for this section when he asks the question, 'What are we looking for in Theological Reflection?'[30] Morgan's study quite rightly asserts a lack of clarity among theological students and theological formation program teachers regarding the purpose of theological reflection. He says that, 'despite the rich and vibrant discussion concerning the theory and practice of theological reflection, it is ironic to note Pattison's observation:

> Students undertaking placements in pastoral studies courses are bidden with monotonous regularity to indulge in theological reflection. This activity has a mystic flavour to it, for the teachers who demand theological reflection for the most part find it very difficult to say what it is that they are looking for.'[31]

In a response to this diffusion Morgan identifies five emerging conceptions of theological reflection:

  i.   Theological reflection as method
  ii. Theological reflection as a means to develop insight
  iii. Theological reflection as a means to inform action
  iv. Theological reflection as consistent thinking
  v.   Theological reflection as critical activity.[32]

---

[25] Ibid.

[26] David Tracy 1987, *Plurality and Ambiguity: Hermeneutics, Religion, Hope*, London: SCM Press Ltd. p. 19.

[27] Ibid., p. 20.

[28] Ibid.

[29] Ibid., p. 7.

[30] Brett Morgan 1999, 'What are we looking for in theological reflection?', *Ministry, Society and Theology*, 13/2, 6–21.

[31] Ibid., 7.

[32] Ibid., 10.

Morgan believes that by understanding these conceptions they may provide a new sense of direction for clarifying what it is teachers are looking for in theological reflection. His article has been of assistance to me, a teacher who teaches a course on 'Theological Reflection on Pastoral Care'. He has sharpened and helped me articulate my understanding of theological reflection. However, while this study is helpful in identifying the different purposes of theological reflection, it does risk fragmenting a holistic understanding of theological reflection. My understanding of the purpose of theological reflection incorporates all of the above conceptions, which range in importance according to their relevance to the particular context. Therefore, the different conceptions or models that Morgan highlights contribute to the overall understanding of the purpose of theological reflection, which is integration. Theological reflection includes method, insight, action, theology and critique. It is difficult to separate these conceptions, as each is part of the theological enterprise. It is with these insights that I state the purpose of theological reflection:

> As a method for integration, theological reflection's primary focus is on what happens at the intersection of what one believes and how one lives out that belief, and the centre of this process is in the discovery of the movement of the spirit of God in human experience. In addition it seeks to know how God's presence makes a difference to one's ministry. At these intersections pastoral supervision is concerned about the congruity between belief and practice.[33]

When I refer to 'one's ministry' I do not interpret these words narrowly. It includes one's total life, which includes theological ministry.

Theological reflection as critical activity

While the congruity between the theory and practice of this stated purpose for theological reflection will be addressed and evaluated later, I will elaborate further on and add to the above definition of theological reflection. It is no easy task to examine what one believes and how one lives that belief. It requires critical and intentional activity, which can be very threatening, but in the end transforming, if a person is willing to engage the process. I have stated earlier (pp. 35ff.) the importance and priority of beginning with experience. I have also indicated that just having experience is not enough to gain insight and knowledge. Patricia A Lamoureux, a practical theologian, says: 'We need to consciously reflect upon it – describe the experience, understand, discuss, and examine it, draw insights, and test them against the insights of others. Otherwise we can just keep repeating experiences, including mistakes, again and again.'[34] This process is critical reflection because theology is critiqued by experience and experience is critiqued

---

[33]   Paver 1996, 'Formation and transformation in theological reflection,' *Ministry, Society and Theology*, 10/2, 94.

[34]   Patricia A Lamoureux 1999, 'An Integrated Approach to Theological Education,' *Theological Education*, 36/1, 145.

by theology. I also would include a cultural component in theological reflection. Further, if theological reflection is holistic and claims to be integrative it will identify, engage and challenge distortions in feelings, perceptions, assumptions, attitudes, knowledge and behaviour. As will be discussed later, self-deception is the enemy of theological reflection, not ambiguity or ambivalence.

Theological reflection is discovering the movement of the spirit of God in human experience

The purpose of theological reflection is to discover God's presence, clues to or signs of God's Spirit in human experience. Practical theologian Mary Ellen Sheehan is more definite when she writes: 'Theological reflection assumes the involvement of God in human history, which mediates his prophetic and healing presence in word and sacrament.' She goes on to say: 'But the experience and recognition of God in history requires interpretation which includes both explanation and understanding as well as commitment to responsible action toward releasing the liberative love of God that constitutes revelation.'[35] As indicated earlier, in theological reflection there are at least three points of interpretation at which God is involved: human experience, religious tradition and culture. It is my belief that God is known only partially in each of these points of interpretation or conversational partners. I believe we do an injustice to the purpose of theological reflection when we neglect some points of interpretation and highlight others. Further, the absence of some conversational partners can imply that all truth about God is discovered in selected conversational partners. Theological reflection demands that all partners be evaluated to determine both the presence and absence of God.

My definition implies that the quality of one's ministry is enhanced when we discover the presence of God. The process of theological reflection helps us to consider what difference God's presence makes in our lives and assists in the 'moment toward insight' about 'God's ongoing revelation in the world'.[36] For Sheehan the governing factor for theological reflection is 'interpretation for change'. She indicates that different models of theological reflection have evolved, but says the goal of these methods is the same; 'to discover the operative theology in the event and to move toward decision and pastoral action'.[37] If this is the case, then the selected models and methods for theological reflection will reflect a diversity of approaches.

The use of the case study reflection mode in theological reflection

Historically, the case study reflection mode has been important for TFE, especially in relation to theological reflection and pastoral supervision. It is often used to

---

[35] Mary Ellen Sheehan 1984, 'Theological reflection on theory–praxis integration', *Pastoral Sciences*, 3, 31.

[36] Lamoureux, 'An Integrated Approach to Theological Education', 145.

[37] Sheehan, *Pastoral Sciences*, p. 31.

great effectiveness in the parish and hospital settings.[38] However, the case study reflection mode is a tool common to all models and methods for theological reflection, as will be seen later.

The case study is an important source for theological reflection as it recovers data in a systematic way for theological reflection. The case study of actual events as a source for learning had its beginnings as a primary educational methodology in the late nineteenth century. It was a method utilized by the law and business schools at Harvard University.[39] Case study reflection used actual historical events as a means of teaching decision-making processes and of assisting students to apply general principles to specific incidents. This method of learning began to influence others to imitate its success. Soon called 'clinical' education, the method was adopted by other vocational disciplines whose theoretical bases were foundational to the academy. Social work embraced case reflection as a primary learning tool, as did CPE, under the leadership of Boisen in cooperation with Richard Cabot, a physician at the Harvard Medical School. Boisen referred to case studies as the 'living human documents'.[40] Case study reflection and its relation to verbatim reporting has deeply influenced the methodology of CPE and field education.

Usually, case study reflection is most effective in a group of six to eight people, although it may also be used in individual supervision where the ministry experience is discussed one to one between the supervisor and the student. The primary overall goal of the case study is to deepen the presenter's self-understanding, to sharpen his or her clarity about the forces that shape the situation of ministry and to increase the presenter's effectiveness when she or he returns to ministry. Practical theologians Jeffrey Mahan and Barbara Troxell and Pastor Carol Allen use the term 'shared wisdom', which describes the collective and collaborative wisdom of case study reflection. It respects human wisdom and the open sharing of the presenter, peer group and the supervisor. Further, they reinforce the role of the peer group in case study reflection. They believe that when writing and discussing a case, 'the presenter is always revealing and concealing' the truth about him or herself and her or his ministry. The peer group's responsibility 'is designed to identify the questions, metaphors, and images, which get under the skin and allow the presenter to bring forth the truth about herself and the ministry in which she is involved'.[41] It is through this process that people are encouraged to locate their strengths and weaknesses in their personhood and ministry. This is true not only for the presenter, but also for the presenter's peers

---

[38]   Peter K. Buttitta 1995, 'Theological reflection in health ministry: A strategy for parish nurses', in James E. Whitehead and Evelyn E. Whitehead (eds), *Method in Ministry*, pp. 112–22.

[39]   William T. Pyle and Mary Alice Seals (eds) 1995, *Experiencing Ministry Supervision*, Nashville: Broadman and Holman, p. 5.

[40]   E. B. Holifield, 'Anton Boisen 1990', in Rodney J. Hunter (ed.) *Dictionary of Pastoral Care and Counseling*, Nashville: Abingdon Press, pp. 104–5.

[41]   Jeffrey H. Mahan et al. (eds) 1993, *Shared Wisdom*, Nashville: Abingdon Press, pp. 20–1.

within the group. It is when we recognize our strengths and weaknesses that we are able to recognize the dichotomies that exist between what we believe and how we practice our ministry.

A case study may also be a written-up conversation that has taken place over a period of time and is usually completed as a ministry is being terminated. Students should provide a great deal of background material at the beginning of the case study. The report will show the ebb and flow of the experience, the dynamics among people in the situation, the various influences on the people involved and the understanding as the case evolved. A student can undertake a case study of an individual or a family or of a non-family group. A religious case study will go into the religious experiences as the individual remembers, understands and relates them, as well as the student's interpretation of the nature of these experiences. Case studies help students deal thoroughly with incidents that take place in their ministry setting. Such studies, which demand an integrative type of examination, show the perceptive ability of students.

The goal of the theological reflection stage of the case study process is interactive dialogue between the case material and our relationship with God. Weaknesses sometimes experienced in case study reflection relate to the lack of explicit attention given to the Christian tradition in regard to the pastoral concern and the difficulty experienced moving from concrete incidents to a broader theological understanding. In fact, the lack of quality theological reflection in case study reflection in both field education and CPE has been a concern for many in these disciplines. In recent years there has been a flurry of material produced to assist the searcher on how one may better do theological reflection. While guidelines for theological reflection are helpful, if we do not have the ability to make life and faith connections, use our imagination and take risks in dealing with the ambiguities of life, then our understanding of theological reflection will be restricted.

The use of models and methods

A model for theological reflection offers a way to structure the conversation. Usually, models highlight the sources of information that are important to insight and decision-making. Theologians Patricia O'Connell Killen and John de Beer indicate the dynamic nature of these sources:

> Sources are aspects of experience ... Even though we separate experience into aspects to make reflection possible, the meaning of any particular event is revealed only when we attend to those aspects or sources and their mutual relationships ... Sources for theology are constructs we put on experience to organise it.[42]

---

[42]   Patricia O'Connell Killen and John de Beer 1994, *The Art of Theological Reflection*, New York: Crossroad, p. 59.

These sources are also points for differing interpretations of the experience. Different models use different ways of dividing the flow of experience and employ different names for similar sources. For example, the Whiteheads name their sources as tradition, culture and personal and corporate experience, while theologian Joe Holland and social justice activist Peter Henriot name their sources as insertion (ministry experience), social analysis, theological reflection and pastoral planning.

The *method* describes the process, dynamic or movement of the reflection. It outlines the stages through which the conversation proceeds. Methods provide a framework for theological reflection. They are maps that can guide us. J. Mueller, a religious educator, uses an everyday working tool to describe method when he says:

> A method is a tool. Like a good multi-purpose screwdriver, a method improves upon what weak fingers and fragile fingernails cannot do. A method extends our abilities, improves upon our limitations, reminds us of forgotten procedures, and allows others to see how we arrived at our conclusions.[43]

The Whiteheads describe the processes of their method as attending, assertion and pastoral response, while for Holland and Henriot, with their sources linking justice and faith, the process is facilitated by asking questions. Who makes the decisions? Who benefits from the decisions? Who bears the cost of the decisions? It is out of a response to questions such as these that theological reflection emerges.

As the Whiteheads indicate, leaving out one or another of these conversational partners may reduce the scope of enquiry, insight and action significantly. While I will be elaborating on the Whitehead model later in this chapter it seems important at this point to highlight the consequences of a theological reflection method that neglects some sources while highlighting others. The Whiteheads illustrate this issue with the following diagram.[44]

---

[43]   J. J. Mueller, SJ 1984, *What Are They Saying About Theological Method?*, New Jersey: Paulist Press, p. 1.

[44]   Whitehead and Whitehead, *Method in Ministry*, p. 83.

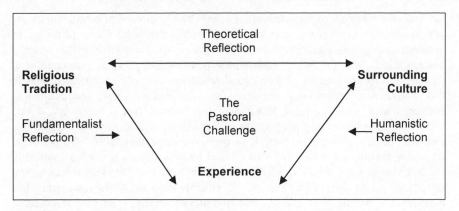

Fig. 2.1   The Whitehead model

The diagram indicates that focusing on person and tradition alone could result in a fundamentalist interpretation, on tradition and culture alone in a purely theoretical interpretation, on culture and person alone in an undifferentiated humanistic interpretation. While it is crucial to have the three conversational partners engage in dialogue in an equal relationship, if the experience of the person is omitted then it becomes an academic mode of theological reflection. If the experience of the person is not included there is no room for transformation or change. In the above diagram the Whiteheads highlight ways in which the mutuality necessary for theological reflection to be effective is lost. However, there are many other ways in which mutuality can be lost. For example, a community can be so influenced by personal experience (its awareness of the patriarchal and misogynist tendencies in the history and current life of the church) that it feels forced to reject the tradition. Overwhelmed by these negative experiences the group is unable to explore the tradition's other (and sometimes contradictory) testimony on women, personal worth, sexuality and human liberation. Here, the conversation concerning women and Christianity breaks off. It is understandable that people develop other models of theological reflection when there is less emphasis or no emphasis on a point of interpretation that they consider important to an understanding of God in their lives.

The diversity of models and methods for theological reflection reflects a diversity of concerns. I can illustrate from my own personal experience for I am constantly reflecting on my own life experience and its place within the context of my Christian faith and the influence of culture. I do not necessarily do this within the context of a group of people. However, I have discovered that when I share the outcome of my reflections with a group of people (community) my understanding of spirituality and community is enhanced. Personal reflection can become individualistic and privatized if there is a refusal to declare the results of at least some of your reflections to your community. I do my community and myself an injustice when I am unwilling to share the outcome of my personal reflections. On the other hand, when I reflect theologically within a group of people I am aware that I am the recipient of the wisdom and diversity of opinions of others, which are not necessarily available to me in my personal reflection. There is room for personal and group theological reflection and each complements the other. I believe this is how the Whiteheads would interpret the personal and communal contribution to the process of theological reflection. As will be indicated later in this book, life experiences demand that we include new and surprising conversational partners in our theological reflection. I would agree that if one understands the theory and the process of theological reflection in its totality, one can start in any place. However, it is my experience that those who advocate beginning theological reflection with biblical texts or church teachings frequently fail to come to terms with experience, which I believe to be the key to theological reflection. As O'Connell Killen and de Beer remind us; 'When we enter our experience – narrate it attentively and non-judgementally – we find it saturated with feeling.'[45] I am aware of the dangers of narrow self-interests and self-deception, which impede theological reflection, but I am also acutely aware of the dangers of decision-making that neglects the value of experience.

Systematic theologian Lucien Richard is more adamant about the place of experience in theology when he writes:

> Man cannot submit ultimately to an authority outside of himself. Truth cannot be attained unless a man is attuned to what goes on within himself ... There can be no dualism of theology and the faith experience. Theology must be a process whereby that experience is reflexively understood, articulated in propositions and embodied in language. There is no thematization and experience, but a thematized experience ... Personal faith invites discovery. The motivational force behind theological reflection is the need to explore the unknown ... It is not easy to establish a balanced relationship between the message and experience. But the more we separate and oppose these two elements, the more we reach an impasse, and the more the integration of classroom theology and field experience becomes impossible.[46]

This impasse to which Richard refers becomes obvious in the TRS and the proposed open-ended curriculum.

The diverse models and methods for theological reflection that will be presented provide another angle of vision for the place of a particular understanding of theological reflection in theological education. I am aware that the angle of vision that results from the use of particular models and methods provides knowledge that is always partial and inadequate, but is, I must say, never false or merely subjective. The outcome of theological reflection may not always be the right action, but it should always be action based upon an informed decision.

I have selected three models and methods that represent different approaches to formation and integration in theological reflection.

---

[45]   O'Connell and de Beer 1967, *The Art of Theological Reflection*, p. 27.

[46]   Lucien Richard 1972, 'The existing malaise in the theologizing of field experience', *Theological Education*, Autumn, 67–70. The language is dated in this article but the truth in it remains.

Experiencing God through ministry – the ministry model[47]

As noted earlier the Whiteheads originated a systematic approach to theological reflection in field education. Their work was formally documented in *Method in Ministry: Theological Reflection and Christian Ministry*, published in 1980 and republished in 1995 with added chapters and a deeper understanding of the listening metaphor. Their work is basic to most subsequent writing on theological reflection.

The model

The Whiteheads begin by saying that: 'Theological reflection in ministry instigates a conversation among three sources of religiously relevant information – the experience of the community of faith, the Christian tradition, and the resources of the culture.'[48] Their own diagram outlines the model.

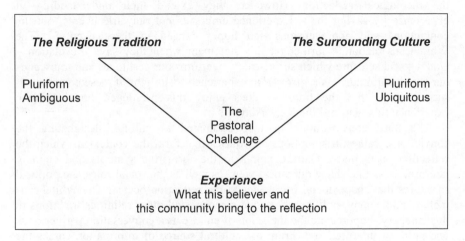

Fig. 2.2   Theological reflection in ministry

The three corners of the diagram correspond to the three sources of theological reflection.[49] The pastoral challenge represents the data for theological reflection. An important criterion for their model is that each pole or source is recognized as plural and ambiguous in its contribution to reflection and action. That is, there may be different interpretations within the religious tradition, for instance, on the matter of recognition and ordination of homosexuals in the life of the church.

The Christian tradition includes Scripture, the history of the church with its own multiple and changing interpretations of the Bible and its own life, which

---

[47]   Named and influenced primarily by James and Evelyn Whitehead.

[48]   Whitehead and Whitehead, *Method in Ministry*, p. 6.

[49]   The three conversation partners involve the Christian Tradition, personal experience and culture, pp. 6-12.

bears on concrete pastoral concerns. The Whiteheads emphasize the importance of 'befriending the tradition', not so much in the sense of intellectual mastery of it, but of developing intimacy with it as a readily available source.[50] The recognition of plurality and ambiguity within the religious tradition gives rise to further feeling as this model concedes 'the voice of our religious heritage enjoys a privileged position'.[51] This is an interesting statement as the Whiteheads' theological conviction is that God resides in the three points of interpretation. In their model God is only partially found in each source; it is through conversation and dialogue with the three sources that a more comprehensive understanding of God's presence is found in this world.

The second conversational partner is the personal experience of the person and the collective experience of the faith communities the person represents. They concede that experience is difficult to define, but for the Whiteheads the starting point for theological reflection usually is experience, which refers to all those ideas, feelings, biases and insights that people and communities bring to the theological reflection. However, they extend their understanding of experience by saying that: 'Experience embraces not only life events, but the convictions and apprehensions and hopes carried in these events.'[52] The Whiteheads elaborate further on this statement when they say: 'Revelation – God's self-disclosure which surprises us, overturns our certitudes and transcends our best imaginings – is *registered* in experience.'[53] In light of these comments it surprises me that the tradition does enjoy this privileged position, with experience 'instigat[ing] the conversation'.[54]

The third conversational partner is named as culture, designating the convictions, values, assumptions and biases that form the context in which the reflection takes place. Culture points to the formative symbols and ongoing interpretations that shape our world view, as well as the social roles and political structures that shape social life in which the reflection occurs. The Whiteheads include philosophy, politics, the social sciences and other religious traditions in this category. I appreciate the inclusion of culture as a conversation partner or as one point of interpretation. From the cultural source of information comes the biases and convictions that are inscribed in our history, philosophy and linguistic past as Australians. Further, our culture is being increasingly influenced and shaped by immigrants and a renewed understanding of what it means to be Aboriginal. For instance, Aboriginal culture is beginning to challenge our traditional understanding of theology. Similarly, we are being shaped by contemporary prejudices about sexuality and personal commitment. I agree with the Whiteheads that we are gifted by the insights of cultural forces such as the social sciences and the women's movement. We have underplayed the significance of the impact of cultural forces that surround us. They have the

---

[50]   Ibid., p. 9.
[51]   Ibid.
[52]   Ibid., p. 43.
[53]   Ibid., p. 45.
[54]   Ibid., p. 9.

possibility of informing or de-forming us; it is for this reason that culture needs to be scrutinized and made accountable in any model that contributes to ministerial reflection and action.

The Method

The method of reflection suggests a process by which we pursue communal discernment.

The first stage in the method is *listening* or *attending*. In fact, listening is the key to theological reflection. Without listening, it is very difficult to proceed. Listening gives credibility to an enterprise. Listening in the context of theological reflection means listening to ourselves, which includes listening to our fears, prejudices and assumptions of what we believe and what we don't believe. It includes what we think and what we feel and invites us to be honest about that as we converse with the tradition, the culture and ourselves. Most importantly, it involves being open to what the other conversational partners have to say to us.

Listening to others requires that we not only listen, but that we are also receptive to what we are hearing. It means taking a non-judgemental attitude to the partner(s) in the conversation. It has been previously indicated that the stance of listening assumes that all partners in the conversation are equal and that there is only a partial understanding of God in the tradition, culture and our own experience. For many, this is a difficult place to start, but it is an essential beginning point in all methods of theological reflection. In fact, there are some who believe the beginning point of listening in reflection to be so essential that they advocate the spiritual discipline of asceticism, which requires an exercise in self-emptying. The discipline of spiritual asceticism has been developed from the *kenosis* (emptiness) understanding of the servanthood of Christ.[55] As Jesus Christ 'empties himself, taking the form of a servant' (Philippians 2:7), so people who undertake theological reflection empty themselves to allow space for discernment of the spirit of God in their human experience. Such a movement of emptying applies whether the person is listening to the tradition, the culture or the stirrings within an individual's own life. It means we empty ourselves of our own agenda, which includes those convictions and prejudices, hopes and distractions that can accompany us and, indeed, prejudice the reflective process. While this advice is almost impossible for many of us to achieve, at least we should be aware of the convictions and prejudices that we take into our theological reflection. A significant element of the challenge of listening, whether to a text or another person, is the suspension of interpretation and judgement until we have thoroughly heard. If we assume the meaning of this text in advance, we fail to listen fully.

The second stage in the process of interpretation is that of *assertion*. By this the Whiteheads mean bringing the perspectives gathered from the three sources of conversation into a lively dialogue of mutual clarification in order to expand and enrich religious insight. It means having the courage to share our convictions and the willingness to be challenged. This process requires a fluidity and flexibility that

---

[55]   Ibid., p. 73.

make us capable of shifting from one viewpoint to another. In perhaps a more aggressive tone narrative theologian George Stroup describes this process as a 'collision of narratives'.[56] In this conversational method of theological reflection, interpretation means the give and take of conversation, teaching and learning, disagreement and conflict. It means offering a viewpoint from my angle of vision in the midst of all the other angles of vision that have been offered. It means asking hard questions, perhaps knowing that there is no answer, or being prepared to receive answers we did not expect. While this stage of interpretation can be a threatening time for participants, people are more likely to change in an environment of hospitality and humility than in a combative atmosphere. It is in this atmosphere of acceptance that, as time goes by, we grow more adept at moving among multiple interpretative viewpoints, comparing and contrasting and integrating them while taking stock of their relative merits.

Once again, the Whiteheads are helpful in identifying three attitudes that assist in the assertion or interpretative stage of theological reflection. These are *self-awareness, self-disclosure* and *self-worth*.[57] By self-awareness they mean that attitude which puts us in touch with the dense and ambiguous information of our own life: Self-disclosure means we are able to expresses ourselves in appropriate ways. It does not mean telling all, but it does require that we are able to describe our experience, share our vision, tell one another what we feel and think about the issues that touch our common life: Self-worth helps us to be assertive. As well as knowing our insights, needs and purposes we must value them and speak of them. By valuing them we help others appreciate them too. The issue of self-worth is an ongoing concern for people undertaking theological reflection, as most people tend to claim less for themselves rather than more. To enter this process of interpretation is to begin to form a pastoral identity. It is, therefore, important that an atmosphere receptive to theological reflection is present in groups.

It is at the point of assertion that theological reflection often stalls or breaks down. Theological reflection is an art, but it is also more than this. It is often a complicated and serious business. It has the potential to change people's theology, if not their lives. The model is simple, but issues of authority can complicate the method. I have witnessed resistance to culture and experience because theology has been the key to a person's personal and religious identity. Theological reflection can be strained for the student when there is a particular authority claim on religious values. However, it is important to note that this model assumes both the presence and the difference of these authorities. It is important for the student to recognise and know that there is leeway in theological reflection. James Whitehead has written *The Practical Play of Theology*, which advocates the importance of play, leeway (how much we can give without regret) and the use of imagination in theological reflection.[58] While he acknowledges theological

---

[56]   George W. Stroup 1981, *The Promise of Narrative Theology*, Student Christian Movement, p. 17.

[57]   Whitehead, *Method in Ministry*, pp. 80–1.

[58]   James D. Whitehead 1987, 'The Practical Play of Theology', in Lewis S. Mudge and James Poling (eds), *Formation and Reflection*, Philadelphia: Fortress Press, pp. 36–54.

reflection as a serious business he encourages us to enjoy ourselves, take risks and to recognize that models and methods are guides for ministerial action and do not tell us all about the place of God in human experience. The information gained by listening we then bring into dialogue with assertion and with the hope that this dynamic interaction will generate insight as to how we should respond.

Pastoral response

The challenge of the third movement of the method is to translate ideas into action. The effectiveness of this stage depends on the quality of the earlier reflection. Integrative pastoral decisions are expressive of and in continuity with the insights obtained from listening and assertion. At this point the Whiteheads indicate a crucial difference between theological decisions and ministerial decisions. It is apparent they are writing for the theological practitioner when they say:

> The minister reflects in order to act. In the face of insufficient information or conflicting facts, a reflection accountable only to the criteria of academic theology can decide not to decide. Instead the theologian can, appropriately, reinitiate the process of reflection in the hope of coming to greater clarity sometime in the future. A ministerial reflection most generally focuses on the question that demands practical resolution now. In many situations the community must act even in the face of partial information.[59]

The last comment infers that theological reflection will not guarantee that the right decisions will always be taken, only that action will be well informed and, potentially, more accurate. I don't believe the Whiteheads intend to minimize the place of academic theology in the process of decision-making; indeed, there are many long-term ethical decisions that need to be mulled over and many decisions have long-term ramifications for the life of the church and society. I would hope that the academic theologians would also give credence to the efficacy of informed ministerial decisions, as they too are crucial to the wellbeing of the people we serve. I have stated that this model is simple, but the method can lack depth if it is not taken seriously. If there is a criticism of this model, it is the lack of structure that exists between the assertion and decision stages.

Adaptation of the model

I have adapted the Whiteheads' model in my ministry in a hospital setting where the social sciences have significant influence. The pastoral concern was focused on a woman with terminal cancer. The tradition was represented by her faith and denominational tradition and I, the chaplain, represented the experience point of interpretation. Doctors, nurses, paramedical staff (psychiatrist, psychologist, occupational and art therapist, social worker) represented the cultural point of interpretation. As chaplain, I was given the responsibility by the medical team to present a case study on this courageous woman to enable the team to reflect on it in

---

[59]   Whitehead and Whitehead, *Method in Ministry*, p. 16.

order to improve our care of her. While the ongoing presentations were not labelled 'theological' they were some of the most significant theological reflections I have ever undertaken. The following case study reflection mode provided an ongoing critical dialogue within a communal setting. It was not only significant for the patient and me, but also for the team.

Patient: Vivienne
Referred by: Everyone
Observations:
Vivienne is a 45-year-old divorced woman who has been a patient on ward for a number of weeks. Vivienne is a long-term patient with a progressive disease and has social, psychological and spiritual issues in her life. She is well known by most staff, who have patiently and loyally cared for her over a long period. She has a very low image of herself emotionally and physically.

Comments:
Vivienne alienates people because she:
• manipulates
• makes carers and family helpless and angry
• is demanding
• creates ambivalence
• divides and conquers through comparisons

Strengths:
• Vivienne is grateful for the care given
• She has insight
• She has a developing sense of humour
• She has a strong denial system
• She is independent and stubborn
• She has a strong religious faith

Pastoral care issues:
• Vivienne's fundamentalist faith has led her to deny her illness for some time. In her view, to admit to her cancer would mean a denial of her faith – 'People with strong faith do not get cancer.' Her former husband also subscribes to this view.
• The gradual recognition that she has cancer has undermined the structure of her faith. 'The Bible says this … [is] good … but what good is it to me?' This ambivalence is the result of a gap between feeling and believing.
• Vivienne's faith is not particularly helpful at the moment because she feels 'empty inside'.
• Vivienne has a great need to know that someone special (one person) loves her. While the visit by her former husband did not completely fulfil her expectations, she feels that the visit was important to her in that it demonstrated that he may still care for her, and in fact, even love her.

My responses:
• Initially I did not like Vivienne, but have come to like and respect her.
• I have resisted her manipulative and divide-and-conquer behaviours.

- I have tried to affirm her faith in a realistic way as she struggles with her ambivalence towards it. Sometimes she asked me to read the Bible and sing hymns with her, which I have done.
- I have acted as a reflector of feelings and thoughts for her.
- Vivienne does not trust men, which includes her current pastor. I have been careful not to intensify that mistrust.
- I suspect that her 'empty feelings' have been with her for most of her life. It may be too late to address this issue. She may die as she has lived. I hope not.
- I have encouraged her pastor and church friends to continue to visit her, as these are the people who have been consistent in her life.
- Vivienne will require ongoing spiritual care once she leaves the hospital.
- I have encouraged and deliberately elicited her mischievous sense of humour.
- I have tried to be her pastor during her stay in hospital.

As chaplain I presented updates on this case study. There was a considerable amount of interaction between the psychiatrist and I. While I agreed with him that there were emotional issues to be dealt with it was my opinion that Vivienne's present crisis was a spiritual one. The reality of her cancer was in conflict with her understanding of her faith. Vivienne took up the invitation to attend one of the team meetings. It was an overwhelming experience for her, but it allowed her to have some say in her care and treatment. Vivienne was eventually transferred to a hospice; she died there. During her time at the hospice I visited her and prayed with her. It was not a peaceful death as she continued to wrestle with a confused understanding of God in her life. The team, upon hearing of her death, spontaneously went to a hotel and celebrated her life and death. Vivienne, in her own way, had touched each of our lives.

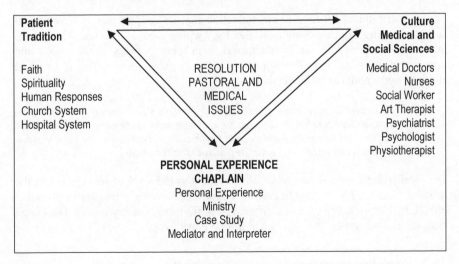

Fig. 2.3   **Ministry model – hospital setting**

Through adapting the ministry model in a hospital setting we are able to identify the following strengths and limitations of this model.

Findings

Strengths

• The case study reflection mode was not only an effective tool for eliciting the important pastoral issues, but it also provided the focus for a spiritual community.
• Vivienne's tradition (personal faith) was not only respected and befriended by the hospital team, but it was also acted upon.
• Vivienne's experience was taken seriously.
• The social sciences (hospital team) deepened and informed our understanding of the woman's diagnosis and prognosis, which resulted in appropriate medical and pastoral action.

Limitations

• There was an overemphasis on personal experience, to the exclusion of a social analysis of the cultural forces within and without the hospital setting (for example, the ethos of the hospital and the negative and positive influences of Vivienne's church and family).

Experiencing God through culture – the praxis model[60]

The ministry model for theological reflection focuses on personal and communal action emerging from an operational theology within a certain context. Contextual interest is sharpened in the praxis model, which has a focus on liberation and transformation of a culture that oppresses and diminishes people. This is a radical and impatient model as it asserts that:

> True Christianity ... must work against such oppressive structures not just seeking to change certain features, but by seeking to supplant them completely. Liberation and transformation, not just gradual development or friendly persuasion, is the only way that men and women can fulfil their call to be genuine children of God.[61]

The model works on the conviction that 'truth is at the level of history, not in the realm of ideas'.[62] The method begins with experience, but the dominant voice is that of culture, culture interpreted in a different way from the ministry model. The model has a distinctive and unique history and it is here that I begin.

---

[60] Credited to Holland, Henriot and Stephen B. Bevans

[61] Stephen B Bevans 1996, *Models of Contextual Theology*, New York: Orbis Books, pp. 66.

[62] Ibid., p. 64.

History of the praxis model[63]

Jon Sobrino, a theologian working in El Salvador, provides an insight into the method of the praxis model by making the point that the most significant difference between what he called 'European theology' and Latin American theology is rooted in a different response to the two moments of modernity. The first moment, characterized by the thoughts of philosophers René Descartes and, especially, Immanuel Kant, introduces the idea of rationality and subjective responsibility. The modern turn to the subject was revolutionary, for then it became clear that 'nothing is either true faith or right morality, which is not our own; and that, in consequence, external authority is, in principle, an unsound basis, and individual judgement, not merely a right but a duty'.[64] The outcome of this revolution in thinking was that theology could no longer seriously argue solely from authority if it was to be credible in the world. 'Proof texting' from the Bible or church teaching was insufficient, and what became necessary was, first, by rigorous use of the historical–critical method, to find out what the church really believed and whether such belief was still necessary. Rational reflection then sought to probe the meaning of what was to be believed.

The second moment Sobrino attributes to Karl Marx. Marx's breakthrough was his discovery that rationality – or intellectual knowledge – was not enough to constitute genuine knowledge. Even personally appropriated knowledge, while better than believing on someone else's authority, was not enough. We know best, Marx insisted, when our knowledge is coupled with and challenged by our action – when we are not just the objects of historical process, but also its subjects. With this understanding theology becomes much more than simply thinking clearly and meaningfully; it becomes a way of articulating one's faith that leads from one's Christian commitments to a particular way of acting and sets the agenda for an even more thoughtful and committed plan of action in the future. Latin Americans, says Sobrino, orient themselves to this understanding of theology. For them, theology finds its fulfilment not in mere 'right thinking' (*orthodoxy*), but in 'right acting' (*orthopraxy*).[65]

When we speak of the praxis model we are speaking about a model in which the central insight is that theology is done not simply by providing relevant expressions of Christian faith, but also by commitment to Christian action. Even more than this, theology is understood as a product of the continual dialogue of these two aspects of Christian life. The praxis model employs a method which, 'in its most profound sense is understood as the unity [integration] of knowledge as activity and knowledge as content'.[66] The two cannot be separated, just as knowing and being cannot be separated. As a method for theological reflection it is reflected-upon action and acted-upon reflection, both rolled into one.

---

[63] I am indebted to Bevans for the historical background to the praxis model.
[64] Bevans, *Models of Contextual Theology*, p. 64.
[65] Ibid., p. 65.
[66] Ibid.

The praxis model is also often referred to as the 'liberation model'. The reason for this is that it has been the political theologians (for example, Jurgen Moltmann) in Europe and the liberation theologians, particularly those in Latin America, who have developed this model in particular ways. The feminist and womanist movements have also taken on the liberation theme to describe their concerns and aims. As closely as the theology of liberation is associated with the praxis model, Stephen Bevans, a missiologist, chooses to continue speaking of it as the praxis model for two reasons. First, he indicates that the context may not necessarily have to take on liberation themes as there are contexts in which structural injustice is not rampant. However, in such instances one could still theologically reflect on one's actions. Second, and perhaps more relevant to our discussion, is that 'the term reveals more clearly than [the] *liberation model* that the specificity of the model is not one of a particular theme, but one of a particular *method*'.[67]

Theoretical structure

The strength of this model is in its method and undergirding theory. The model and method provide a systematic and probing tool, which guarantees an outcome for theological reflection. Bevans suggests it be seen as a process of 'faith seeking intelligent action'.[68] The intelligence is inherent in its philosophical history, but I would want to go further and say that the intelligence is in the method or the process. The intelligence is that the method stems from actions and struggles and works out of a theoretical base (social analysis being one expression) that illuminates and examines these actions. While the ministry model addresses these issues in the assertion and ministry decision stages of the method, it is not as incisive or systematic; nor does it act with the depth of the praxis model. It is by acting and then reflecting on that action in faith that practitioners of the praxis model believe one can develop a theology that is truly relevant to a particular context.

It is clear that the praxis methodology is committed to privileging marginal perspectives – primarily that of the poor. Theologians Holland and Henriot outline their perspectives and biases because they feel strongly that the type of social analysis for pastoral action today 'should be heavily value-laden'.[69] The integrating aim of their method is to link faith and justice and, to this end, they have developed a method called 'the pastoral circle'.[70] They choose a circle to suggest that the process is ongoing. 'It is related to what has been called the "hermeneutic circle", or the method of interpretation that sees new questions continually raised to challenge older theories by the force of new situations.'[71] Four moments form the pastoral circle.

---

[67]   Ibid., p. 66.

[68]   Ibid., p. 67.

[69]   Joe Holland and Peter Henriot 1992, *Social Analysis-Linking Faith and Justice*, New York: Orbis Books, p. 6 – First edition 1980.

[70]   The pastoral circle involves four moments: Insertion (experience), social analysis, theological reflection and pastoral planning. pp. 8-9.

[71]   Ibid., p. 8.

The pastoral circle

Experience is the basis for the analysis. The first moment is *insertion* into the lived experience of individuals and communities. People's feelings and responses to what is happening in their lives constitute the data for reflection. Taking people's experience seriously as the locus of religiously significant information demands that we reflect upon experience from a participant's perspective. This is similar to the listening or attending process in the ministry model, but in this model the listening is focused on answers to specific questions.

> Where and with whom are we locating ourselves as we begin ourselves, as we begin our process? Whose experience is being considered? Are there groups that are 'left out' when experience is discussed? Does the experience of the poor and oppressed have a privileged role to play in the process?[72]

The experiences of people and communities must be understood in the richness of all their interrelationships.

The second moment involves a critical *social analysis* of the situation. Data gathered from the economic, social, political and cultural arenas are analyzed to discover linkages, to identify causes and to plan for action. We remember that the personal is political and ask: Who benefits from the situation? Who pays for it – economically, physically, psychologically or spiritually? Who wins? Who loses? How did the system, institution, situation, develop? What values are exhibited? Holland and Henriot state that: 'Social analysis can be defined as the effort to obtain a more complete picture of the social situation by exploring its *historical and structural relationships.*'[73] Philip Berryman is a little sharper in his definition when he says the praxis theory is constructed 'as a tool for cutting through the appearance and getting at the heart of things'.[74]

Social analysis explores reality in a variety of dimensions. Sometimes it focuses on isolated issues, such as immigration, the homeless or inflation. At other times it focuses on the policies that address these issues, such as population control, housing policy and monetary control. Reaching beyond issues, policies and structures, social analysis ultimately focuses on systems. Holland and Henriot write: 'The questions posed by social analysis unmask the underlying values that shape the perspectives and decisions of those acting within a given situation.'[75]

The third moment is *theological reflection*. As we have seen in the models and methods for theological reflection there is a strong link between, and dialogue with, the other sources for interpretation: Praxis models are no different. For Holland and Henriot the link between faith and justice requires that the outcome of theological reflection emerges from analysis, questions and new insights. It is their contention that: 'The Word of God brought to bear upon the situation raises new questions,

---

[72] Ibid., p. 9.
[73] Holland and Henriot, *Social Analysis*, p. 14.
[74] Philip Berryman 1987, *Liberation Theology*, Chicago: Myer, Stone, p. 85.
[75] Holland and Henriot, *Social Analysis*, p. 15.

suggests new insights, and opens new responses.'[76] However, they do not outline a process by which to achieve those goals. In a refreshingly frank admission the authors state that 'the theological reflection we need is difficult to find in North America'.[77] Once again, they suggest a framework for theological reflection, but they are hesitant themselves to undertake this task. Their remarks are designed to generate a local theology for the American context rather than import a process 'to our particular cultural environment'.[78]

Holland and Henriot emphasize that social analysis has a close connection with theological reflection. In the pastoral circle the two are closely related, effectively linking faith with justice. In the actual practice of analysis in a pastoral situation the theological and the social interpenetrate. It is for this reason that they suggest we begin our social analysis with certain theological presuppositions, that is, that we have values and biases, which come from our faith and from the tradition of the Christian community. These shape and orient our questions. They also assert that we practise our theological reflection with some implicit sociological understandings, concerning, for example, the structure of the church and the relationship of culture and the Word of God. These implicit sociological and theological assumptions and understandings, they believe, are influenced by 'root metaphors'.[79] They suggest that there are two root metaphors that compete for our loyalty and understanding of our view of life. These are the mechanistic root metaphor and the artistic root metaphor. Ideally, the mechanistic drive in society seeks to free humanity from its chains to nature and tradition. But the drive of the machine (or technology) has now become all-consuming. It is dissolving the nation's spiritual depth, converting people to objects and becoming increasingly destructive. Designed to free humanity, the mechanistic (or technological) society is now trying to make humanity and the earth into its slaves, but is at risk of destroying both.

Against this root metaphor a second root metaphor is emerging as an antidote to protect the preciousness of humanity and the earth. It is the artistic root metaphor which, rather than seeing society as a scientific machine, proposes a vision of society as a work of art, flowing from the creativity of rooted communities in solidarity with each other. It is this emphasis on root metaphors, Holland and Henriot contend, that helps us to understand the interpenetrating of the social and the theological and so brings together the creative strains in the understanding of social realities and religious dimensions.[80] It is not clear in their understanding of theological reflection whether 'theologizing' takes place in each moment of the pastoral circle. Bevans removes some of this uncertainty by advocating the integration of analysis and the Bible and tradition in his configuration of the praxis model. He suggests a spiral figure with the following points of interpretation:

---

[76]   Ibid., p. 9.

[77]   Ibid., p. 93.

[78]   Robert J. Schreiter 1996, *Constructing Local Theologies*, New York: Orbis Books. In this book Schreiter develops models and methods for constructing local theologies.

[79]   Holland and Henriot, *Social Analysis*, p. xvi.

[80]   Ibid., xviii-xxi.

- committed action
- reflection
  - analysis of action and situation
  - rereading the Bible and tradition
- committed and intelligent action (praxis).[81]

In this configuration the theological reflection part of the spiral would come from an integrated analysis of all the issues under scrutiny. I am one of those people who believe that theologizing takes place in the whole process. Bevans, in discussing where theology is located in this praxis process, says:

> One might do better to think of theologizing as taking place in the entire process. As one acts, one knows in a way that is only augmented by reflection ... and as one acts more consciously, one knows even more clearly. The articulation of faith is in intelligent action (praxis) itself.[82]

The fourth moment in the circle is *pastoral planning*. This moment requires not rashness, but carefully planned and executed action. The questions here are: How might things be different? What can we do to make them different? This moment takes seriously the obligation to act, but just as seriously the obligation to take intelligent action. What do we think will really facilitate change in an oppressive situation? What can we do to redeem, heal and liberate? What is the ministry to which God is calling us? Holland and Henriot remind us that a response to action in a particular situation brings about new experiences. These experiences in turn call for further mediation through insertion, analysis, reflection and planning. Therefore, the pastoral circle continues without final conclusion. In fact, it is more of a spiral than a circle, so that each approach does not simply retrace old steps, but breaks new ground.

Culture and its relationship to faith

In the ministry model, culture is given equal status with tradition and experience. Culture in the ministry model includes philosophy, politics, the social sciences and other religious traditions and all or any of these may have a positive or negative influence on the outcome of theological reflection. While the ministry model includes culture as an interpretative pole, in actual practice it is the conversation partner who receives less attention than the other two partners and when it is included, it is recognized often in the form of human values and behaviours.

The praxis model places greater emphasis on cultural and social change, which includes political and economic systems, and assumes that any articulation of faith cannot be politically or economically neutral. The praxis model affirms the basic goodness of creation and the continued presence of God's Spirit in the world and history. Holland states:

---

[81]   Bevans, *Models of Contextual Theology*, pp. 68–9.
[82]   Ibid., p. 69–70.

The deepest source of cultural energies, indeed the deepest source of all human creativity, flows from *participation in divine creativity* [Holland's emphasis]. The creativity of human culture is humanity's participation in the creative Spirit of God who brooded over the waters in Genesis and still moves with the depths of human civilization.[83]

His language is just as striking when he describes the destructive side of culture: 'But in the crises of our present civilization these energies of creativity are being converted on a massive scale into energies of destruction.'[84] It is at the intersection of creativity and destruction in our culture that the praxis model focuses its interests.

This model proposes a rereading of the Gospel and Christian tradition within particular contexts, coupled with communal reflection on ways to develop more of a community sense as a way of correcting some of the destructive forces within our culture.

An understanding of revelation

The ministry model affirms the partial understanding of God in each of the three conversation partners. It is through critical dialogue with the human and the divine operating in the three conversation partners that we attempt to discover the presence of God in human experience in order that we might act. The praxis model understands revelation as 'the presence of God in history – in the events of everyday life, in social and economic structures, in situations of oppression'.[85] The praxis model is hospitable in that 'God's presence is one of beckoning and invitation, calling men and women of faith to locate God and cooperate with God in God's work of healing, reconciling, liberating'.[86] Further, all women and men are equally invited to locate God's presence in history. Theological reflection is not just the priority of professional theologians; it is also a communal exercise in which all men and women are called to theologize. This praxis model of theology has seen a development in basic ecclesial communities and Bible sharing groups, from where a theology emerges that belongs not to one individual but also to the community as a whole.

Adaptation of the model

The praxis model has been adapted and modified by the SUMP, established as a cooperative effort by the UCTC and the Hotham Uniting Church Parish Mission.[87]

---

[83]   Holland and Henriot, *Social Analysis*, p. xiii.
[84]   Ibid.
[85]   Bevans, *Models of Contextual Theology*, p. 68.
[86]   Ibid.
[87]   A copy of the handbook is available from me. SUMP has been accredited by the Victorian Association for Theological Education and is accredited for the degree of the BTheol by the MCD. The teaching faculty at UCTC has also successfully evaluated it. The supervisory team of SUMP has been appointed to the adjunct teaching staff at UCTC.

Students from UCTC can receive credit for field education toward their BTheol degree. SUMP has provided the UCTC and the TFE program with an opportunity to be involved in a different educational program than that of the methodology of CPE.

The work of Holland and Henriot has been important to SUMP, for social analysis is one voice that contributes to the theological reflection conversation on the practice of urban ministry. However, these authors struggle to present a less complicated way of conducting social analysis and theological reflection based on this methodology. It is for this reason they have included in the revised edition of their book a new chapter on a practical methodology that includes a way of undertaking theological reflection.[88] The key to the presentation of the social analysis component of SUMP lies in the creative presentation of the material by the pastoral supervisor. It is the supervisor's warmth and understanding of the process that enables this program to work. The social analysis in SUMP unmasks oppressive voices through the use of case studies of pastoral events, networking assignments, reading, placements and evaluations.

One effective tool in the program is liturgy. Participants are required to present a liturgy that is linked to their placements, and then to reflect on its importance for the course. We find that these tools for social analysis unmask humanity's enormous capacity for self-justification and, in doing so, may save us from being captive to the taken-for-granted justifications of urban life. The task of theological reflection in urban ministry is to deepen our awareness of God's purposes in creation, to confess the fallen-ness or alienation of the urban situation in which we minister and to identify and respond to God's calling for us to participate in God's redemptive work. To engage in social analysis is often overwhelming for practitioners within the program, but we find that the very depth of this struggle provides insight into the experiences of those whose lives are constrained by these factors. In being open to the process of social analysis, urban ministry participants are encouraged to wait upon God. Social analysis does not determine strategies or actions. Rather, it is driven by a question that comes out of engagement and marshals information and understandings that contribute to the question. The information is then brought into a conversation with material derived from a process of spiritual discernment and reflection upon Scripture, tradition and the current experience of the church. The process of spiritual discernment used in SUMP is based on the writings of Walter Wink in his trilogy on the Powers.[89] The theological reflection conversation between the three voices of Scripture, tradition and experience proceeds by way of correlation, disjunction and imagination. The outcome of this reflection is a decision of faith, whether it is to act, to reflect further or to change the question in light of new insight.

---

[88] Holland and Henriot, *Social Analysis*, pp. 95–105.

[89] Walter Wink 1986, *Naming the Powers*, Philadelphia: Fortress Press; see also *Unmasking the Powers*, Philadelphia: Fortress Press, 1986, and *Engaging the Powers*, Philadelphia: Fortress Press, 1992.

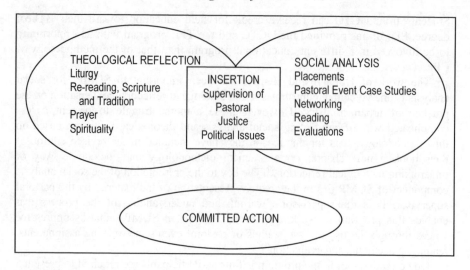

Fig. 2.4   Praxis model – supervised urban ministry

Through adapting the praxis model in SUMP we are able to identify the following strengths and limitations of the model.

Findings

Strengths

- Social analysis is an effective method in unmasking the injustice of oppressive systems and structures, especially as it relates to the poor and the oppressed in society. The method as critical reflection is more detailed and effective than the ministry model.
- The method engages the participants in the struggle of injustice and oppression in society. There is a strong emphasis on the potential for redemption and evil in culture.
- The model makes a connection between faith and justice

Limitations

- The model diminishes the importance of personal experience and places more emphasis on corporate experience.
- The experience of SUMP indicates that the model is too scientific and overwhelming; it also lacks warmth. Spirituality and systematic theologian Ronald Rolheister speaks of the importance of the 'mellowness of heart and spirit' when understanding the ministry of social justice.[90] Rolheister says we will not succeed in this ministry if our actions issue forth from anger and guilt.

---

[90]   Ronald Rolheiser 1999, *The Holy Longing*, New York: Doubleday, pp. 66–7.

It is important to have a grateful heart. The key to these difficulties is the role of the pastoral supervisor who can provide the warmth, a grateful heart and skills to present the intricacies of the model in a creative and simple way. However, it is sometimes difficult to have a grateful heart when you are oppressed.

- Some of our participants are put off because of its Marxist origins and because the method sometimes gets too close to the oppression in their own institutions, the church. To act may have severe repercussions, a cost too much to contemplate.
- My criticism of the model is that it concentrates on what is negative in society and does not recognize manifestations of grace in society.

Holland and Henriot acknowledge that the social analysis methodology is complicated and therefore they propose a simpler terminology. They warn that the following methodology requires some background if this simpler approach is used.

Social analysis: a practical methodology

1. What do you notice about our situation here today? What are people experiencing?
2. What changes have occurred in the last twenty years? What have been the most important events?
3. What influence does money have in our situation? Why?
4. Who makes the most important decisions around here? Why?
5. What are the most important relationships people have here? Why?
6. What are the most important traditions of the people? Why?
7. What do people want most in life? Why?
8. What will things be like in ten years if they keep on going in the same way? Why?
9. What are the most important causes of the way things are today? Why?
10. What did you learn from all of this?[91]

Experiencing God through personal experience – the transcendental model[92]

Mark 2:21–22 can introduce this model of theological reflection.

No one sews a piece of unshrunk cloth on an old cloak; otherwise, the patch pulls away from it, the new from the old, and a worse tear is made. And no one puts new wine into old wineskins; otherwise, the wine will burst the skins, and the wine is lost, and so are the skins; but one puts new wine into fresh wineskins.

---

[91]   Holland and Henriot, *Social Analysis*, p. 102.
[92]   The source of the transcendental model is in the work of Bevans and theologians Bernard Lonergan and Sallie McFague but has been further developed by myself.

This parable provides a key insight into the transcendental model of theological reflection. There are some things we cannot understand without a complete change of mind. They demand a radical change of perception, a radical change in perspective. Until we make this shift, whatever we try to understand will defy our understanding. It is only as we transcend ourselves, reach out and open ourselves and, indeed, risk ourselves, that some understanding emerges.

The term *transcendental* is meant to refer to the transcendental method that was pioneered by Kant in the eighteenth century and developed in this century by thinkers, such as Joseph Marechal, Pierre Rousselot, Karl Rahner and Bernard Lonergan,[93] all of whom had the conviction that the 'knowing subject is intimately involved in determining reality's basic shape'.[94] This philosophy was a basic shift from one which postulated that reality could only be known 'out there', independent of human knowing. Lonergan believes that: 'Genuine objectivity is the fruit of authentic subjectivity. It is to be attained only by authentic subjectivity.'[95] I understand this to mean that beginning with oneself can shape truth and reality.

The model and the adaptation

While I have been influenced in an understanding of this approach by the work of Bevans, Lonergan and, especially, the insights of McFague in her book *Speaking in Parables*,[96] the substantial insights I outline below are my own work. I have developed and refined this model because of the way other models neglect inner experience and spirituality. The transcendental model attends to spirituality without neglecting critical analysis, social justice and the need for change.

I have written earlier on my understanding of experience and its potential to create a new type of openness, emancipation from some prior certainty or settled self-understanding. My life and history have been radically changed as a result of often-painful experiences, which have in turn opened up new experiences. I have striven in my life for unity of life and thought. In many ways this model is a personal testimony and so, in keeping with the philosophy of this model, I begin with myself.[97]

Beginning with oneself

I have always begun with myself in theological reflection. Indeed, Bevans says:

---

[93] See Otto Muck 1968, *The Transcendental Method*, New York: Herder & Herder, for a thorough and comprehensive discussion of the whole movement in Marechal and his successors.

[94] Bevans, *Models of Contextual Theology*, p. 98.

[95] Bernard Lonergan 1972, *Method in Theology*, New York: Herder & Herder, p. 292.

[96] Sallie McFague, 1975 *Speaking in Parables*, Philadelphia: Fortress Press.

[97] This model has been adapted as it has provided a framework for my deepest concerns for people and expresses most eloquently the ongoing conversation between human beings and God.

A fundamental presupposition of the transcendental model is that one begins to theologize ... not by focusing on the essence of the gospel message or of tradition as such, nor even trying to thematize or analyze culture or expressions of culture in language. Rather, the starting point is transcendental, concerned with one's own religious experience and one's own experience of oneself.[98]

Using Lonergan's terms I begin my theology with the Authentic Subject.[99] It is important to state that when I say I begin my theological reflection with myself, I do not operate in a vacuum. Very much to the contrary. In beginning with myself (as subject) I have to acknowledge that I have been determined at every turn by my context. I am precisely who I am because of my history, because I exist at this particular time, because I am a recipient of a particular cultural heritage, because I had a particular set of parents and have a particular religious experience, because I have a particular amount of education, and so forth.[100] What seems at first glance to be a personal and individual model is in fact an extremely communal model. Counsellor and psychotherapist Carl Rogers is right when he says that: 'The most personal is the most general.'[101] It is my experience that when you begin with yourself people have a point of identification and, while they might not completely share your world view, they are put in touch with some deep-seated issues in their own lives. However, beginning with myself involves more than a point of identification for others. It also derives from a strong vocational drive that is passionate about relationships between God and human beings in order that people may know the presence of God in their lives more fully. Further, the theological issues that are of great concern for myself and others are not off the top of my head, but are worked through the agony and passion of my own life and through my commitment to the lives of others.[102] These beliefs shape my personal life, my ministry and my relationship with God.

Let me illustrate this from some of my history. My ministry as chaplain to the Peter MacCallum Cancer Institute, Melbourne, from 1975–86 taught me the importance of moving from the search for certitude to a search for understanding. Due to simultaneous personal and faith crises I was in danger of disintegrating, but in the end this time turned out to be a seminal formational period in my life. My first marriage was breaking down and the effects of the insidious disease cancer and the impact it had on people who I had grown to love were challenging my understanding of and belief in God. There were periods of time when I felt evil was going to win. It was a long painful experience.

---

[98]   Bevans, *Models of Contextual Theology*, p. 98.

[99]   Lonergan, *Method in Theology*, p. 292.

[100]   Bevans, *Models of Contextual Theology*, p.98. Bevans sets the scene for this communal model.

[101]   Carl Rogers 1961, *On Becoming a Person: A therapist's view of psychotherapy*, Boston: Houghton Mifflin, p. 25.

[102]   McFague 1975, *Speaking in Parables*, pp. 157–61. McFague has been influential in my understanding of autobiography and its use in my life.

Lonergan captures this struggle and its implications for theology in his essay 'Theology in Its New Context', in which he speaks of how contemporary theology has undergone a shift from being a deductive to an empirical science. What this means is that:

> Where before the step from premises to conclusions was brief, simple, and certain, today the steps from data to interpretation are long, arduous, and at best, probable. An empirical science does not demonstrate. It accumulates information, develops understanding.[103]

This is my understanding of the process in developing a theology. It was during this time of crises that I was forced to attend to the dynamic of my own consciousness. Had I not attended to my own being I would not have survived. I was inauthentic and this was reflected in my incongruence. It was a hesitant and painful acknowledgement, but I finally admitted that I was in trouble. This admission grew into an irrepressible desire to know what was happening to me – personally, in my ministry and in my understanding of God. The theme of the crisis that transcended my personhood, ministry and faith was that of vulnerability. Only as I incorporated the essence and meaning of vulnerability into these three areas could I be satisfied that I was an authentic person.

It was during this time that I developed a keen sense of what was involved in a Theology of the Cross. This continues to be a challenge, and struggle for me. I came to the conclusion from my Peter MacCallum Cancer Institute experience that, for my faith to be genuine, I had not only to be open myself, but also to be open to the forces that were intimidating me. Basically, it meant letting go of my control.

An understanding of revelation

This model contends that beginning with one's authentic self is to know that God's revelation is not out there. Revelation is not in the words of Scripture, the doctrines of tradition; nor is it hidden within the networks of culture. In this view God's revelation takes place within human experience. I experience God's revelation as I am as open to the words of Scripture as read or proclaimed as I am open to the values embodied in a cultural tradition.

The emphasis is on openness to receive this love. In this view revelation is understood as an event, not as content. It is something that happens when a person opens up to reality. Theology happens, in this view, as a person struggles more authentically to articulate and live an ongoing relationship with God, other people, culture and the creation. Revelation occurs in the giving and receiving of love. Bevans states that the core of this model, in which the emphasis in theology is on activity and process, is also 'about a careful but passionate search for authenticity of expression of one's religious and cultural identity'.[104]

---

[103] David Tracy 1970, *The Achievement of Bernard Lonergan*, New York: Herder & Herder, p. 80.

[104] Bevans, *Models of Contextual Theology*, p. 101.

The challenge to authenticity

What I discovered was that to begin my theology with my authentic self was not without its dangers. The enemy of authenticity is not ambiguity or ambivalence, but incongruity, focused in self-deception.[105] New Testament scholar Dan O. Via Jnr. outlines three literary examples of self-deception, which I believe not only undermines one's selfhood, but also, for our purposes, the theological reflection method. All three are related to personhood, ministry and one's relationship with God.

Reinhold Niebuhr and honest dishonesty

Theologian Reinhold Niebuhr postulates that pride is the fundamental sin, more basic than sensuality.[106] When we try to overcome insecurity by a will to power we transgress the limits of creatureliness. We fall into pride when we try to raise our finite capacities to the absolute.[107] Niebuhr says: 'Closely related to the pride which seems to rest upon the possession of either the ordinary or some extraordinary measure of human freedom and self-mastery, is the lust for power which has pride as its end.'[108] Pride is closely connected to self-deception. In self-love people make inordinate claims for themselves, knowing them to be inappropriate and which they can justify only by deceiving themselves. Via says: 'The dynamic or motive of self-deception is the need to justify what is unjustifiable – claims of inordinate power, knowledge and righteousness.'[109] Of particular interest for schools of higher learning and, in particular, theological education is Niebuhr's assertion that intellectual pride can be prompted by a sense of insecurity.[110] Further, he says: 'Intellectual pride [knowledge] is thus the pride of reason which forgets that it is involved in a temporal process and imagines itself in complete transcendence over history.'[111] According to Niebuhr self-deception is concealing from me 'my limitations because I cannot bear the pain of being caught in the visible, conscious dishonesty of claiming more knowledge, righteousness, or power, than I have'.[112] For the purposes of theological reflection, self-deception is claiming too much for yourself as a person and as a pastor in the ministry situation. It is laying claim to your strengths and not acknowledging your weaknesses.

---

[105] Dan O. Via *Self-Deception and Wholeness*, Minneapolis: Fortress Press.

[106] Reinhold Niebuhr 1949, *The Nature and Destiny of Man*, Vol. 1, New York: Charles Scribner, pp. 186–207.

[107] Ibid., pp. 203–7.

[108] Ibid., p. 189.

[109] Via, *Self-Deception and Wholeness*, 7.

[110] Niebuhr, *The Nature and Destiny of Man,* 190.

[111] Ibid., p. 195.

[112] Via., *Self-Deception and Wholeness*, p. 7.

Jean-Paul Sartre and bad faith

For French philosopher Jean-Paul Sartre self-deception is lying to oneself.[113] Self-deception is grounded in the proposition that human reality is at once facticity (fixed state) and transcendence. Facticity for Sartre is that which is fixed in a human being, that is, the past of human reality is fixed and cannot be changed. Transcendence, on the other hand, is a process whereby human reality goes beyond the given in a further project of itself. These two elements of facticity and transcendence ought to be capable of coordination. Bad faith fails to coordinate facticity and transcendence. It seeks to affirm their identity while preserving their differences.[114] But in transcendence I am not subject to all I am (the fixed given of being) and I have the potential to be something other than it.[115] And so self-deception is the felt desire to escape the burden and anguish of freedom, to escape being condemned to freedom, to turn my becoming someone through my choices into something already fixed. Sartre's view of self-deception is concealing from 'myself my flaws, apparently, simply because I cannot bear to acknowledge my fault but also because I cannot bear the uncertainty of being more than my flaws'.[116] For the purposes of theological reflection this understanding of self-deception is shown in claiming too little for yourself. In this example self-deception is claiming your weaknesses and giving little or no attention to your strengths or potential.

Herbert Fingarette and the disavowal of 'selves'

For philosopher Herbert Fingarette the self-deceiver is a person who lies to himself and others and believes his own lie, although he knows in his heart he is not being true to himself. People practise this form of self-deception in order to avoid the inner pain of seeing truth, particularly to escape from seeing themselves in contradiction with their normative view.[117] The result of this form of self-deception is that people do not know themselves; there is diffusion in identity. Fingarette says the person engaged in self deceptive practices will try to develop an elaborate cover story as a protection from having to spell out what that person has been doing, from having to face up to life. He uses the word 'engagements', by which he means a person's conduct, aims, hope, fears, perceptions and memories. These self-engagements play a central role in understanding the formation of a life story.[118] According to Fingarette the reason self-deceivers will not acknowledge or incorporate these often disruptive, disharmonious and painful engagements is that they present too great a threat to their present conception of selfhood; such a spelling out of these engagements, therefore,

---

[113] Jean-Paul Sartre 1956, *Being and Nothingness* (trans. H.E. Barnes), New York: Philosophical Library, pp. 49, 56.

[114] Ibid., pp. 56–7.

[115] Ibid., pp. 63–4.

[116] Via, *Self-Deception*, p. 9.

[117] Ibid., p. 10.

[118] Herbert Fingarette 1977, *Self Deception*, London: Routledge and Kegan Paul, p. 40.

is habitually avoided. He says: 'What the self-deceiver specifically lacks is not concern or integrity but some combination of courage and a way of seeing how to approach his probable dilemma without disaster to himself'.[119] Simply put, the self-deceiver refuses to avow these engagements as his or her own.[120] If they were acknowledged they would be a threat to that person's present identity. Self-deception, by this definition, if not attended to can distort our understanding of God, ministry, spirituality and ourselves. Via makes a startling claim, but a relevant one for theological reflection, when he says: 'If the mind is thoroughly integrated and transparently in touch with itself, self-deception is impossible.'[121]

The issue here is not just whether one has a narrative; the issue is whether we have one that is authentic and genuine, one that can sustain us in reality, one that has dealt with and incorporated our memories into our very being and frees us from having to continue to make one up. Self-deception has an impact on our authentic selves and, indeed, on our relationship with God.

The relevance of the concept of self-deception for this particular method for theological reflection is significant, but there are implications for all models of theological reflection. In each model it is necessary to speak, declare, uncover, own, embrace and acknowledge our own self-deceptions. I particularly respond to Via's claim that self-deception has the goal of overcoming pain, embarrassment, self-contradiction, and the possibility that it is linked with power. The implications for theological reflection concern the challenge of finding the safe sacred place to reveal to our own selves and to others our self-deceptions that allow the Gospel to address us, and the power of the Spirit to transform us.

Pastoral theologian Neil Pembroke, in his book *The Art of Listening*, cites arguments that refute the concept of a unitary or authentic self.[122] I acknowledge that the current debate on the authentic self is complicated and warrants a deeper discussion and attention than it is given here. For the purposes of this model it is sufficient to say that some would argue that there has been a dramatic shift from a focus on the authentic self to an exploration of the self in terms of subpersonalities. He says: 'While older theories worked with the metaphors of cohesive self, core self and authentic self, post-modern theories throw up images of sub-selves, possible selves and a community of selves.'[123]

Pembroke cites the work of psychologist Hazel Markus and behavioural scientist Paula Nurius, who have developed a theory of possible selves.[124] 'Possible selves' refers to how individuals might construct their future existence. In any vision of their potential selves are people's hopes and dreams – along with their fears and anxieties. A possible self is the ideal self a person dreams of. However, it can be a self she is

---

[119]   Ibid., p. 47, 143.

[120]   Ibid., p. 73, 53, 88.

[121]   Via, *Self-Deception*, p. 17.

[122]   Neil Pembroke 2000, *The Art of Listening*, Grand Rapids: William B. Eerdmans, pp. 94–6.

[123]   Ibid., p. 94.

[124]   H. Markus and P. Nurius 1986, 'Possible selves', *American Psychologist*, No. 9, 41: Cited in Pembroke, *The Art of Listening*, September, p. 95.

afraid of becoming. The possible selves might include a variation of selves, such as the successful self, the rich self, the creative self or the thin self. While Pembroke would agree that there has been a shift in the way the Self is theoretically constructed I agree with his contention that it is a mistake to overemphasize the differences in approach between earlier and more recent theorists. In Pembroke's view, 'psychological theorists have always worked with the community model of the Self'.[125] While there are differences of opinion between the traditional approach and post-modern theories of the self 'all have a communitarian dimension in their construction of the Self'.[126] The important issue is that these possible selves, grandiose self or subselves are integrated into the community of the Self.

Since the onset of my current cancer I have been confronted with some unexpected selves in my life. Some have come as a surprise and have contained some intensity. I have experienced the impotent self, the irritable self, the messy self, the inferior self and the isolated self. I am aware that some of these other selves are partly due to the treatment of my cancer, but I do wonder if some of these selves are really 'me'. Fingarette believes it is crucial to avow or integrate these subselves into the community of the self. As will be seen the community of the selves is an important ingredient in the transcendental model of theological reflection. For me self-deception is my understanding of sin.

The integration of my selves in the community of the self

In 1998 I was diagnosed with an aggressive prostate cancer, one of many thousands of Australian men who are diagnosed each year with this disease. A radical prostatectomy was performed in November of that year, after which I was placed on hormone treatment. Fortunately, the treatment contained the cancer, but in the process knocked me around. Then, in 2000, by mutual consent, the doctor and I agreed to suspend treatment. My prostate-specific antigen (PSA) reading, taken in February 2005, has doubled from what it was in 2003, indicating disease activity in my body once again. In August 2003 I was diagnosed with and operated upon for bowel cancer; I subsequently completed a six-month course of chemotherapy.

It is difficult to understand the meaning of having two cancers in my body. What implications have these diagnoses had for me as a person, as a minister and for my faith? I believe that the formational experiences of 1975–78 when I was chaplain at the Peter MacCallum Cancer Centre prepared me to face what I have faced and what I need to face. But, of course, there have been times when I have not been sure of my personal or professional identity; initially, the cancer destabilized me, which is hardly surprising.

So, what are the new personal, ministry and theological insights that I have reached as a result of being diagnosed with a second primary cancer? I share with you some of my reflections.

---

[125] Pembroke, *The Art of Listening*, p. 94,
[126] Ibid., p. 95.

The tension between distance and closeness

As a chaplain I was deeply involved in the lives of people with cancer. At times my involvement was so deep that I imagined I myself had cancer. But I didn't and, over a period of time, I was able to care for people while at the same time keeping cancer at a distance. Today I have cancer. Two primary tumours have invaded my body. What does it mean to take ownership of this cancer and yet at the same time keep it at a distance? It was only as I opened myself to my cancer and to other people that I began to feel a sense of authenticity and integrity.

During a teaching session in 2000 I discovered that I had been distancing my cancer, ignoring its presence within me, which was just as troubling as allowing my cancer to get too close. I came to realize that I had been disembodying my cancer, which was contrary to what I believed about the incarnation and integration. Simply, I have given it equal status with the other influences in my life. The first cancer I eventually came to consider as an additional conversational partner in my theological reflection. It does not dominate, but it is an influence, as are the other partners. It is not surprising, therefore, that the initial cancer had subtle influences on my teaching role. Can you imagine the conversation? The cancer cells saying 'I'm here to offer you pastoral care'? (I have come to let you know that your life is finite.) Or a statement of a theological nature, such as 'I am here to prove that God created evil.' My response, after a long discussion, has been, 'I don't believe my God creates cancer.' Or, 'If you do this for me, I will not multiply as quickly as I am supposed to', to which my response is, 'I am not ready to bargain with you.'

While I am still coming to terms with my second cancer and its place in my life and that of my family I am acutely aware of the physical toll. At the moment it is too close to me to ascertain its emotional and spiritual impact. It is painful maintaining the tension between closeness and distance. Like the hormone treatment, the chemotherapy is fragmenting my spirit; at times I am someone I do not know. Time will tell. I have begun to bargain – if I can balance these two cancers I hope to be given some years to live.

There is one consistent theme in my life. While the cancer cells are an important conversation partner, there are also other conversation partners ('other selves') who provide a different message: my faith, the love for and from my partner Marlene, my children, family and friends and my deep understanding of the sacrament of Holy Communion. To know that I am loved and can reach out in love is the sustaining point in my life.

I will now spell out the Biblical and professional implications of this journey.

An integrated approach to a theology of ministry

Richard is correct when he says: 'Theology must be a process whereby that experience is reflexively understood, articulated in propositions and embodied in language.'[127] I will now spell out in language some propositions about my theology

---

[127]   Richard, 'The existing malaise of the theologizing of field experience', pp. 67–70.

that are a result of my personal experiences. These are articulated under the general theme of vulnerability and strength and specifically addressed in my response to the development of a Biblical theology of ministry and its implications for the actual practice of ministry.

A biblical theology of ministry[128]

The personal theme of vulnerability and strength has had a profound influence on my theology of ministry. Many of the Christian gospel values are expressed in paradoxes. A paradox is a seemingly absurd or self-contradictory statement that is or may be true. One such example in the value of the Christian gospel is expressed in the paradox that strength comes through weakness. It was the Apostle Paul who developed and extended the theme of strength and weaknesses in his theology of the cross, which was initiated by the death of Jesus Christ. Paul writes from a background of much physical pain and ministering and leading a young church that continually challenged his authority. Paul, when talking to the Lord about the reasons why he was experiencing all this pain, complained so much that the Lord said to him: 'My grace is sufficient for you, for my power is made perfect in weakness.'[129] This paradoxical reference to weakness and power is at the very core of this theology. The theology began with the initiative of God in the incarnation of Jesus Christ. In the incarnation Jesus became poor and experienced the ultimate poverty – weakness and death: 'For he was crucified in weakness, but lives in the power of God. For we are weak in him, but in dealing with you we shall live with him by the power of God.'[130] The implications for Paul of Christ's incarnation and death meant that he understood living and dying in a new way. However, for Paul, the crucifixion was not the final word in the life of Jesus. True, he died on the cross in weakness, but he lives by the power of God and we who share his weakness shall by the power of God live with him in service.

In Paul there is interplay of weakness and strength, death and life. We are weak in him, but we shall live with him, by the power of God. The crucifixion of Jesus was not the final word in the life of Jesus, but the crucifixion and its implications seem to be the essential word, before the final word. In other words, before these can be the final word we must experience the power of the cross in our lives. Paul is saying:

---

[128] In advocating a theology of the cross I am in no way stating that this is the only way that God can be known. I am aware that some people find and know God in a theology of glory. The problem arises when one is emphatic that God can only be known through one of these expressions. I am also aware that I could be charged with propagating a split in the theory–praxis debate by advocating the importance of the theology of the cross as a prerequisite for experiencing the resurrection. An understanding of the meaning of the cross and resurrection occurs in dialogue with each other. Both need the other in order to understand God's comprehensive place in our lives. The two-way relationship is akin to Charles Wood's discussion on vision and discernment, on which I elaborate in Chapter 5.

[129] 2 Corinthians, 12:9, 1952 *Revised Standard Version*, New York: William Collins, p. 175.

[130] Ibid., 13:4, p. 176.

'Before the power of the resurrection can become effective in my life, I need to grasp the redemptive nature of the cross', that is, its finiteness, weakness and vulnerability. At a pastoral level I have a concern for many people of faith who, when death looms, are so keen to experience the resurrection, they bypass the one essential that is a precondition for their resurrection – the redemptive nature of the cross. I don't say this lightly, or as a judgement, as many of us struggle to understand the issues of life and death. It is indeed a struggle sometimes to fully comprehend the redemptive nature of the cross when you are there in the middle. However, Paul is convinced of two things:

- It is in human weakness that the power of the gospel is most clearly shown
- Human weakness is not a thing to be tolerated, but an essential ingredient of his Christianity.

This was the issue that lay behind Paul's wrestling with the false apostles and the Corinthian church. The false apostles presented strong credentials for their claims. The disturbances in the church were centred on the parishioners who claimed to be strong. These people wanted Paul to produce letters of authority, but he refused. The Corinthians, according to Paul, failed to understand him, because they failed to understand Jesus. The church at Corinth had not yet discovered the Christ who proclaimed the Lord as crucified – finite and vulnerable.

Before I discuss the professional implications to be drawn from this theology I will draw some implications from how such a theology would operate in my own life experience.

The theme of weakness and strength has significant meaning for my broken body and the Eucharist. What does it mean to have a broken body? I know my body is broken. Two cancers have invaded it. It has been cut, a foreign substance controls it. A foreign body has been inserted in an artery near my heart where there was a blockage. My body tires easily. I know something is not right. It is an impotent body. What does it mean to be a man with a broken, impotent body? What does it mean for a man and a woman who love each other very deeply?

However, my body has sacramental meaning when you place it in the context of Jesus' words: 'This is my body that is [broken] for you. Do this in remembrance of me.'[131] What do these words mean for my relationship to the church? Each time I re-present my weakened, broken body in the context of the Eucharist and offer it to the Lord, whose own body has been broken for me, I experience the mystical love of God. My human spirit meets the divine spirit – there is a unity of spirit. My body is renewed and my love of God and for my community is renewed. My body continues to be stretched and broken by the two cancers. Even so, the meaning of the sacrament of the Eucharist continues to have greater meaning for me. Recently, within this safe environment, I was able to ask the question of the broken Body of Christ: Why do I have two cancers in my body? I have discovered that asking the right questions at the right time is the beginning of the healing process. At this point I do not understand

---

[131] 1 Corinthians, 11: 24 1989, *New Revised Standard Version*, New York: Oxford University Press, p. 181. Other ancient authorities read 'broken for'.

and probably will never understand, but I do have the desire to continue the conversation.

Bernard Lonergan believes God's grace is radical and is expressed as 'being in love', and that:

> such a dynamic state of loving occurs as a gift, so affecting the human capacity for self-transcendence that it becomes an unrestricted self-surrender to the giver of the gift. The unconditional experience of loving and being loved pervades all levels of consciousness … the gift of love occurs as something of a holy disruption in the routine flow of life.[132]

This understanding of a holy disruption in the routine flow life is akin to Gadamer's understanding and my understanding of experience: 'For experience to be an experience it must run counter to our expectations.'[133] In Gadamer's view we have a social science interpretation of experience, whereas in Lonergan we have a theological understanding. To theologically experience and act on this radical grace of God means that there are consequences for all of one's life.[134] To experience this love (this 'holy disruption'), according to Lonergan, brings us to the point where we sense the dismantling of our former limited horizons, only to be drawn into an unrestricted horizon illuminated by the love of God. At this point I am seeking a new horizon in my life; hopefully, it may occur as I allow the radical grace of God to pervade all of my life. The Apostle Paul speaks of the grace of God that comes through human weakness. As Lonergan speaks of it, this radical grace of God is something to be anticipated, experienced and cherished.

Professional implications for a theology of ministry

Experiencing some of the treatments for cancer rather than just observing the treatments on other people has deepened my understanding of the importance of power and strength versus vulnerability. In ministry to the person with cancer, we are caring for people who are not strong and in many circumstances are not going to change or regain their health. What are the ministry implications for people undergoing treatment and the symbolism of these treatments? There are no easy answers.

Pastoral identity is enhanced when we stand with people offering them our vulnerability – not our strength. It is not that people should not be strengthened. That is not the issue. Our world is preoccupied with ambition, rapid change, the desire for quick answers and easy solutions. In fact, our world is aggressive in its demand for quick change and quick answers and, when they are not forthcoming, there is a tendency for people to run away from the realities of everyday life or attempt to change them as quickly as possible. A demonstration of strength, it is thought, is the key to solving our world's problems.

Sometimes our medical technology symbolizes that strength. Think for a moment

---

[132] Anthony J. Kelly, CSSR and Francis J. Moloney SDB 2003, *Experiencing God in the Gospel of John*, New York: Paulist Press, pp. 5.

[133] See pages 35–38.

[134] See appendix 1 for an integrated approach to experience as developed in this book.

of the aggressive treatments that are given to people with cancer. All are symbols of strength and have militaristic overtones.

Radiotherapy uses penetrating rays to kill the tumour.
Chemotherapy is a chemical that invades the whole body system to attack cancer cells.
Surgery is an exorcism of the tumour.
Immunology is fighting fire with fire.
Hormone treatment places a foreign substance in the body to reduce the levels of testosterone in the body, which feeds the cancer.

These conventional forms of treatment are symbols of power and strength. While I acknowledge that we need these symbols of strength, my concern is for the people of peace. It is interesting to note that, for many in post-September 11 America, Jesus the avenging militaristic warrior is replacing Jesus the gentle saviour. The warrior Jesus confronts the vulnerable Jesus.

If strength and power are overemphasized and the predominant feelings of vulnerability and powerlessness are neglected, the result is desolation, loneliness and fear. To fully understand what it means to be vulnerable in the presence of God can have a profound effect on our ministry to people with cancer. It is when we meet their vulnerability with our vulnerability and not with strength and power that ministry becomes alive and effective.

The issues of strength and vulnerability as partners are important in our pastoral care and theological reflection and must be kept in tension. Theologian Dorothee Soelle, when faced with the power and might of nuclear weapons, wrote a poem that reinforces the importance of keeping the tension between power and vulnerability.

The Window of Vulnerability

The window of vulnerability
must be closed
so the military say
to justify the arms race
my skin
is a window of vulnerability
without moisture, without touching
I must die
The window of vulnerability
is being walled up
my land
cannot live
we need light
so we can think
we need air
so we can breathe
we need a window
open toward heaven.[135]

---

[135] Dorothee Soelle 1990, *The Window of Vulnerability*, Minneapolis: Fortress Press, pp. vii.

The transcendental model

The transcendental model operates only when we are open and vulnerable and willing to engage those influences, which come before us.

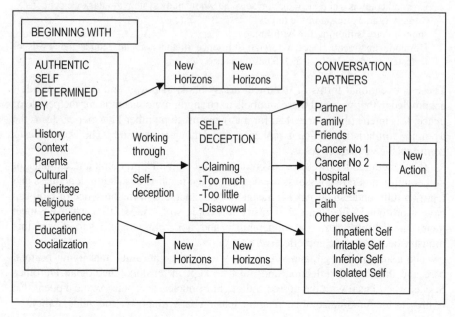

Fig. 2.5   Transcendental model – John Paver

From my experience of this model in my life I outline some of its strengths and limitations.

Findings

Strengths

- The model begins with the inner experience of the person. The beginning with one's self locates the context and culture of God's love in a person's life.
- This model not only calls for integration and integrity in a person's life, but also insists that these two characteristics are present in all social, cultural, professional and political domains of the person's life.
- The model takes seriously the spiritual life of the person.
- Social analysis is expressed in detecting the self-deception that occurs in the life of the person, society and culture.
- The model uses the autobiographical case study reflection to elaborate and deepen the experiences of the person.

Limitations

- It is difficult to lead an authentic life in a world full of self-deception and people who deceive us.
- There is a danger that this model can be too subjective and, therefore, open to the whims of individualism and a spiritualizing of experience.
- It is difficult for some to make a shift from thinking of theology as some kind of content to be studied to thinking of it as the actual activity of an authentic believer.
- There is the danger of claiming too little for yourself, thereby not claiming your full strength and potential.

The three models of theological reflection – a comparison

The table below gives a brief comparison of the three models (ministry, praxis and transcendental) outlined above:

Table 2.1 The three models for theological reflection – a comparison

Model	Dominant Voice	Values	Revelation	Outcome
Ministry	Ministry experience	Inclusive	Faith is centered in the activities of the believing people-religious tradition	Communal discernment-Informed Action
Praxis	Cultural experience	Marginal perspective - poor and oppressed	Understands Revelation as the presence of God in history – in the events of everyday life, in social and economic structures, in situations of oppression	Social analysis Diagnostic tool - social cultural and structural change
Transcendental	Personal experience (authentic self)	Strong vocational drive – people may know the presence of God in their lives more	God's revelation takes place within human experience - Emphasis is on openness to receive God and people's love	Seeking new horizons to renew commitment to God and people

Chapter 3

Pastoral supervision – a vehicle for theological reflection

The attempts to heal the division between theology and practice met with limited success. Although TFE is an accepted part of the curriculum in most theological schools its integrative influence continues to be marginal. This failure arises in part from a lack of credible models for theological reflection, which in turn is linked with the lack of adequate supervision in many TFE programs. It is to the contribution of pastoral supervision to the formation process that I now turn.

The place of pastoral supervision in the formation process

Pastoral theologian Kenneth Pohly's definition of pastoral supervision picks up most of the ingredients of the formation process:

> Pastoral supervision is a method of doing and reflecting on ministry in which a supervisor (teacher) and one or more supervisees (learners) covenant together to reflect critically on their ministry as a way of growing in self-awareness, ministering competence, theological understanding, and Christian commitment.[1]

His definition includes personal awareness, ministry skills, Christian commitment and theological understanding. In Pohly's 1993 edition he does not include the term 'spirituality' and his book does not indicate why it was excluded. This exclusion surprises me, especially when autobiography and self-deception have a central place in his model of theological reflection. However, in his revised 2001 edition there are specific references to the term 'spirituality' and in this edition he says, '*Spirituality* is an issue that demands attention … [it is] the search for a spirituality that can both satisfy the soul and transform our lifestyle'.[2] While he does not explicitly use the term 'spirituality', in Chapter 6 he states his belief that spirituality is imbedded in his model of theological reflection as it is in the whole of his book.[3]

---

[1] Kenneth Pohly 2001, *The Ministry of Supervision: Transforming the rough places*, Franklin, TN: Providence House, pp. 107–8.

[2] Ibid., p. 90.

[3] Ibid., pp. 151–75.

On the surface Pohly is reluctant to precisely define or use the term 'spirituality', but the deeper reason may be in his struggle to define the purpose of pastoral supervision. We are given an insight into the process of his thinking in a paper presented by Pohly and Margaret Evans at a symposium on the integration of supervision. In their paper they conclude that: 'The purpose of pastoral supervision is formational.'[4] The purpose of formation in pastoral supervision is focused on the integration between 'belief and action'.[5] If Pohly believes that spirituality has to do with being an integrated person in the fullest sense, his model of theological reflection in Chapter 6 is abundant with authenticity and integrity. He is more specific in his understanding of this spiritual integration in his personal definition of Christian commitment, which, he says, is 'a giving of myself to the living of a spirit-filled life, which for me takes place within the Christian framework – a life consistent with and guided by one's relationship with God through Christ'.[6]

Pohly's distinction between supervision and pastoral supervision has guided me. For the purpose of this study I define pastoral supervision as a method that reflects on particular acts of ministry in order to grow in theological understanding. Theological understanding is developed through the art of theological reflection.

The process of preparation for ministry usually includes six dimensions: academic formation, spiritual direction, ministerial formation (which includes personal identity, pastoral identity and pastoral leadership), pastoral supervision and theological reflection, and denominational ecclesiology. The aim is to immerse the student in this holistic formation process with the hope that, at the end of the theological training, students will be sufficiently formed to begin their ministry. Of course, formation is a life-long process and continues after students complete their theological studies. Careful support of new ministers through supervision and mentoring in the years following theological school is also necessary in order to continue the process of formation. Further, if formation is to be holistic, we need to find more effective ways of linking the academic study of theology with the other formation partners.

It has already been stated that there is a problem of fragmentation within theological education. Pastoral supervision makes the claim that because of its integrative nature it has the ability to promote the integration of academic formation and ministerial formation.

This chapter argues that pastoral supervision provides an integrative force for a number of the elements of the formation process. However, pastoral supervision is also aware of the dangers of claiming too much or too little in its contribution to

---

[4]   Kenneth H. Pohly & Marilyn L. Evans, 1997, 'The Multidisciplinary Nature of Pastoral Supervision: Integrating Supervision, Counseling and Spiritual Direction', *Journal of Supervision and Training in Ministry*, 18, 57.

[5]   Pohly, *The Ministry of Supervision*, p. 90.

[6]   I am appreciative of Kenneth Pohly's clarification of the term 'Christian commitment'. This clarification occurred through personal correspondence in which he queried my interpretation of these words.

the formation process. I believe that, historically, too much responsibility has been placed on TFE to direct the formation process. This has not been helpful in understanding TFE and will not change until the theological colleges are clear about their goals and the place of field education within the theological enterprise.

Theological reflection comes in a variety of models and methods and has its own inbuilt processes, regardless of whether supervision is involved. You do not have to have training in pastoral supervision to undertake theological reflection – it is undertaken by Christian people daily without consciously being aware of supervisory skills or models and methods for theological reflection. However, in a theological institution where people are being formed and trained for leadership in the church and the community, pastoral supervision as a vehicle for theological reflection creates insight, understanding and the depth required for such leadership. Pastoral supervision has a body of educational and theological knowledge that enables it to undertake such a task. It is my hope that the experience of pastoral supervision, especially within the context of theological reflection, will equip students to have some ability to self-supervise their ministry upon graduation.

For some, supervision is theological reflection. However, this is a general statement and needs clarification. The many models of and methods for theological reflection and pastoral supervision need to be adept in enabling these models to be used in such a way that they will achieve what they are expected to achieve. As an aid for theological reflection, supervision is a method of integration, with the primary focus on what happens at the intersection of what one believes and how one lives out that belief. At these intersections supervision is concerned with the congruity between belief and practice. The test of the quality of supervision is the way the supervisor offers and uses the appropriate skills and how the supervisor models congruity in his or her life and teaching. Theological reflection is to be centred in discovering one's operative theology as it unfolds in human experience. There is a dynamic quality to theological reflection, which does not tolerate mere repetition and is more concerned with interpretation leading to change. It recognises that the goal of theological reflection is transformation rather than restoration and so there is a close mutual relationship between theological reflection and pastoral supervision, although each is separate and each has a particular responsibility for promoting integration.

It is with these understandings of pastoral supervision that I will now develop an educational model of supervision for theological reflection and then outline the characteristics of supervision that make it a vehicle for theological reflection.

An educational model of supervision for theological reflection

CPE and TFE have provided leadership in developing educational models of supervision, and yet, both movements have struggled to produce an educational model specifically related to theological reflection. I am aware that there is considerable discussion and sometimes controversy about developing an integrative educational model for theological reflection.[7] The theological reflection process requires a particular educational model. The TFE program at UCTC has a comprehensive training program for pastoral supervisors that includes educational and supervision models for TFE, but has not, up until this point, developed models specifically for theological reflection. While I have appreciated theological field educator Donald Beisswenger's insight into the educational process of a number of supervisory modes, his examples do not specifically locate a model for theological reflection.

Beisswenger's grid shows seven modes of supervision in field education: work – evaluator, instructor, apprentice, trainer, resource, consultant and spiritual guide[8] – and 'dominant educational mechanisms' in terms of five factors (primary goal, supervisor's task, focus of attention, dynamics and locus of dominant control). A particular mode, utilizing the five factors appropriate to that mode, constitutes a model of supervision. Beisswenger points out that schools tend to use one or a combination of modes, with one usually being dominant. I have adapted Beisswenger's structure in order to develop my own educational model of supervision for theological reflection.

An educational model for supervision for theological reflection requires at least four prerequisites for students to function effectively in it. Ideally, the model is most effective in the latter part of their training after they have acquired some understanding and coherence of the following requirements.

Prerequisites

• Skill development
• Personal growth
• Cultural and social awareness
• Theological awareness.

Skill development

The emphasis here is on the development of particular skills within the field education placement. This could involve learning techniques and approaches to pastoral care and counselling, conducting marriages and funerals, worship and administration. The educational method is didactic and experiential. The supervisor can also model techniques and approaches for the student. The goal of supervision is to develop skills, rather than develop how the students feel about each other. Skill development is important for the theological model, as the outcome of most models usually requires skill implementation. Psychologist Antony Williams

---

[7]   Pohly, *The Ministry of Supervision*, pp. 93–9. These pages outline a number of educational approaches for supervision.

[8]   Donald F. Beisswenger 1974, 'Differentiating modes of supervision in TFE', *Theological Education*, 11/1, 58.

names these skills 'procedural knowledge'. Speaking from a psychotherapeutic model and highlighting the importance of wisdom in supervision he says:

> [w]ise clinicians need a rich procedural knowledge – how to do things; after all, they are not scholars as such, but people who act in a world with other people. They are in the field of decisions, judgments and practices that have to be made by clients in the face of uncertainty, ambiguity and complexity.[9]

The rich procedural knowledge of the supervisor also includes challenging skills, involving self-disclosure, appropriate confrontation and immediacy. Warmth, genuineness, and empathy are also crucial supervisory qualities, although I believe these are inherent in the personality of the supervisor rather than skills to be learned.

Personal growth

In personal growth the emphasis is upon developing insight, affective sensitivity and interpersonal functioning. Ministry students are encouraged to use their intuition, to see through situations. They are encouraged to understand their own life stories in order to understand other people's narratives and to understand why they have developed these particular narratives. Perhaps the most important personal insight for the student is to recognize ambiguity as fundamental to the nature of things, as intrinsic to human life, rather than as the exception. The goal of supervision is that students become aware of their strengths and weaknesses and recognize the dangers of self-deception.

As we've already seen, this is crucial for authentic theological reflection. Normally personal growth is a high priority for students today, but what is often lacking is the ability to bring this personal growth and awareness to their ministry. Therefore the focus in supervisory sessions must be not only on students' personal growth, but also on how they use this in order to assist other people to grow. The CPE movement is at its best in promoting personal, pastoral and professional growth. The methods used provide a link between the pastor's wellbeing and that of the patient or client. For some students some aspects of personal growth and insight are lacking, so counselling and/or psychotherapy may be required.

Cultural and social awareness

There is a tendency in some field education programs to limit the focus of activity, reflection and supervision to skills development and personal growth, neglecting the way social and public forces and structures can profoundly influence the understanding and practice of ministry. I believe that there are few programs that would consider cultural and social awareness as being part of the theological

---

[9]   Antony Williams 1999, 'Clinical Wisdom – A major goal of supervision', *Psychotherapy in Australia*, 6/1, November, 28.

reflection process. As we've already noted, the praxis model is difficult and threatening to implement as it examines the broader cultural, social, political and economic factors pertinent to the situation. Theological field educator Russell Seabright believes that: 'Each student should have the experience of reflecting upon the "tyrannies", the insurmountables, having his/her consciousness about it reach new dimensions, and engage in activity designed to transform it.'[10] Practical theologian Lynn Rhodes continues to be concerned about power, role and authority for women in the life of the church, believing that institutions and churches still carry within them basic sexist and patriarchal modes of meaning and forms of ministry and that what we do as supervisors is shaped by that reality. Rhodes writes that the supervisor should have skills of social analysis, including power analysis, and that it is critical that women learn to analyze power relationships.[11]

Theological awareness

It is crucial that students bring their formal academic learning and knowledge to the theological reflection enterprise. Crucial to the theological reflection process is their knowledge and understanding of biblical and systematic theology and ecclesiology.

While students vary in their development in these prerequisites it is important that they have attained some level of skill, personal growth and cultural and theological awareness in the process for theological reflection to function. I am also assuming that theological reflection is best done in a community and that the following dominant educational processes reflect this.

Dominant educational processes

Theory

Action/reflection model of learning, beginning with experience as discussed in Chapter 2.

Goals

The goals are to foster critical enquiry and to discern the movement of God in human experience in order that the student becomes a more effective minister.

---

[10] Russell Seabright 1984, 'A model of supervision for the integration of social awareness and ministry functioning during a year of internship in Lutheran theological education', unpublished DMin project for United Theological Seminary, Dayton, pp. 146–65.

[11] Lynn Rhodes 1991, 'Sexual ethics: power, role and authority in field education supervision', paper presented at the 21st Biennial ATFE Conference, Denver.

Supervisor's task

The supervisor's task is to encourage students to reflect theologically through conversation rather than argument or competition. The adoption and adaptation of some of the teaching methods from the social sciences has enhanced the supervisory process. Not the least has been the clinical rhombus of Ekstein and Wallerstein.[12] Their approach is popularly known in CPE circles as 'parallel process'. The parallel process describes how a supervisor, student or client's anxiety causes impasses to develop between supervisor and student or between student and client. Particular importance is placed on the impasse that develops initially between student and client and how this impasse can be resolved in supervision. Indeed, for Mueller and Kell, resolution of impasses becomes the central focus of supervision.

> According to our paradigm of supervision, all three sources of conflict and anxiety – the client in relation to others, the client and therapist in relation to each other, and the therapist and supervisor in relation to each other – must find a way into the supervisory relationship if it is to be productive. The way in which the supervisor interacts with the therapist or assists him to cope with the conflict generated in each of these relationships as the conflicts unfold, merge and interact, defines the supervisory process. Unless all three sources of conflict and their interaction become part of the process, supervision will provide no new dimensions to the development of the therapist that can't be obtained with less expenditure of time, energy, and emotional commitment elsewhere.[13]

Supervisors who use the parallel process concept will greatly strengthen the students' understanding of interactional patterns and help them to resolve their impasses with clients. Further, the use of the parallel process will highlight the interactional patterns between the personal and communal experience of the student minister, the tradition and the culture. Sometimes, when their views are threatened, there is a great amount of anxiety, resistance and lack of trust in the theological reflection process among students. An appropriate understanding of the parallel process and use of skills by the supervisor to break down this impasse can lead to an opening up by the student and a renewal of engagement. This process has been discussed at length because it is not only an effective supervisory method in that it works, but it also occurs within the normal relationship between supervisor, student and the person being helped; it does not have to be understood pathologically. It happens because people are human. This is an important statement because much of what has occurred in the supervisory process has been psychotherapeutically driven.

Another of the supervisor's tasks is to assist in identifying the voices in

---

[12]   R. Ekstein and R. S. Wallerstein 1976, *Supervision in Social Work*, New York: Columbia University Press.

[13]   W. J. Mueller and B L Kell 1972, *Coping with Conflict: Supervising counselors and psychotherapists*, New York: Appleton-Century-Crofts, p. 7.

the theological reflection group with the hope that the group becomes a spontaneous theological reflection community, rather than a group that just talks about theological reflection. The supervisor also provides students with reading material on models and methods for theological reflection.

Specific focus of the group

The focus is upon theological reflection on case studies and life experiences as well as on critical readings of models of theological reflection.

Overall focus of the group

The group develops the resources named as the four prerequisites and enhances them by linking them with the three partners of personal and communal experience, the tradition and the culture. The focus of the group is on process and its partners are viewed as a mutually interdependent unit in which each affects the other through critical reflection. The outcome is that students will develop their own preferred models for theological reflection.

Relationship

There has been much discussion in supervision of the relationship between supervisor and student. Because of the mutuality emphasized in this model there is a temptation to claim a peer relationship between supervisor and student. However, there are two hindrances to this claim. The first is that the theological institution requires an evaluation process, one that prevents supervisor and student from ever attaining true peer or colleague relationships. This tension between evaluation and supervision remains, but its import is reduced when the supervisor is genuinely willing to enter the process with the students and be as accountable as they are. When the supervisor is willing to stand beside and be with students, a collaborative relationship develops in which the supervisor and students are a mutually interdependent unit. This is crucial for the process of theological reflection. Furthermore, the collaborative relationship allows students to develop an internal sense of evaluation through self-evaluation, rather than being wholly dependent on the external evaluation established by the theological institution. Unless the evaluation is internalized it is unlikely that the students will integrate that which has been imposed upon them.

The second issue that modifies collegial relationships derives from the assumption that a supervisor has skills, knowledge and competence to which a student aspires. Through this process of supervision the student gains access to that knowledge and competence. The student may not completely access all that the supervisor has to offer, but the supervisor is responsible for providing as many opportunities as possible for learning. This educational view of supervision reminds us that supervision is a process taking place between two people who are not peers. It also reminds us that the task of the student is to move toward peership, while the task of the supervisor is to provide opportunities for that movement. Counsellor and theological educator Kenneth Mitchell says, 'peerhood is not the *nature* of supervision, but the goal of supervision'.[14]

Clearly, supervisors have competence and knowledge about ministry that students do not. This was self-evident in my time of directing a CPE program in a hospital setting. Not only was I more competent in pastoral care to patients, but I was also legally responsible for students in the hospital. I am sure my modelling of pastoral care enabled them to be more effective pastors, however, my knowledge is limited though it has been enhanced and deepened by the collaborative relationships I enjoy with students. A reduced hierarchy between supervisor and student encourages the student to become more active and responsible during supervision.

Control

At this point I see the relationship between the supervisor and the student as a collaborative one, with some institutional restraints that modify a peer relationship. The significance of this relationship is that the supervisor and the student function as a mutually interdependent unit.

Having established an integrative educational base for supervision I will now describe the characteristics of pastoral supervision and their place within theological reflection.

Characteristics of supervision that facilitate integration

What makes supervision pastoral? The scope of this book will not permit an in depth discussion on this question, but it is enough to say that: 'The ministry of pastoral supervision, as related to Christ's own oversight and shepherding, seems to have been taking place in the life of the church since near its beginning.'[15] The concept and basis for pastoral supervision is its Christian heritage.

Pastoral and ethical boundaries

Pastoral supervision is something that Christians do as part of their ministry, whatever that ministry may be. But it is pastoral in function as well as office in the sense of its shepherding nature, that is, its care giving. If this basic care is not present then supervision is not pastoral. Nancy Ramsay, a pastoral theologian,

---

[14] Kenneth R. Mitchell 1990, 'Ethical issues in supervision: justice, authority, equality,' *Journal of Supervision and Training in Ministry*, 12, 158.

[15] Pohly, *The Ministry of Supervision*, p. 14. In pp. 9–22 Pohly provides a biblical basis for pastoral supervision.

extends the metaphor of shepherd to include trustee, which incorporates the privilege and responsibility that students entrust to the supervisor.[16] According to Scripture, the shepherd is to assure safety and justice for the vulnerable. Supervision must be a context in which the vulnerability of the troubled is protected. Supervisors assure students that the boundaries – personal and sexual – will never be violated. Trustee similarly conveys that one is worthy of trust – a trust that is more than safekeeping and just action. It also includes modelling an ethical vision that is trustworthy. Pastoral supervision involves shaping a student's ethical standards for the practice of ministry.

While pastoral supervision is concerned with assisting the student to respect other people's boundaries, it is also concerned for the student's own personal boundaries. Pastoral supervision therefore addresses the delicate balance involved in being what pastoral theologian Glen Asquith calls a 'wounded healer' for others.[17] Oglesby, a pastoral theologian, points out that being present to others and available to others in pastoral relationships can result in 'the erosion of the self'.[18] Supervision helps the student pastor to set appropriate boundaries in such a way that the relationship itself becomes a healing source. The pastoral supervisory relationship can provide the student with a model of love that sets limits, but which also enables the student to experience a vital, healing relationship.

Even though the symbolism has been reduced in today's world, the pastoral office still has symbolic meaning for many. Urban Holmes III speaks of the pastor in terms of the archetypal figure of the shaman, whose role in history has left 'the image of the one who mediates between the people and the spirits' buried within our consciousness and thus affects our relationship with people.[19] Coming to terms with this symbolic power in the lives of others is an issue of pastoral identity, and hence an issue for the supervisory relationship. Students may deny, minimize or even maximize the impact of this symbolic power because of the anxiety it often produces in others and the particular responsibilities it brings. Pastoral supervision seeks to enable students to appropriately claim this identity and power and integrate it into their self-concept. This is done in part by the way in which the supervisor models the appropriate use of his or her own identity and power in the supervisory relationship. The test of the quality of supervision is centred in how the supervisor offers and uses the appropriate skills and models congruity in his or her life and teaching. For instance, if the supervisor believes that supervision is

---

[16]   Nancy Ramsay 1991, 'Pastoral supervision: a theological resource for ministry', *Journal of Supervision and Training in Ministry*, 13, 193.

[17]   Glen H. Asquith 1991, 'Pastoral theology and supervision: An integrative approach', *Journal of Supervision and Training in Ministry*, 13, 166.

[18]   William Oglesby 1980, *Biblical Themes for Pastoral Care*, Nashville: Abingdon, p. 196.

[19]   Urban Holmes III 1978, *The Priest in Community*, New York: Seabury, pp. 79–81. This reference was cited in Glen H. Asquith 1991, 'Pastoral theology and supervision: An integrative approach', *Journal of Supervision and Training in Ministry*, 13, 166.

relational, then the supervisor is called upon to exercise his or her power relationally rather than unilaterally. This means that the supervisor is called on to be part of the process rather than being outside of it. When authenticity–congruity is modelled by the supervisor and when students experience this first hand they begin to form a solid, integrative sense of their own pastoral identity from the inside out, an identity that will be different and distinct from the supervisor's. This will occur in an enduring and reliable form through the process of internalization, not imitation, so what will be internalized is the experience of the supervisor being with the student.

Pastoral supervision operates most effectively at the intersections

Pastoral supervision encourages dialogue, reflection, critique, interpretation, correlation, encouragement and evaluation. It can take a leadership role or it can stay in the background. It has a history of respect for the tradition, culture and the personal experience of the minister and encourages dialogue between these three sources. However, the gifts of pastoral supervision are most usefully exercised at the intersections of life's situations. Supervision works best when seeking to connect perspectives and qualities that are separated by our religious and secular culture: judgement/grace, fear/faith, conformity/rebellion, being/doing, feeling/thinking, subject/object. Pastoral supervision is comfortable with being at the intersection of doing and reflection and, particularly, the historical tension between classical theology and practical theology. It is at these intersections that the possibility of integration occurs. As an aid for theological reflection, supervision is a method of integration whose primary focus is on what happens at the intersection of what one believes and how one lives out that belief. At these intersections supervision is concerned with the congruity between belief and practice.

Pastoral supervision is reflective

Supervision occurs within a conversation in which students reflect critically on their personhood, ministry and faith. While there are identifiable stages through which this conversation normally flows the objective is for students to confront themselves in ministry as a way of making appropriate faith (action) statements. It is reflective in that the supervisors assist the students to see themselves and their ministry more accurately, clearly and creatively. It is important for students to know who they are, why they do things and how they relate to other people. The analogy of the mirror is helpful here.[20] Supervision is like holding a mirror before the students so they can see how others perceive them. As some mirrors are convex and some concave, every person offers a different perspective to participants.

---

[20] Doran McCarty 1986, *Supervising Ministry Students*, Atlanta: Home Mission Board, Southern Baptist Convention, p. 10.

Mirrors may be feedback from authority figures or reflection from peers. The concept of mirrors makes students responsible for their own future. Having seen themselves, some students decide to make the changes they need to make. The process of reflection enables students to take ownership of what they see reflected back to them from another angle of vision. It is when students take ownership and responsibility for decisions and for their future that the possibility of integration occurs.

Pastoral supervision is revelatory

One of the goals of pastoral supervision is to promote honesty. Supervision is tolerant of the students' weaknesses and shortcomings. It understands, but does not tolerate, dishonesty and self-deception. These mitigate against wholeness and promote fragmentation, which, as we have seen, is already rampant in the theological enterprise. Pastoral supervision calls for authenticity and integrity. Pastoral supervision is aware of the subtleties of some self-deception and seeks to address these issues in the supervisory relationship. It provides a disciplined way of examining who we are, where we come from and where we are going. Its function is to encourage openness to culture, experience and tradition in order to find a place where God reveals God's self. God continues to work in our lives, bringing new and creative ways into being in us. Pastoral supervision provides a process that can enable people to reflect on the movement of the spirit of God in their lives.

Pastoral supervision is confessional

Pastoral supervision is confessional in the sense that, in advocating wholeness, it requires that students not only acknowledge and face their strengths and weaknesses, but also accept and integrate them. The Apostle Paul illustrates such a confession in his statement: 'I do not understand my own actions. For I do not do what I want, but I do the very thing I hate.'[21] Paul knew himself and was able to address his strengths and weaknesses. Through his confession and God's grace he was not only able to minister and care for people, but also to open himself to transformation. It is only as students confess their weaknesses and strengths that the whole person can be addressed in the supervisory relationship. The task of supervision is to bring the person to wholeness and health.

The idea of pastoral supervision as confession is explored in an article written by theologian William Close on hermeneutics and identity formation:

> Belonging not to 'explanation' but to 'understanding', identity statements emerge as symbolic confessions at the end of the hermeneutical exercise. Like all confessions they draw together the whole person and those parts of the setting with which the person has

---

[21]   Romans 7:15

meshed horizons and say of the hermeneutical process, 'It is finished'. Whatever pastoral activity the intern has been about, whatever mastery of ministry's craft the intern has achieved, at some point the interpretative process shifts to the language of identity and through symbol or metaphor the meaning of the whole – a temporary meaning to be sure – is confessed.[22]

Pastoral supervision is covenantal

Pohly uses the term 'the right to fail' to describe the essence of the covenantal relationship in pastoral supervision.[23] He relates this to the field education learning document, which is called a 'learning covenant' rather than a 'learning contract'. Generally, a contract connotes legal enforcement. Pastoral supervision has adopted the Biblical word 'covenant' because the agreement between two people or a group of people is more than a legal agreement. The supervisory covenant is a commitment to life and growth. It is a statement, often written, of intent, which binds the supervisor–student–group in a mutually agreed upon process to see that particular segments of ministry are undertaken and, together with life experiences, reflected upon. In this sense the agreement is legal – it has the elements of accountability and mutuality. However, because such a covenant runs the risk of being inadequate by some standards, limited by a lack of vision, perhaps impossible to fulfil because we expect too much or because of a mismatch between supervisor and student or placement and student, the covenant may be broken.

It is with such an understanding that we refer in supervision to the right to fail. In my experience if we try to enforce the contract we create anger, frustration and mediocrity. Covenant does not eliminate failure; however, instead of reinforcing the failure that many people in any case feel, we give people the right to fail and, hopefully, to learn from this experience. We renegotiate the covenant in more realistic terms and use it as an opportunity for growth and new life.[24]

A belief in the future

The becoming human process that is provided for and actively encouraged in pastoral supervision specifically implies a belief in the future. God is always the God in front of us. The present moment is not locked in, not finished. It is open to the future and, for this reason, we are able to trust process; to grow means to allow for future change, optimistically, hopefully. In spite of the current struggle there is hope of becoming a more integrated person and a more effective pastor. There is present in pastoral supervision a vision of and towards the future.[25]

---

[22] William J. Close 1983, 'Pastoral hermeneutics and field education,' *Key Resources IV*, 184.

[23] Pohly, *Transforming the Rough Places*, p. 144.

[24] Ibid., p. 144.

[25] The work of Dean Olafsen is acknowledged for this insight. Dean writes of supervision as being 'eschatological' in an article entitled 'The process of supervision as a

Pastoral supervision is contextual

Pastoral supervision is contextual and operates at many different levels of ministry, within and outside the church. The key to pastoral supervision is the facilitation of theological reflection in these different contexts.

These pastoral, ethical, intersectional, reflective, revelatory, confessional, covenantal, future and contextual characteristics of pastoral supervision have a deep influence on the way it seeks to facilitate integration in theological reflection.

Formation, theology and pastoral supervision

My understanding of pastoral supervision can be expressed in a series of assertions. To think and feel about theology, culture and supervision is to engage in theological reflection. And to engage in theological reflection is always to proceed contextually and inductively from experience. Each of these assertions represents a particular stance within the debates concerning theological education, theological reflection and pastoral supervision that have been reviewed in this book. I am committed to the case study approach, not least because of the priority it gives to experience. I also believe that defining moments in pastoral supervision occur when experience runs counter to expectations.

These critical moments are surprising and often challenge beliefs and formation.[26] They are points of departure from what has hitherto been known. They are often subtle and personal and dealing with them requires great sensitivity and perception on the part of the supervisor. The integrity of this kind of theological reflection requires a reciprocal and mutual relationship with the students and may require appropriate self-disclosure by the pastoral supervisor, always within ethical boundaries and with concern for the use of power and authority.

I cannot claim originality in using the term 'critical moments', nor can I claim originality in asserting 'that it is precisely this critical component of formation that provides the way to authentic practical theological reflection'.[27] However, I can claim its truth in my own life and ministry and my responses of pastoral supervision to these critical moments. While, for the above reasons, I can identify many critical moments in the ministry of students, I will illustrate a critical moment in a ministry with which I was involved.

I was presenting to my faculty colleagues at a seminar on work in progress relating to my understanding and purpose of theological reflection. Specifically,

means of ministry formation', *Ministry, Society and Theology*, Vol. 8, No. 2, 88-97, November 1994.

[26]   A. J. Van Den Blink and James N Poling 1991, 'Theology and supervision', *Journal of Supervision and Training in Ministry*, 13, 257–73.

[27]   Ibid., 261. The above volume contains a number of articles on a symposium entitled 'Theology and Supervision'. These critical moments are also known as 'convictional moments', 'holy moments' and the 'lived moment'.

the title of the paper was 'The Art of Theological Reflection'. The subtitle was 'How do I encounter God today?' The paper was a reflection on my cancer and its impact on my faith. I was nervous and anxious about presenting this paper because I feared that some of my colleagues might intellectualize and critically dissect it, thus jeopardizing the personal integrity of my effort. I was also struggling in my confidence to present a paper that would be accepted academically and be of publishable quality. I feared judgement. I read the paper and was surprised to realise that my colleagues were listening attentively. My confidence increased to the extent that I was able to speak with little reference to my text. I addressed the issue of self-deception and its threat to authenticity and theological reflection. I was nearly home. Then I came to the section headed 'A broken body'. I read the words:

> 'What does it mean to have a broken body? While I am in remission and feeling quite well – I know my body is broken. It has been cut; a foreign substance has been placed in my body. It tires easily; I know something is not right. It is an impotent body. What does it mean to be a man with a broken, impotent body?'

At this point, I could not go any further. Tears came to my eyes and I placed my hand over them. It seemed ages before I looked up and faced my colleagues. Some had their heads down, but I could feel their care; others were looking at me, some with tears in their eyes. There were neither words nor an attempt to interpret what was happening to me, let alone them. Their deep empathy allowed me to complete my words.

> 'What does it mean for a man and a women who love each other deeply? However, it has sacramental meaning when you place it in the context of Jesus' words: "This is my body, broken for you."'

During this critical time I was feeling the full impact of my physical and sexual impotence. I was also feeling hopeless and helpless because nothing could be done medically to reverse the impotence. I had talked about my impotence, but in the instant I had taken ownership of it I felt its overwhelming impact. At this moment I came face to face with my God.

I completed reading my paper. There was a depth of silence for many minutes, and then, words of deep appreciation issued. After a time the critical and theological reflection commenced. One colleague remarked: 'This has been an existential moment; it made me think of the impotence of Christ on the cross.' Another colleague wondered about the Christology in this experience. A number examined the place of self-deception in their own lives, while another colleague wanted to understand more the method we employed in my TRS. The response from my colleagues was a mixture of inductive and deductive thinking.[28]

---

[28]   John E. Paver, 'The art of theological reflection', unpublished paper presented to Theological Hall faculty, Melbourne, 2 May 2000.

Critical reflection

I have undertaken a considerable amount of critical reflection since this critical moment. A colleague, while being supportive, asked some probing questions concerning my methodology. If I had been more immediate in my responses I would have pointed out to my colleague that what had been occurring in this interdisciplinary seminar was a living reminder of the method used in the TRS. Or, to my colleague who classified this critical moment as an existential moment I could have said that it was an existential moment, but it was more. For me it was a deeply felt spiritual moment in which my spirit met the spirit of God. Another colleague was also concerned about my method being true to the Christian tradition. In retrospect I could have pointed out that in the presence of this company did they not think that the presence of the Spirit of Jesus was fully alive and encapsulated in this moment?

The critical moment and authentic theological reflection

This critical incident has allowed me, through being faced with reality, to take ownership of my impotence and the helplessness I felt to change this situation. It has given me a deeper insight into people who, for many reasons other than sexual, feel impotent and unable to change things. It has touched my sense of social justice for those people who feel impotent to change things. However, it was the unconditional presence of my colleagues that gave me hope. This is a good lesson for all pastoral supervisors. I am aware that this moment could have been destroyed if my colleagues had entered into didactic and speculative theological reflection, but the spiritual moment came first and the critical theological reflection followed.

This case study illustrates that for theological reflection to have real meaning it must begin with such a critical incident. Even so, the above example illustrates that it is not enough to believe that one is proceeding inductively when starting with the case material itself. Theological reflection must start inductively from these critical incidents. And so formation, theology and the immediacy of the spiritual insight come together to make possible the emergence of new theological convictions about the nature of God.

It is the spiritual component of this critical moment that provides a way for authentic theological reflection.[29] There has been considerable debate about the place of pastoral supervision and its ability to facilitate spiritual direction in the formation process. One view is that it is difficult to accommodate the spiritual

---

[29]   These critical moments are a Divine–human encounter and are poignantly and ultimately represented in the meaning of the Eucharist. The meaning of the critical moment is only one expression of spirituality, but in my opinion plays a significant role in the student's formation processes.

dimension of formation within the supervisory process. While there are common features in theological reflection and spiritual direction, such as a concern for integration and a valuing of vulnerability, pastoral supervision has a pedagogical difficulty in simultaneously fostering spiritual growth and critical theological reflection. Pastoral supervision's primary focus is facilitating the student's education for ministry.[30] While there is a variety of forms of spiritual direction, 'the common theme is walking with people as they develop their relationship with God. The task is to open the structure and space in which the seeker can learn and grow'.[31] If integration and the issue of vulnerability are part of spirituality, which I believe to be so, and are present in these critical moments, then pastoral supervision has a responsibility to address these issues. Again, it should be noted that the claim is that the spirituality present in this critical moment provides an avenue for authentic theological reflection.

However, spiritual direction includes more than integration and vulnerability. In order to pay due respect to the wholeness of spiritual direction, it should be placed in another section of the formation program and a spiritual director appointed to give oversight to the program. In order to avoid further fragmentation of the formation process, the spiritual director would need to understand the importance of integration and vulnerability to spirituality.

Pastoral supervision requires sensitivity in locating these critical moments. My critical moment was obvious; others are not. Pastoral theologians Van den Blink and James Poling describe such a subtle moment in the ministry of a student when they write:

> There was, however, a discrepancy in her behaviour. She was not the kind of woman who found it difficult to express feeling. And yet in this instance, so briefly as to escape the attention of most in the group, she had not been able to acknowledge her emotion openly.[32]

It was the pastoral supervisor who picked up on the brief discrepancy in the woman's behaviour. Upon recognizing this discrepancy and acknowledging this emotion she got in touch with a deep despair in herself, which was a profoundly sad conviction that there was no hope and that all the ministerial activity was only masking that reality.[33] It often takes great skill on the part of the pastoral supervisor to assist the student through the anxiety of the moment. The moment can easily be lost by the anxiety contained within it.

It is for this reason that another pastoral theologian, John Patton, believes that at these critical moments 'one must "bracket" all speculative and constructive

---

[30] Herbert Anderson 1984, 'Forming a pastoral *habitus*: A rich tapestry with many threads', *Journal of Supervision and Training in Ministry*, 15, 234.

[31] 'Being Professional and Honouring the Pastoral Relationship', support document for the Interim Code of Ethics, Melbourne: UCA, 1997, p. 9.

[32] Van Den Blink and Poling, 'Theology and supervision', 262.

[33] Ibid.

views of the event so that there can be disciplined "seeing".[34] These critical moments can be subverted by moving from the inductive to the deductive, where critical reflection prevails. If this moment is being threatened it is the responsibility of pastoral supervision to hold on to it through direct intervention.

Central to all critical reflection is judgement. I feared judgement by my colleagues' evaluation of my presentation, but the eventual outcome was an abundance of grace. In all evaluation we experience judgement and grace. For our students there is often more judgement than grace. From a theological point of view evaluation reveals and activates both God's judgement and grace. The message of the Bible is clear: judgement and grace are realities of our experience and they come to us uniquely when we confront Jesus' life and teachings, death and resurrection. Jesus judges and restores us. It is in these terms that we experience pastoral supervision. Pohly grasps the truth of this when he says:

> We come under judgement every time we bring a piece of our life experience to another person or [a] group for reflection. To share the events of brokenness, division, hostility, failure, doubt, and indecision which mark our ministry – or even those moments of joy and success to be celebrated – is to lay ourselves open to the criticism of our colleagues as well as God. None of us enjoys having our colleagues evaluate a sermon we have preached, a situation we have bungled, or communication that has broken down. That can be frightening, anxiety-producing, intimidating; it is certainly an invitation to judgement. It can also be challenging, restorative, and exhilarating. It becomes this when grace is experienced as well as judgement. We experience grace every time we discover that others have the same problems and questions; whenever we find that we are accepted and loved not only for who we are but because we have been willing to reveal a part of ourselves for others to know and appreciate; each time we are affirmed as a person and minister who is struggling with the key human issues. We come under grace in all those moments when we feel the support and trust of our colleagues who are now able to give themselves to us because we have given ourselves to them.[35]

Students experiencing pastoral supervision will encounter both judgement and grace, each of which is a key to growth in the development of ministry.

It is important to recognize that pastoral supervision acts as a facilitator or vehicle for theological reflection. It has a body of educational and theological knowledge that enables it to undertake this task. I have outlined some of the art and science involved in such an undertaking in those critical moments in a person's life. This body of knowledge continues to be made available in the critical reflection that is required in the different models described for theological reflection. It will become apparent in Chapter 4 where I describe its processes in the TRS.

---

[34] Patton, *From Ministry to Theology*, p. 37.
[35] Pohly, *The Ministry of Supervision*, pp. 149-150.

Learning as a life-long process in supervision

In addressing the issue of lifelong learning for the minister, there are many opportunities today for ongoing post-ordination learning and refreshment courses for ministers: ongoing supervision, CPE, short term programmes in continuing education, spiritual direction, doctor of ministry programs and further theological education study, to name a few. I have highlighted two aspects of supervision in order that the full benefit of supervision is made available to the minister.

Train-the-trainers program in pastoral supervision

Increasingly, church bodies are providing post-ordination supervision for their ministers. Some are developing organized train-the-trainer programs where selected people are trained to train others in some of the art and skills in pastoral supervision.[36] This training does not equip the participant to be a professional supervisor, but does provide the necessary resources to assist ministers in a particular context. In general terms at the conclusion of the training participants will be:

* equipped to train people in their synods/presbyteries/constituencies in theological practice and the skills in pastoral supervision
* familiar with the components of pastoral supervision
* alert to the issues and skills necessary for effective pastoral supervision

The outcome of this training is to equip people to be trainers for people engaged in pastoral supervision. The people who are selected for training will already have the following interests and capacities, and they are people:

* who have a vital interest in pastoral supervision and education
* who already have reflective insight and skills in pastoral supervision
* who are committed to ongoing education in pastoral supervision in synods/presbyteries/constituencies

The benefit of this type of programme is that it provides a structured way in which to train supervisors who will in turn continue to train supervisors in their particular region/s. It also provides an ongoing 'pool' of supervisors.

Supervision to address the issues of transference and countertransference

Supervision provides an opportunity to address the impact of transference and countertransference on our personal and pastoral relationships. I am aware that

---

[36] One such programme has been developed by the UCA. Ministerial Education Commission 2002. *Participant's Booklet: Peer supervision material.*

these two phenomena have been largely neglected or avoided in the pastoral care literature over the last decade.[37]

In my opinion the church has paid a high price for this neglect in the area of transference love and sexual dangers. Whilst I do not wish to elaborate in this book on the sometimes-complicated issues of transference and countertransference, it is sufficient to say that unresolved past issues could have a negative impact on the minister's relationship with those for whom she/he cares. Likewise, the person coming to the minister for pastoral care can impose past negative experiences onto the minister. Sometimes complications may arise and it may be necessary for the minister to seek help from a psychiatrist or counsellor to deal with these matters.

Clinical Pastoral Educator Graeme Gibbons believes that negative transferences can be counteracted through positive transference. Gibbons highlights this positive aspect of transference in ministry when both supervisor and supervisee bring both transference and countertransference to the relationship.[38] He identifies three elements of transference or needs important to the supervisor and supervisee relationship: mirroring, idealizing and twinship. He defines mirroring as embracing the need to be nurtured, valued, recognized and accepted; idealization as the supervisee's need to merge with the strength and calmness of the supervisor; and twinship as a requirement of the supervisor to offer a quality of essential likeness with which the supervisee can identify and feel at home. Gibbons believes it is important for the supervisor to respond to these three needs, as they are important for the establishment of the personal identity of the minister.

However, having noted this about positive transference, the point needs to be made that these positive transferences in supervision and therapy are temporary homes of love which are preparation for a new understanding of love in any relationship with other and God. We may need these safe, insightful, interpretative and understanding places before we can venture into the immediate and sometimes dangerous world.

Whilst there are dangers in idealizing transference in relationships it must be acknowledged that the above insights are more productive than some negative approaches to transference and countertransference.[39] Whilst not all will engage in therapy during their time of ministry, for many it has been an essential ingredient for a holistic and integrated life.

---

[37] Until quite recently there has been an absence of pastoral care literature on this topic in USA and Australia since the mid 1980s. The UK and New Zealand have paid more attention to the impact of transference and countertransference on personal and pastoral relationships during this period.

[38] Graeme Gibbons, "A good supervisor is able to do" *Supervision: Introducing a process of reflection on ministry experience.* From the document of the UCA: *Supervising the Supervisor.* Gibbons work is based on the insights of Heinz Kohut, the founder of the self psychology movement.

[39] See John E. Paver, *The impact of Transference and Countertransference on Ministry and Pastoral Supervision,* Unpublished paper, 2002. In this paper I discuss a number of approaches to transference, which includes a theological rationale.

Chapter 4

An integrated approach to theological education through the theological reflection seminar[1]

The Theological Reflection Seminar is a coursework unit accredited in the Bachelor of Theology program of the MCD. It draws upon the three basic models (see Chapter 2) and others like them to offer an overview of the topic that will equip students to develop their own model of theological reflection.

Before introducing the TRS, I will sketch how it has emerged from my own experience as a CPE supervisor making a transition into the theological world as field educator.

This journey, which has been crucial to my personal, pastoral and professional identity, is documented in a paper I presented to a CPE gathering in 1997.[2] CPE taught me accountability in supervision, and was formative in that it sought for congruence between my identity as a minister and my acts of ministry. My entry into theological education was by no means easy. A number of factors contributed to my difficulties. While it began as a way of supplementing the church's pastoral education, CPE has existed for more than a half century outside the formal structures of theological education and the church. I would be the first to admit that, during my extensive training in CPE, there was a freedom to experiment and to develop an identity, which may not have happened if CPE was related to the formal structures of the church. However, when I moved into theological education my accountability shifted from the hospital setting to that of the church. Further, my context changed from a clinical setting to a church institution with multiple settings. Issues of accountability and contextual changes are not insignificant issues. While there is evidence that the ASPEA is attempting to develop more significant relationships with the church, the fact remains that the setting is mainly clinical and the issue of accountability has not changed. I continue to pride myself on being a clinician in the sense that I require clinical evidence before I act and will not make a pastoral diagnosis until I have differentiated the evidence before me. I have shown in Chapter 2 that the data collection method of the case study is

---

[1]   A copy of the student handout is in Appendix 2.

[2]   Paver, 1997, 'The place of supervision in theological education', paper presented at a seminar at the Austin Hospital, Melbourne in August, honouring thirty years of CPE at this centre. The paper was a response to a paper presented by the Reverend Roy Bradley, who founded the centre in 1967.

effective in determining the quality of a ministry, whether it is in CPE or field education.

I cannot speak of supervision in CPE without also speaking of theology and the clinical setting. Boisen's original intention to create a more experiential way of studying theology runs as a thread through the CPE story. It is present within the standards of the ASPEA, but this component has often become lost in the more personal interests of self-understanding and professional development based on psychotherapeutic principles rather than theological principles. While I cannot speak with authority about North American CPE models, there is evidence in Victoria that the theological nature of supervision is receiving attention.[3]

Nevertheless, I continued to grapple with the human and the divine as I developed my program of TFE. In order to make this program more theological I began reading the literature and associated literature around the debate on curriculum reform reviewed in Chapter 1 (some of which has been included in the *TRS Handbook*). I researched the history of the struggle to develop models for pastoral supervision and theological enquiry in field education in North America and in Australia. I read a multitude of publications on experiential theological reflection and some of the emerging literature on new models for pastoral supervision.

Out of this background I developed the TRS for ministry students at UCTC. Coupled with this new development was the establishment of the SUMP (see Chapter 2). While the program is not compulsory for ministry students at UCTC a significant number of these students have completed the course. The TRS and the SUMP are efforts to modify the curriculum at UCTC. Each offers a way to heal the division between theory and practice through engaging in new theological models for ministry.

Chapters 2 and 3 proposed that theological reflection is a method of integration for theological education, with pastoral supervision being the vehicle for facilitating the integration. This hypothesis was tested in developing the TRS.

---

[3]   Sister Julie O'Brien, Director of CPE at the Mercy Hospital for Women, East Melbourne, has developed a model for theological reflection that she uses in her program and which has been used elsewhere. I am also aware that Stephen S. Ames has been active in the development of theological methods within ASPEA. These have been public declarations of the use of theological reflection in programs. I would be less than honest if I did not acknowledge that many supervisors do have visible biblical and ecclesial components within their programs, with some transformative results. In my experience what is missing is a consistent model of theological enquiry. Joan Hemenway's publication, *Inside the Circle* (1966, Journal of Pastoral Care Publications) attempts to address the theological perspectives in CPE. In my opinion she does not go far enough. When I speak of theological enquiry and its use in the action reflection model of learning I am referring to the interaction of at least three poles of interpretation – tradition, culture and experience – all focused on pastoral or ministry experience. Further, I would also include a methodology that addresses how these poles of interpretation interact with each other.

History of the theological reflection seminar model

The TRS was initially a non-degree unit in the field education requirements for the UCTC ministry candidates, but it soon became accredited as a unit in the Bachelor of Theology degree, thereby enabling private students to undertake the unit. While previously there had been a theological reflection process in the field education program, it was primarily contained within the individual supervision meeting with the student. It was the assessment of a number of our faculty, though, that some of our supervisors were not proficient in the art of theological reflection and, in addition, there was a concern that there was not a communal model for theological reflection.

While I may have questioned their understanding of the art of theological reflection I took their comments seriously and conducted a TRS for pastoral supervisors and for ministry students during the first theological reflection program in 1995. Feedback from supervisors and students was overwhelmingly affirmative. It was an innovation for the students and the supervisors in that it not only took their theological study seriously, but it also attended to their personal experience. Basically, it was an attempt to get their hearts and heads together. For many it was a new way of doing theology, creating a community in which people felt free to trust themselves and others to offer their opinions. It was not, however, an uncritical community as it called for accountability, evaluation and congruence, but it was a community in which people were not afraid of failure and, if they did fail, they learnt (in most cases) from this experience. This initial program was largely unstructured and became the prototype for a structured TRS developed in 1996. To a large extent the format remains the same today.

The structure

The aim of the course is to:

> introduce students to different models and methods for theological reflection on the experience of pastoral ministry with a view of a critical appreciation of them. Students will present a ministry and a life experience of their own on which to reflect. It is expected that students will develop their own model and method for theological reflection. This unit will be conducted on a seminar basis, with students sharing reading, presenting reports and case studies.[4]

In order to undertake the unit students are normally required to have completed one year of theological studies and have some significant ministry experience. The unit assumes that students have completed an approved placement in field education and, for the purposes of reflection, preferably are engaging in an approved concurrent field education placement. Consideration is given to students who are not in a concurrent field education placement, but who have had significant field

---

[4]   'TRS on pastoral care', in *UFT Handbook*, 1999.

education experience. The latter provision allows those students who are not in the ministry stream to enrol for this unit.

The unit usually falls midway in students' theological training. Educationally, such placement relies on their having acquired some skill development, personal growth, cultural and theological awareness on which to build in the TRS.

The unit runs for eleven or twelve weeks and the class contact time is three hours per week. In the first hour of each session students provide a critique of a model for theological reflection and receive feedback from their peers. In the second and third hours students break up into small groups and present ministry case studies and life experience material. Each student is expected to present three written reports (or some other creative presentation), and then write an essay on her or his model for theological reflection.

The course is assessed in the following way:

One reading report providing a critique on a model for theological
reflection   (20%)
Two reports each of 750 words on theological reflection   (40%)
One 1500 word essay on the student's model for theological reflection   (40%)

Seminar leaders

The TRS is a holistic, integrative and interdisciplinary process that seeks to reflect this in the choice of seminar leaders. As I am the founder of the TRS, the program reflects my understanding of theological reflection and pastoral supervision. For this reason it is important to have at least one leader committed to the processes of pastoral supervision. The TRS has been co-led at different times by a New Testament scholar, a spiritual director and a feminist scholar. Each of these co-leaders has been committed to inductive learning, but the TRS has also appreciated the inclusion of their theoretical perspective. It is my opinion that if the TRS is to be integrative and interdisciplinary it either needs to alter its format or seek ways to involve all members of faculty in a creative manner.[5] While more will be said later in this chapter regarding the place of supervision, the responsibilities of the leaders are to facilitate the group process, to provide some theoretical input at the beginning and to engage with students at some of the teachable moments along the way. For this reason it is important to have leaders from other theological disciplines who can provide a range of insights for interpretation and clarification.

TRS leaders are not expected to be experts, to have a complete understanding of personal and communal experience, to have a complete knowledge of the Christian tradition or to have a complete insight into the murky and highly ambiguous impact of cultural forces on our lives. It is essential that the leaders

---

[5]   Rev. Colin Hunter, Director, TFE, Whitley College, Parkville, invites all members of faculty in turn to present their model of theological reflection. The feedback is positive for this supervisory training program and for the members of faculty involved.

have an understanding of this particular methodology of theological reflection, the processes of which have been outlined in the models and methods of theological reflection and pastoral supervision. I am aware of Klink's stinging remarks made in the early formation days when he said that field work seminars may communicate knowledge, but unless attention was given to the formation of the group as colleagues in the process the experience essential for any place of supervision would be lost. Leaders are therefore expected to be inside rather than outside the process.

Leaders should not be exempt from the possibility of change and transformation that can occur if one takes the theological reflection process seriously. While the assessment requirements of the institution do place some distance between the leaders and the students, it is my belief that when the leaders become part of the process this distance is largely overcome.

There are three stages to the TRS. Stage one requires each student to critique of a model of theological reflection chosen from the *Handbook*. In stage two students reflect theologically on ministry and life experiences in which they have been engaged. It is out of the engagement with these two stages that the student develops his or her own model of theological reflection in stage three.

The three stages of the seminar/case studies

Stage 1

The TRS offers three introductory articles on theological reflection and fifteen papers on models or issues relating to theological reflection. The papers are categorized into four sections: the ministry model, the praxis model, the transcendental model and the academic model. There are, however, papers offering variations on each model from which the student can select. For instance, the praxis model (see Chapter 2) highlights social justice as a concern, while in the TRS I also included as variants feminist theologian Letty Russell's understanding of feminist issues, the challenging Aboriginal theology developed by the Rainbow Spirit elders and Poling's insight into the silent voices of the sexually abused. The transcendental model is given further variety by the autobiographical and biographical insights of neurologist Oliver Sacks, Sallie McFague and myself. Pohly's insights in his narrative approach to ministry and Kinast's work in his theological reflection on John's Gospel complement the ministry model. I have included the insightful discussions of theological education by Charles Wood and religious educator Thomas Groome because of their understanding of the fragmentation within theological education.[6]

---

[6]   Paver 2000, *TRS Handbook*. The handbook has been compiled by Paver and has been added to and subtracted from over the last four years. The authors cited and their articles represent some of the models for theological reflection contained in the handbook. Details of these publications are in Appendix 1.

Students are expected to present a critical reading report of 1000 words (which may include a creative presentation) of one of these models from the *Handbook*. The critical report is presented to the TRS group for feedback. The supervisor reviews the report and returns it with appropriate comments. The feedback from supervisor and students is often helpful to the student presenting and important for the ongoing integrative process.

Students are encouraged to engage the model for theological reflection rather than write a review of their selected reading from the *TRS Handbook*. When students have done this there have been some surprising results. For example, one student selected and wrote a critique on Wood's excellent and often erudite book *Vision and Discernment*. The student's introductory and preliminary statements were a scathing denunciation of methodologies used in educational institutions, especially in theological education.[7] The student contended that academia was exclusive, cognitive and resistant to the value of personal experience. She pleaded for more lateral thinking and room for the use of one's imagination. At the end of this outburst she nervously asked whether she should proceed. I am sure she was expecting condemnation. To her surprise the group affirmed her honesty and encouraged her to keep on reading from her prepared text.

What followed was an excellent, constructive and critical engagement with the book. The crucial point for this student was Wood's method of theological reflection, involving as it does a dialectical relationship between vision and discernment in each of the theological disciplines, which, he believes, will bridge the gap between theory and practice. She warmed to the metaphors and illustrations used in this section because, 'That is how I think best. I like to use my imagination and have my imagination challenged. One of the fundamental flaws with Wood's method is that he presupposes that all theological students think like he does. Analytically.' The student supports her argument by saying that Wood is so caught up in his 'vision' (theory, seeing connections) that his 'discernment' (the particularity of his expression and his aim) suffers. Her conclusion is somewhat ironic in that she makes a plea for student voices to be heard over the 'clinically intellectual babble of the published theologians', but then says:

> We need them if only to disagree with them and as a result, begin to find the seeds of our own beliefs and our own voices. So if that has been one of the intentions of Wood; to begin theological students thinking about their own methods and theological voice, then he has succeeded with me.

In this presentation there was interplay of personal experience (student), the culture (the theological institution) and educational methodology. While the Christian tradition figured largely in the text of the paper it was in the background of the student's concern. The crucial turning point for the student was having her 'voice' validated by the group and the supervisor. The action of the group embodied the educational philosophy of the TRS, and allowed her to move on and make a

---

7   I have received permission from each person included in this study to use his or her materials for the benefit of this research.

constructive contribution to her colleagues and the ongoing life of the seminar. The student not only learnt from this event that some aspects of her theological study contained and encouraged both theoretical and experiential learning, but also that she could have a 'theological voice' in the more classical aspects of theology.

Stage 2

This stage focuses upon a case study reflection report on a ministry and the presentation of a life experience.[8] The case study reflection on a pastoral ministry involves a written report on a ministry in which the student has been involved. Students are encouraged to include in verbatim form part of a conversation they have had with a person. While some students comment on the difficulty of writing about a significant ministry experience so compactly, the method does provide a concrete text to anchor the interaction. This case study report on the conversation enables the group and the supervisor to judge the actual quality of the ministry. The case study report involves known and observed information about the person. For example: Who is this person and what did you know about him or her before this encounter? (Examples: age, gender, race, marital status, sibling rank, parents, children, religious beliefs, social concerns, political allegiance.) The observed information includes physical appearance, setting and a description of the student's responses to this information. Perhaps the key to the collation of this information is the effectual response by the student to it. (Examples: Was the person interesting, boring, attractive, repulsive, enjoyable? Did this person make you anxious? Did you find yourself engaged, turned off or withdrawing?) This information can be of assistance to the student, peers and the pastoral supervisor when assessing the quality of the pastoral ministry. It can also be an indicator of any incongruence that may occur between the student's claims and the theological reflection assessment.

Following the verbatim account of the pastoral conversation comes a reflective assessment of the pastoral conversation and an assessment of the ministry leading to theological reflection on the ministry. It is the incorporation of all the above factors that enables the student and the group to proceed to the theological reflection section of the case study reflection report. Questions asked in this section include:

- What theological issues emerged from the event and/or conversation?
- Where do you see the redeeming activity of God in this event?
- What biblical events seem parallel to your reported ministry?
- In what ways are the two similar?
- Can you identify the model of theological reflection used in this case study?

---

[8]   I have documented the history of the case study reflection method in Chapter 2. The above information on the case study reflects the particularity of its use for this particular seminar.

It integrates this knowledge, but it also connects it with matters of wisdom and the heart. Therefore, the case study reflection structure is concerned with all parts of the person.

Crucial to the development of theological reflection is often the incongruence between the religious images or images of God and humanity that emerge from the pastoral conversation and those recorded in the student's theological reflection. While the focus is on the effectiveness of pastoral care given to the person, the TRS also attends to issues for the student that may have been detrimental to or have enhanced her or his ministry. It is often revealed that the student's learnt ministry is at odds with that operative in a particular pastoral ministry. Frequently it is within these tensions that the presence of the spirit of God is discovered.

Students' ministry experience

This tension can be seen in a ministry student's pastoral conversation with a depressed elderly man who had been homeless and now required intensive medical care. The student, who was undertaking a field education placement at The Lodge, a care facility, was asked by the social caseworker to visit this particular man in hospital. The social worker had established a good relationship with this man, who had enjoyed her visits. But her increased responsibilities did not permit her to visit as frequently as she might have wished. The social worker informed the student that the man had been feeling rather depressed in the past few days since his return from a bowel operation. The student, who was in his late twenties, was intellectually bright and a quiet leader. He indicates in the background material to his case study that this elderly man 'is one of my favourites, as much as my professionalism permits me to have them'. The conversation centred on the mutuality of care. While the man was depressed and 'had precious little to live for', he had a gift of hospitality in welcoming people. When the student entered the room he was greeted with the words: 'Welcome home, S!' The student's pastoral care was so perceptive and astute that he picked up the theme of hospitality and (I believe genuinely) said:

S[tudent]1: Every time I come here I see you and it cheers me up. Every time I walk past you say hello to me and it always makes me feel good.

C[lient]2: (His face burst again into an open smile). Hey, that's just what Peter [another house carer] said yesterday, I said 'Welcome home' to him and he said that I made his day.

The student reinforced his worth by saying, 'You are very important to this place, you know.' He replied:

C3: Oh I don't know. Sometimes, I think I have got precious little to live for. Ellen cheered me up when she said that you people loved me, and that's worth something, I guess. I really enjoyed the flowers.

It was the student's impression that the man's ability to keep on going was based on other people's appreciation of his hospitality and the knowledge that, no matter how bad things became, there were people who genuinely loved him. The student reinforced this hope in the quality of pastoral care that he offered. However, the crucial point for the student came when the man enquired, 'How is your study going?' The student made a notation in brackets ('I confessed it wasn't going all that well, until I realized he really did not need to hear all about me and changed the subject'). As the student read these words I noted a look of despair.

The student's reflection centred on the man's low opinion of himself and how the man's open nature often belied those feelings. The student's theological reflection was based on Genesis II, which informed him that God takes delight in the love shared between people as expressions of his love for us. The translation of this insight for the student's understanding of God's presence in this ministry was based on the mutuality and reciprocity of love between people and God, which can give life meaning.

The student's response to the positive feedback from the group was flat. His response to a caring enquiry about his study was met with very few words. The group discussion was completed with some caring comments from me to the student.

> I don't know who the real S is! It sounds as though you are as depressed as your client. You taught us today the importance of reciprocal love. You also highlighted the most important truth, 'If you know you are loved you can go on'.

I said I did not wish to intrude on his personal life, but if he wished to talk about anything I would be available to do so. I also responded with comments on his case study:

> This is how I experience you – loving, competent and caring – that is the side I see – I also see a person that is not available – perhaps that is the private side that needs to be respected. However, all of one's personhood needs to be embraced for ministry identity. For instance, are you (or were you) as depressed as the client was? I don't want an answer from you, but simply to say that all of one's life needs to be acknowledged in such a way, because in the end it could have a significant impact on your understanding of theology and yourself as minister. You may know your self, and if this is true you may need to allow that to be visible to God in order to discern the movement of the spirit of God in your life.

He did come and see me. I felt great warmth for him as he spoke deeply of his despair in his personal relationships and how this was affecting other parts of his life. It wasn't a long conversation, but it was a significant one. He sought professional help as a result of which, in my opinion, his life has changed significantly. He is more open and quite different. He has a different dress persona, has ended a long-term relationship and sought a new direction in ministry. He responds more openly to people and to God.

While it is dangerous to claim too much I would like to think that this critical incident and the events that followed were significant for his ongoing life and ministry. As noted earlier, self-deception can also be present when one claims too little for oneself. I am in no doubt that there were other factors, influences and people who contributed to S's new direction, but I would claim that in this presentation and the proceeding ministry event not only were there people present, but God was also present. Only as he brought this slice of life before God could he begin to see the impact it had on other parts of his life. The client received from the student's ministry comfort and the knowledge that people loved him. This is a worthwhile outcome for any pastoral ministry. The unexpected outcome for the student from the process was the beginning of something new in his life.

Overall, these case study presentations, discussions and sometimes dynamic interaction reveal a wide range of student learning. The pluralism of theologies operative in the situation concern:

- the image of God, Christ, church, justice, ministry
- the congruence and incongruence of the student's own learnt ministry with that operative in pastoral ministry
- the level of ability to identify the central issues involved – for example, gender, power, authority, conflict, etc.
- the level of adequacy of pastoral judgement
- the ability or inability to identify what is going on in the situation and the ability to offer genuine care
- the degree of ease and judgement in such interpersonal skills as presence, attending, listening, feeling and translating what is really going on in the event
- the level of ability in communicating one's faith commitment; understanding the purpose and process involved in coming to action as well as being able to evaluate the ministry for its effectiveness.

It seems the more that is discovered and explored in the group and the more that the members of the group trust each other, the more students will develop and articulate their ministry in an ongoing, dynamic way.

Students' life experience

The second part of stage 2 is the presentation on a student's life experience, one they chose themselves. The presentations have included a variety of forms – poetry, Scripture, autobiography, biography, art, film, liturgy, wedding, funeral, etc. The rationale behind this presentation is that as students are encouraged to give free rein to their creativity and imagination, it enables them to present something close to their hearts. It also gives the message that God is present in ways other than ministry and supervision. This section is theological reflection because we are seeking to discover God's presence through clues to or signs of divine reality in human experience. God's word may be hidden among the details of nature and the experiences of men and women. As Rahner describes it, God is the mystery and depth dimension of human experiences such as love, friendship, death and hope.[9] Even loneliness, suffering, violence or disappointment can be revelatory moments, opening us to the transcendent. The students are not provided with an outline of expectations for this 750-word report, but the topic can be expressed in the form of their choice. This section has provided some of the most powerful and exciting pieces of theological reflection – and some of the worst. It separates those who understand the methodology of theological reflection from those who do not, or who struggle to understand.

One of the students from a religious order, a woman with extensive ministry experience, presented a theological reflection on the film *Dead Man Walking*. The film tells the story of a religious pastoral worker, Helen Prejean, who became involved with Matthew, a convicted rapist and killer. At first he asks her assistance in his appeal for clemency against his death sentence. When this fails she is led to befriend him as he faces execution. The student's presentation drew the group into a drama that highlighted the human and theological issues of judgement and grace. It took this form because the student placed herself in the centre of the text. In so doing she was attempting to discover who she was and where God was in this process. (Often, in the reading of autobiographies and biographies, we find out who we are and what we stand for.) This student presented a drama that was full of images, ambiguities, ambivalence, contrasting attitudes and polarization. The student was deeply disturbed by:

- the horror of a brutal rape and senseless murder of two teenagers
- the calculated, deliberate execution of this man by the state
- the people who cried for what they saw was their rightful revenge, as well as those who, shocked by that cry, sought the abolition of the death penalty.

Both groups considered themselves to be faithful followers of Jesus.

The film disturbed her so much that it pushed her to consider the place of God in such horrendous circumstances. We journeyed with her as she asserted that: 'There is no place where the divine presence will not dwell.' She clung to the Scriptural belief ('at times with tenacity lest I let go') that each one of us is made in the image and likeness of God. The student conducted a dialogue with the human and divine issues in the film through the relationship with Matthew and Sister Helen, the interactions between Helen and the parents of Matthew's victims and the dilemma of capital punishment. The following excerpts from her presentation illustrate her pain and investment in the dynamics of what is occurring in the film:

> I felt that the film could be viewed from three levels.
> The first level shows the relationship between Matthew and Sister Helen, which develops from acquaintance to intimacy. Matthew finally says, 'It seems I had to die to find love.' I wept for Matthew at times. However, the film always keeps

---

[9]   Patricia A. Lamoureux 1999, 'An integrated approach to theological education', cited in *Theological Education*, 36/1, 145.

before you (and never lets you forget) the brutality of his rape and the murder of two young people. It is vividly and fearfully portrayed.

Helen commits herself to Matthew. The priest, an official chaplain, tells her that her job is to ensure that this man prepares worthily for death. For him this means that her task as minister is to lead him to receive the sacraments, which will be his 'ticket for eternal life'. However, Helen sets herself another goal: she offers Matthew the possibility of dying with dignity by refusing to allow him to play the victim or to maintain his defensive macho arrogance. She consistently leads him towards accepting responsibility for his actions.

> She sets herself to love this man – the effort of love. It is clear, unambiguous love, which, while acknowledging his sinfulness and weakness, will not judge it. Nurtured by her, he eventually finds the courage to accept the truth of his own life. His honesty gives him dignity and inner peace. He is able to say, 'I am sorry.' This is salvation.
>
> On the second level we find the story of the interaction between Helen and the parents of his victims. We are given a clear portrayal of the effects the tragedy has on their [the victims'] lives. Helen is caught between their grief and her stance for Matthew. The right to grieve is deeply appreciated. However, when they call for revenge and choose to watch Matthew's execution, I was reminded of Jesus' words: 'Let the one who is without sin cast the first stone.' By witnessing the execution they hoped to find relief for their own grief. I felt extremely distressed for them.
>
> On the third level we are faced with the dilemma of capital punishment. I am affronted by this concept. It is difficult for me to remain unbiased. As he dies, Matthew says, 'I believe that all killing is wrong – the killing I did and the killing that you are doing now.'

The student, through Helen Prejean, engages in a running debate with some of the attitudes of people in her own tradition who use proof texts from Scripture to support the death penalty. While she can understand the response from the culture to this violence, she is sickened by the violence of the crowd demanding someone's death and cannot condone this reprehensible behaviour. Pushed to her limits and out of her depth, she identifies with Helen and the need to acknowledge that she too is sometimes scared as she describes faith 'like a giant leap into darkness'. However, like Prejean, on these occasions she finds friends who surround and encourage her. Perhaps the key to the student's struggle and her strong identification with Helen Prejean is reflected in the scene after Matthew's burial:

> After Matthew's burial Helen meets the father of one of the murdered teenagers in the cemetery. 'I don't know why I am here,' he said. 'I wish I had as much faith as you.' She replied, 'I find faith hard too.' That is my story too, it is also the stuff of my commitment.

This presentation depicted vividly the student's struggle to be true to the Gospel values, as she understands them, and her vocation, to which she is deeply committed. At the end of the seminar the student handed out a single page with a photograph of Matthew, grim faced, looking ahead, with Helen, her face full of concern and sadness, a caring hand placed on Matthew's shoulder. At the top of the photograph is a quotation from Dag Hammarskjold: 'Life only demands from you the strength you possess. Only one feat is possible – not to have run away.' The student did not run away from her struggle and continued her dialogue with the Christian tradition and culture, only to discover a deeper understanding of God's presence in the world.

In stepping out and sometimes affirming, at other times challenging, the values inherent in the Christian tradition and culture her presentation modelled for others in the TRS group a perspective on commitment to a religious vocation and the outworking of this commitment. Her stepping out and beginning with her authentic self is at the heart of her model for theological reflection. Each time she does her understanding of the presence of God in the world not only deepens, but also sometimes changes. While she does not give a name to her model for theological reflection it has some similarities and ingredients of the transcendental model, which was outlined in Chapter 2.

I have outlined the methodology for the two stages of the TRS on Pastoral Care and offered three examples that illustrate the methodology of the stages. I am aware that they represent only a small portion of the many presentations of the TRSs life. It is out of this experience – the critique of models and then reflecting theologically on their ministry together with a life experience that students – hopefully – develop their own model for theological reflection. This has been the experience for some groups, although for others it has not been as successful. Reasons for this will be discussed in the evaluation of the TRS.

Stage 3

This is the culmination of the other two stages, assisting students to develop their own model for theological reflection. Students by now have been exposed to many theoretical models of theological reflection and have shared life experience in their ministry presentations to the seminar group. They are now expected to write a 1500-word essay on their own model for theological reflection. The essay is not presented to the class for feedback, but handed to the seminar leader for comments and an overall grade.

To illustrate Stage 3, I present two contrasting models for theological reflection from two people with different ecclesiastical, cultural and theological positions. What each has in common, however, is the seriousness and integrity with which they have approached their task. Each has considerable life and ministry experience and both are in the ministry stream, each representing different traditions. Each used the resources offered to them in the TRS, drawing upon their ministry and personal experiences in developing their models.

The first model for theological reflection could be identified as a ministry model. The student makes strong claims to be an evangelical Christian. His beliefs include the authority of Scripture, although not fundamentalism; the majesty of Jesus Christ; the Lordship of the Holy Spirit; the need for personal conversion and evangelism. 'Without the undergirding of these fundamental beliefs, theological reflection to me is like a ship broken free from its moorings in a storm.' The seminar provided quite a challenge to him as its methodology was threatening and generated resistance. I was aware that he had received some negative responses from some of his peers in other classes for his theological views. While my theological position was quite different from his, I had a great respect for him as a person and for the strength of his conviction. The integrity of the student would not allow him to resist the process, and he worked with the process within the bounds of his strong doctrinal position. Below is a summary of his model for theological reflection:

Primary sources for reflecting: knowing God and making God known

Preparation for reflecting on ministry: Reflection on one's relationship with God through prayer and calling on the Holy Spirit for guidance.

Resources for theological reflection

Use of one's imagination and moral imagination in decision making, which involves the suspension of judgement.

- Theological reflection in Scripture is particularly directed toward the person of Jesus Christ, in whose life and ministry we encounter what it is to live in relationship to God and one another. The Bible's ethical teachings reflect and nurture wholeness and direct us on our journey towards growth in the virtue of love, which fulfils all of the requirements of the law.
- The tradition requires that one works within the orthodox beliefs of the reformed tradition.
- The social sciences: psychology can provide insight for our ministry to people with psychological problems.
- Theology assists in understanding the interconnectedness of the whole creation, which assists in understanding pastoral relationships in the light of the many relationships that bring life or destruction to people.
- One's own experience and the experience of others are important resources for theological reflection.

Within the working of the student's orthodox and evangelical beliefs there was genuine movement in gaining insight into the value of new resources for theological reflection and a change in attitude to some delicate pastoral issues. The new learning for him was the insights received from classes in Christian ethics, the social sciences (seminar reading) and the thoughts of Jurgen Moltmann in his theology class. He discovered that these disciplines not only have an influence on how one understands the complexity of human relationships, but that they can also be of assistance in the way one offers pastoral care to people.

The test of these new insights came in his field education placement where he was confronted with the issue of homosexuality. It would be fair to say that, up until this point, the student had not only rejected homosexuality as being sinful, but also rejected the person as being a sinner; later the student rejected only the act as being sinful. In his theological reflection paper he indicated the importance of the insights of author Philip Keane in his book *Christian Ethics and Imagination*, which explores the work of the moral imagination in decision making. In this work judgement is suspended to enable traditional insights and new insights to play, in the hope that a fuller understanding will be reached. The student wrote:

> This process reminded me of my reflections during my field education placement. It was here that I found myself suspending my traditional understandings and allowing experience and new insights to come together, in the hope of coming to a fuller understanding of homosexuality.

The suspension of traditional understanding allowed him to care deeply for a number of homosexual men who had AIDS. His verbatim account of his ministry was moving. Through this experience he did gain a fuller understanding of the epidemiology of homosexuality, but he also acknowledged that God's inclusive love for all people includes homosexuals. His view of Scripture could or would not allow him to change his belief that homosexuality was a sin against God. While some might consider this a small shift in his belief system, it was a genuine and integrated shift that will be reflected in his pastoral care ministry as he genuinely loves and cares for people.

Although the method of reflection was not clearly stated in his paper there was enough evidence to suggest that there was an ongoing dialogue involving the various resources, which he acknowledges as being part of his model.

The second presentation combined aspects of the praxis and transcendental models for theological reflection. This presentation was concerned with issues of justice in educational methodology; it also spoke to the student's struggle to live an authentic life in the midst of cultural confusion.

The student as a Koori woman was striving for an identity in a communal home of understanding where she offers her ministry.[10] A ministry candidate for the priesthood, she has not had an easy journey in her chosen vocation. Her model for theological reflection provided some insight into the reason for this uneasy journey. She requested that she be allowed to choose a book for the stage 1 presentation. Her critical reflection was on *God's Wrathful Children*, by Willa Boesak. The essence of this book speaks to a theology of the land. Her ministry presentation involved a ministry to a person with Alzheimer's disease. Her life experience paper was based on a personal account of her family history and her struggle to find an identity for herself. The elements of all these presentations infiltrate her final paper, her model for theological reflection.

She began with the 'Why?' of her model. She was critical of Charles Wood's intellectual method of theological reflection, which emphasizes understanding and meaning. She said that understanding is only part of the process of her model and preferred 'language that images knowingness', which means 'experiencing a deeper life force within us, knowing ourselves as more alive, more deeply

---

[10]   The term 'Koori' is used for an Australian Aboriginal of South Eastern Australia. For more information see www.koori.usyd.edu.au

integrated into our bodies'. In citing the influence of Veronica Brady she said, 'It is not just meaning we are after, which is more an exercise of the mind, it is "presence" that human life is questing after.' This understanding of knowing and presence was illustrated in an experience in her ministry placement to an aged care facility for dementia patients. In this place she discovered that human life is fragile. 'We struggle to understand the reason why we exist.' She failed to stay with the fear as 'it shuddered at the very core of who I am. What if life does not matter? For a moment we live, then die and is that all there is?' However, she soon discovered that:

> To ask why, opens us to the mystery that is life. We may never be sure of what the motivation behind creation is, but through my struggle to give my life meaning and substance I discovered human life is not a problem to be solved but a mystery to be enjoyed.

Part of the mystery to be enjoyed was the meaning of her presence in the aged care facility.

This mystery of life was further highlighted with her acknowledgment that all humanity is part of a living and dynamic world in which we are all interconnected. She did not expand on this implication for her model, but simply indicated she wished to develop a deeper understanding of how connected and interrelated human beings are to each other and the environment.

The student proceeded to relate how her model has operated in her own life. Her model is based on living a fully incarnated life. Her search for understanding and truth through education and religion, while promising so much, failed to provide an answer to the meaning of life. She described four phases.

1. The recognition that there was something wrong in her life. This recognition occurred when she collapsed, critically ill, alone and isolated. She spent many months alone and quiet in hospital. It was during this time that she reflected on the incongruity in her life and 'began a journey back into my history, a painful, confronting pilgrimage that opened up charnel houses full of skeletons and shadows that began to draw together the weft and weave of my story'.
2. It was during this journey that she discovered she had built a world of self-deception. She had built a cover story that prevented her:

> ... from having to face up to my many weaknesses, face up to my life as it really was. I had created many lies and spent large amounts of energy maintaining them. But through exploring my humanity, learning to live with myself as broken and fragile, headed for death, I discovered that what I had been looking for was waiting within me all the time. There was nothing I needed to do.

3. The restoration of her life meant learning to live with herself, accepting herself. She took ownership of the lies, truths and insecurities. In doing so, 'I now know myself as a child of creation, a beloved child of God.' The journey to recognition of this relationship with God was not just an individual journey; it also involved others from her Koori community. 'I saw myself in others, I

began to understand the delicate bond between us and between our environment. As a Koori woman and mother this was important to my identity. I knew forgiveness by acceptance.'

4. This continuing restoration required a sharing and sacramental community. She needed a group of people to share the struggle. She also needed a sacramental community because: 'We are sacramental people. Our brokenness is the brokenness of the bread, the symbol of the life of Christ. Christ points us to the presence of the divine in our lives and in the environment, and authenticates our humility as humans in the cosmos.' She has chosen the Anglican tradition in which to live out this communal and sacramental community.

The 'How?', or process, of this continuing journey is crucial to her model for theological reflection. The journey indicated in her model begins with being able to enter the silence within us and remain in it. To enter an event from the silence in the body and take time to brood on it, to come to know oneself as part of the process of the reflection, is, she said, 'to fill it with my life. To make it mine.' For her this is the meaning of integration. She says the use of Scripture and other resources are important in order to fill the event with other images and ways of understanding so that a conversation can be established with communities and any other people involved in the event or its analysis. She says: 'I may not own my life, but I am fully responsible to live it.'

I have chosen to present this reflection on her life journey rather than present the more ordered and formal presentation of her model for theological reflection. Her reflection shows the complexities and sometimes horrendous struggles of her being true to herself while at the same time studying in an educational system which, in many ways, is diametrically opposed to the very core of her cultural beliefs and understanding. Further, her approach to spirituality and theology can stand in tension with the tradition to which she is committed.

It was a privilege to enter her world, a world I struggled to understand at times. What I did understand was the integrity of her personal, cultural, spiritual and faith journey. The strength of her model is that her God is within, not determined by any outside forces that people may want to impose on her. She has been ordained into the priesthood and I hope her words at the conclusion of her account still dwell within: 'My model I pray will help me live more truly and deeply with myself, with my family, with others, with creation and with our Creator in relationships that are always dynamic.' If she can say 'yes' to even part of this, the outcome of her participation will be significant.

Pastoral supervision – its place within the theological reflection seminar

The characteristics of pastoral supervision outlined in Chapter 3 are deeply ingrained in my understanding of the theory, theology and practice of pastoral supervision. Its effect on me over the years has been a formative and transformative experience; its incarnational and relational nature will no longer allow me to stand outside and remain uncommitted. Its evaluative nature reveals and activates God's judgement and grace. Its covenantal nature gives the student the right to fail and to learn from that failure. Pastoral supervision is more often exercised at the intersections of success–failure, judgement–grace and congruity–incongruity. My supervisory style is concerned with warmth, genuineness and immediacy in the supervisory relationship. It encourages a balance between appropriate and genuine affirmation and confrontation. I use the word 'genuine' because contrived affirmation and confrontation does not promote authenticity; nor does it encourage people to take responsibility for themselves. I use my gifts and skills and delegate power to empower other people. I understand dependency and security needs and the subtle issues of transference and countertransference in relationships. I work diligently and use my supervisory skills to develop relationships of independence and interdependence. I encourage people to take responsibility for themselves in order that they can take responsibility for others. I believe passion and hope are kept alive in one's life and ministry by a vision for the future.

Central to this vision is the recognition that ambiguity is fundamental to the nature of my faith. However, I am aware that, for many, security is fundamental to the nature of their faith. This difference in perspective requires a respect for people's genuine beliefs. I have a respect for the social sciences to inform my pastoral supervision, but not to define it. Therefore, I model my beliefs naturally and use the skills inherent in the psychotherapeutic theory of the parallel process[11] that enables people to see how impasses can develop between them and how they can be resolved.

Resistance and theological resistance

One of my roles as pastoral supervisor is to highlight the congruity–incongruity between what the students believe and how they practise their actual ministry. I push them to state their espoused theology and how this matches their particular style of ministry.

Of course, the composition of people in each TRS group is different and the supervisory dynamics and issues can also be different. A recent group was composed of people from a number of cultures and the gender balance was equal. Initially, it seemed it was going to be an exciting group with which to work. The co-leader was a religious sister whose specialty was spiritual direction and who was at this particular time director of a community day centre for people unemployed and homeless. However, it soon became obvious that there were a number of students who were vocal and passionate about theology, especially systematic theology. Their assertiveness, which sometimes bordered on aggression, was a disruptive influence to the process of the TRS as it provoked anxiety among other members of the group, causing them to retreat to their familiar and defensive

---

[11] John Foskett and David Lyall 1988, *Helping the Helpers*, London: SPCK, pp. 114–34.

systems. Those people entering the theological reflection process from the theological position were quick to point out that our post-modern society had diminished the tradition and therefore the social sciences and the influence of the culture had to be viewed with suspicion. In fact, if any interpretation was to occur it was to be on the 'turf' of theology and the tradition. Their hostility was expressed towards a sociologist who was invited as a guest speaker. Fortunately or unfortunately, his response to them was just as assertive: I am not sure that there was much learning that day.

Those entering the theological reflection process from experience and cultural positions resisted the stress placed on the importance of theology; they were also intimidated by the knowledge of the theologians. They had the potential to model the best in theological reflection, but spent most of their time challenging the assertions of those who wanted a systematic theological voice to dominate the theological reflection process.

Up until this particular TRS the majority of people in the seminar groups were open to the process. So much learning and integration occurred as a result. The composition of this group made for a different dynamic. In addition, the co-leader was new to the process and, while she felt what was happening would be good in the end, she too was shaken by the strong assertions made by some of the students.

The position of pastoral supervision and the pastoral supervisor was continually tested. I felt I was caught in the middle, wanting to affirm the validity of each position. I found it difficult to hold and contain the anxieties that most students were experiencing when faced with new learning and change.[12] As a pastoral supervisor I was aware on the one hand of the tension of shielding students from too much anxiety, which could impede learning and, on the other hand, allowing people to face their anxieties with all the attending risks. The polarities were named as the inclusion of the validity of experience in the theological reflection process and the importance of the inclusion of systematic theology in the process. In this instance I was attempting to contain the anxieties of the students in order to allow them to undertake the risks and the new learning that might emerge as a result. However, I too had my own anxieties – I was intimidated by the 'superior' and sometimes valid knowledge of the theologians.

Some of the students were playing the game of 'If you knew Tillich like I know Tillich'. In this particular game a student may display a superior or more up-to-date theological knowledge than the supervisor.[13] My most effective supervision occurred when I trusted myself to find my voice and assert my authority with a plea to the students to listen to the voices of culture, experience and theology that were equally represented in the group and were impacting on the theological reflection process. I asked that each person not only listen carefully to the other, but also clarify, if necessary, something that was not clear to them before asserting their position. Basic to any model of theological reflection is that of listening.

I also knew that these voices of assertion and aggression were coming from a

---

[12]   Winnicott, in his book *The Family and Individual Development* (Tavistock, 1965), develops this concept of holding of care in the development of children.

[13]   Foskett and Lyall, *Helping the Helpers*, p. 120.

position of fear and insecurity. Up until this point I contended that when the students experienced the authenticity and congruity of the pastoral supervisor at first hand they would begin to form a solid, integrative sense of their own pastoral identity from the inside out and develop an identity that would be different and distinct from my own. This would occur in an enduring and reliable form through the process of internalization, not imitation. What would be internalized is the experience of my being with the student. However, I found it difficult to be with many of the students due to their resistance to the process.

Trust began to develop within the group and people tentatively began to listen to each other, but we ran out of time. The final essays were either devoid of passion (cognitive) or too defensive (of their position) or deceptive (pretending that change had taken place in order to pass the course). There were, however, a number of students who had the strength to engage the process and deliver a final paper that reflected insight and change. One student in particular, who initially claimed that experience was the only influence shaping her view of life, was in the end able to claim and embrace the influence of culture and theology on her interpretation of life and ministry. She continues to blossom in her academic and formation studies.

The evaluations of this particular seminar were surprisingly positive and thoughtful, although in some cases predictable. Perhaps the most significant evaluation came from one of the more open theologians who said as part of her evaluation: 'This course has been the most difficult course so far in my theological training, but it also has been one of the most challenging (oral evaluation).' In general, the evaluations over the years have been positive and indicate the importance of this integrative course for students within the theological education curriculum.

I have also come to a new level of understanding of the term 'resistance' through my direct experience of the praxis model of theological reflection and through my involvement in SUMP. Previously I viewed resistance as a negative response to authority, assuming that this authority issue needed to be addressed before one was able to work with a particular supervisor or institution. While this may be true in the medical model of care I have come to recognize the need for a ministry of resistance that is connected with oppression or injustice. In fact, it is in the area of social analysis, which unearths social and cultural injustice, in which my supervision has developed.

This is why some writers and practitioners would challenge the primacy of the concept of transformation and its connection with oppression. Christine Smith, a liturgist, characterizes the debate when she writes of preaching and its relationship to resistance:

> It is crucial to name this kind of preaching *a ministry of resistance* [Smith's emphasis] rather than a ministry of transformation. Though a transformed world is the ultimate hope that undergirds such a ministry, if preachers listen carefully to the oppressed voices surrounding them, that will discern that the language of survival, struggle, and resistance is what permeates these messages of indictment and hope, not the language of transformation. Transformative language assumes a certain measure of privilege and

power that neither accurately describes nor reflects the lived realities of oppressed people.[14]

The issue of resistance to oppression in our society today raises not only anxiety for the student, but also the supervisor. I am more comfortable with the term 'transformation' than the word 'resistance'. The Third World theologians have made the church very uncomfortable with their emphasis on resistance. However, I believe that genuine transformation may need to be preceded by genuine resistance, especially where oppression is involved. While I do and have used the legitimate term 'transformation' to indicate a radical change in a person's life, I detect at times some incongruence between the claim and the actual reality. Pastoral supervision needs to acknowledge and affirm genuine resistance just as it does genuine transformation. However, it also has a responsibility to point out in both cases where there are discrepancies between the claim and the reality. It is here that students can learn about dichotomy and its divisive effects on their lives and ministry and that of others.

Observations

There have been some changes in the educational and philosophical positions of the TRS. From the experience described above I have become acutely aware of the importance of providing in theological reflection groups a safe structure for discussing potentially threatening differences in belief and behaviour. I also believe there has been too much emphasis on the integration of theory and practice within the theological reflection process. This dichotomy, which is represented by knowledge and experience, confuses the students. I have noted that many of our students in attempting to integrate their academic study with the practice of ministry lose their passion. They are caught at the intersection of cognitive and feeling positions and are often unable to proceed further. Charles M. Wood is correct when he says theological enquiry engages the whole person. He speaks of this activity as a process of 'transformation'.[15] However, this process will not occur through a paradigm, which tends to perpetuate the dichotomy between academic and practical disciplines and therefore fragments the 'whole' person who engages it.[16]

The illustrations that are provided in this chapter and in Chapter 3 are evidence of a more holistic approach to theological reflection. This means that all of these aspects of the student's life become part of the theological reflection process, which, in turn, becomes a more dynamic process.

From an educational and curriculum point of view the UCA *Report into Ministerial Education* should also be included in the TRS *Handbook* in order that the students might be engaged in curriculum reform. This would provide a local

---

[14]   Christine M. Smith 1996, 'Preaching as an art of resistance', in Christie Conzad Neuger (ed.), *The Arts of Ministry*, Louisville: Westminster /John Knox Press, p. 193.

[15]   Wood, *Vision and Discernment*, p. 59.

[16]   Ibid., pp. 63–5.

context for students as they engage models and methods for theological reflection with the eventual aim of developing their own model for theological reflection.

Many students struggle with the processes required to undertake a course of this nature. Often this is due to the curriculum split between knowledge and experience. More attention needs to be given to the educational entrance requirements not only for students but also for some seminar leaders who are not conversant with the educational processes employed in the TRS.

Perhaps the greatest limit on the effectiveness of the TRS in curriculum reform is the lack of knowledge or interest of some faculty members. For some its aim and purpose is not clear, and for others it is not 'academic'. However, there are a number of my colleagues who have been involved and others who have registered good feedback from students and this provides encouragement. Perhaps my greatest encouragement came from a faculty member at a recent meeting on the structure of the curriculum when she said 'we need to make more connections between knowledge and wisdom'.

Reviewing the strengths and limitations of the TRS and the overall response from students has been most encouraging. For the minority it is unimportant but for the majority it is important, and for a significant number of these it has been the most crucial development for their ongoing formation as ministers.

While the Ministerial Education Report had shortcomings the clear message from the report is that theological education must be shaped to meet the context and goals for mission and ministry. The report is critical of the ' "classic" approach that is linear in its movement, commencing with core knowledge, moving to practical knowledge and then applied knowledge'. Instead it asserts:

> A curriculum expressing an integrated approach based upon inter-disciplinary engagement with the 'core' subjects would be one that emphasised an ongoing conversation with culture and experience, tradition and the church and our scriptural centre[17]

It is my claim that such an approach in fact constitutes an understanding of theological reflection as practised by the numerous theological reflection models outlined earlier and incorporated in the TRS. The report indicates that the purpose of this integrated approach to theological education is not only to alleviate the dichotomy between theory and practice, but also to prepare ministers more effectively for the work of mission and ministry of the church. I have argued that the TRS makes a significant contribution to this understanding of theological education by defining and practising theological reflection as critical activity (developing pastoral effectiveness) and in discovering the movement of the Spirit of God in human experience. Further, I have argued strongly that pastoral supervision is a vehicle that facilitates integration in theological reflection. This concept of pastoral supervision as a vehicle for integration is not, however, envisaged in the report.

The report is also concerned that ministers are not being prepared to minister in

---

[17]   Report of the Task Group to Review Ministerial Education within the UCA.

a post-Christian society. While these findings do not use the term 'post-Christian' to describe the status of our society, it is intrinsic to an understanding of theological reflection that its process is dynamic rather than static. It is concerned about living one's faith in a changing and ambiguous world rather than in a world where certitude prevails. I argued in the development of the transcendental model for theological reflection that ambiguity was not the enemy of authenticity and integration, but rather of incongruity focused in self-deception. Theological reflection is concerned with transformation rather than restoration. Therefore, the TRS can be seen to be concerned about preparing ministers for ministry in a post-Christian age.

Chapter 5

Structural integration within the theological institution – a case study

In addressing the processes being undertaken by the UCTC to implement the spirit of the Ministerial Education Commission's recommendations into the curriculum, I will reflect on the place of the TRS within the curriculum. It is sufficient to comment at this point that, within the formation program, TFE has enjoyed a high profile for many years, but in recent years the hours have been reduced in order to allow space for other facets of the program. TFE also has a high profile in the recommendations of the *Ministerial Education Report*. Prior to implementing the recommendations in the present curriculum the field education requirement for ministry students was two years of field education, which is equivalent to two subjects plus one unit of theological reflection.

Proposal for a new core curriculum and faculty responses

Three members of faculty were appointed to prepare a proposal for the implementation of the recommendations for Phase 2 of the core curriculum. Members of the committee were the Dean, a moral theologian and myself, Director of Field Education, as convenor of the committee. We produced a document that met the broad objectives of the new core curriculum. The following extract gives the major thrust of our proposal:

> In order to meet the need for students to have a basic understanding of the fundamentals of theology that ministry requires, it is proposed that the first part of the course consist in a series of discipline-based introductory courses. These introductory courses would aim to provide students with an overview of the subject, awareness of the key issues in the field, alertness to the key issues that form the relationship to other fields and knowledge of the resources available to pursue independent learning in the subject. Set within the framework of encouraging students to develop an integrative approach to theological study, the first year would consist of the more foundational disciplines of biblical studies, systematic theology, church history, pastoral theology and Christian education. In the first year, there would also be a three-week pre-sessional introductory course in pastoral care and counselling. There would be no Field Education placements in this first year to enable students to focus on theological study. As students enter field placements in the second year, the first half of the second year would focus upon the more integrative subjects of liturgy and Christian ethics (and theological reflection in the second semester).

The second half of the course would be very flexible both as to course format and student choice. The central aims of this half of the course are to enable students to develop their particular gifts and to further the objective of theological integration.

This program focuses upon theological integration through academic, experiential, and reflective opportunities. While the first semester of the second year ethics, liturgy, and theological reflection, will place a particular emphasis on it.[1]

Whilst this extract indicates the committee's concern to develop an integrative core curriculum, it also recognizes that all disciplines have a constructive part to play in this process of integration.

The response of the Faculty

The core curriculum committee invited written feedback from faculty eliciting a wide range of responses which expressed a certain amount of resistance to our proposal as well as legitimate concerns. The responses represented elements of shared and differing visions of theological and ministerial education. Because of the importance of developing a shared vision that all members of faculty could enthusiastically pursue, we recommended that faculty find some extended and dedicated time away from our immediate context and seek to develop such a vision. The value of such a focused discussion is that while there was a diversity of responses they nevertheless suggested the possibility that developing a common vision for a new core curriculum could be achieved.

In seeking the services of a suitably qualified independent facilitator for the discussions we approached and interviewed many eligible people but for many reasons they were not available. Finally, faculty agreed that a member of the core curriculum committee be the facilitator.

We met as a faculty for two days to discuss the proposal in order to negotiate an outcome. The two-day meeting was an enlightening time as we entered into the give and take of developing a new curriculum. I was encouraged by the compromises, generosity and graciousness of my colleagues in the hard decisions that had to be made in those two days. We agreed to a new curriculum and, although what we ended up with was somewhat different from the one the committee had proposed, the spirit of recognizing each other's contribution was retained. The new proposal included not only more interdisciplinary teaching, but also the intention of developing more integrative courses.

During the development of the new curriculum I reluctantly chose to relinquish the TRS as a compulsory unit for ordination requirements. I did so because it seemed at the time that faculty was committed to most of the integrative processes inherent in the seminar. Further, the decision was consistent with the position I had already espoused publicly:

---

[1] John E. Paver, Rufus Black and Gwen Ince, 1999, 'Core Curriculum Proposal', unpublished document relating to the implementation of the UCA Report at the Uniting Church Theological College, Melbourne, Australia. The above is a short summary and the full text can be found in Appendix 3.

I wish to state that field education does provide an important space to assist the integrating process, but it is not our responsibility alone! I am convinced that the total curriculum and faculty have responsibility for integration. Field Educators have their role to play, but we cannot assume this task alone, because it will not work! It must be shared by all faculty, and find a place in all courses. The problem of fragmentation cannot be solved in any other way![2]

I believed that at the conclusion of these two days, faculty as a whole had taken responsibility for the process of integration. Unfortunately, this perception did not last for long as some faculty members, in the days following the meeting, came to believe in all conscience that they could not subscribe to some of the decisions made. The erosion of our new curriculum had begun. We have subsequently had many core curriculum meetings without coming to any conclusions. The existing curriculum continues and theological integration is heavily dependent upon the TRS.

Critical reflection on faculty responses

In retrospect, the original core curriculum committee did not pay sufficient attention to the educational processes necessary to undertake the integrative style of learning that we were advocating, nor did we fully comprehend the impact that our proposal might have on our theological partners (Jesuit Theological College and Trinity (Anglican) Theological School). Further, we did not refer explicitly to the recent debates on theological education. It would be fair to say that the majority of faculty was not conversant with this literature. I certainly have not previously articulated the educational and theological framework that undergirds the TRS.

Would it have made any difference had this been done? Since June 2001 the UCTC debate has been Athens and Berlin revisited.[3] There is a clear division between academic theology and practice. Subsequent to the two-day meeting this division was accentuated by an attempt to marginalize TFE by programming it outside the semester period, an action that would allow more room for academic subjects during the semester. If successful TFE would be marginalized and hence the integrative style of learning we were advocating jeopardised. A flicker of hope for ongoing discussions surfaced at a curriculum meeting held in September 2001, when a member of faculty suggested we should be investigating the connection between knowledge and wisdom. I thought: 'Perhaps we are moving towards the position that Farley holds.' The comment was not taken up as too few were interested in the connection between wisdom and knowledge.

In the most recent discussions, however, there was a modest breakthrough. Faculty was asked to respond to a curriculum proposal initiated by the principal of

---

[2]   Paver, 1999, 'Field Education'. p.5.

[3]   Kelsey, *Between Athens and Berlin*. Numerous references are made to this book in Chapter 1. The terms 'Athens' and 'Berlin' represent two very different and, in Kelsey's opinion, ultimately irreconcilable models of excellent education. For the purpose of this discussion these two models are identified as theory ('Berlin') and practice ('Athens').

UCTC. One colleague, in a faculty meeting, relayed a message from a student naively describing an arm of practical theology as 'mere feeling'. It was a critical moment for me as the comment was made in the context of developing a new curriculum. In the meeting I made a strong plea that a coherent body of knowledge informs all aspects of practical theology. I indicated that this colleague's comment was out of date and did nothing to further our discussions. I took a strong stand for the place of practical theology and its place within the curriculum.

Only those who were present can answer whether my stand had any lasting influence. A new core curriculum committee is in the process of developing four options for discussion. The one I favour most resembles Charles Wood's model, which advocates interdisciplinary teaching with an emphasis on vision and discernment, where there is an attempt to understand the impact that each of our disciplines has on the others and the implications this has for our teaching and learning. There is no doubt in my mind that we respect each other's professional abilities; perhaps this will be the beginning of mutual respect for each of our disciplines.

It appears that the TRS might remain intact, but be taught with more interdisciplinary input. The number of field education placements will be reduced slightly, but the options to be provided may well be more creative for the students. The discussion continues and the outcome will not be known for a number of months. Since my retirement the ministry studies and TFE positions have been separated placing in danger the integration processes that developed when they were unified. Further, little has changed in the theological structure in my institution.

'A depth of sorrow' – my responses and recommendations

My leadership style is to listen pastorally to all sides of an issue with the aim that the process leads to an acceptable outcome for all. It is a costly approach, as one enters people's souls. It is at the point of implementing the decisions that pastoral care becomes subservient to the administrative concerns. This process has, over the years, not only stood me in good stead, but has enabled me to develop pastoral care departments and theological programs. Rightly or wrongly, in the case of implementing the decisions faculty had agreed upon during the curriculum days, my pastoral heart dominated my administrative responsibilities. This was due in part to the pain and tension that I experienced in many faculty members. Decision makers draw a fine line between good pastoral care and the creative management needed in good decision-making. The initial decision by faculty may have been implemented if I had been faithful to my understanding of decision-making.

Further, my plea to faculty members involved in the two curriculum days not to discuss issues with other members outside of the group was not agreed upon. In my view, this decision led to some members of faculty coalescing which eventually resulted in a number of faculty individually approaching the principal stating in all conscience they could not go ahead with the decisions made. This action took the decision outside of the group-agreed decision and therefore was a form of resistance.

The classical forms of resistance to supervision and pastoral care have been discussed elsewhere, but it is not unfair to say that all members of faculty were anxious about change taking place during this process of decision making and, further, that there was a perceived threat that power and authority would be undermined if this proposal went ahead. [4]

This leads me to the question: Is resistance in theological education different from the classical forms of resistance found elsewhere? Theologian Matthew Lamb, in his presentation to the Catholic Theological Society of America, believes that the core of many debates in theological education is the theory–praxis issue. He says:

> The relationship of theory and practice goes right to the core of the entire philosophical enterprise: it involves the relations of consciousness to being, of subject to object, of idea to reality, of word to deed, of meaning to history. Similarly, in theology, this relationship goes beyond a discussion of contemplative or active ways of life to raise such fundamental issues to the relations of faith to love, of church to world, of orthodoxy to orthopraxy, of salvation to liberation, of religion to political concerns, of historical and systematic to moral and pastoral theology.[5]

If Lamb is correct, and I believe he is, then there is much at stake for the future of theological education in the theory–praxis debate. The intensity of the debate and the pain experienced by many faculty members would suggest that the relationship of theory and practice is at the core of theological education. One can understand the historical emotions that emerge in this debate as well as the resistance on both sides of the issue. However, Wood, in addressing the risk of 'one-dimensionality' in identifying theology exclusively with one's dimension or theological discipline, says that this is not just 'short-sightedness' or an act of arrogance – as a rule. Rather, he says:

> It is rooted in an awareness of the tendency of those engaged in theology to evade or distort certain of its demands as they attempt to satisfy others: to pursue 'authenticity' at the expense of 'relevance' … It is understandable if some theologians liken this situation to that of a person attempting to serve two masters, and draw the expected conclusion: you must choose one.[6]

It was in this conflicting pain that my pastoral heart ruled over my administrative responsibilities.

---

[4]   See Chapter 4, pp. 118–122; Foskett and Lyall, *Helping The Helpers*, pp. 114–34; David Myler 1979, 'Resistance to clinical learning: four biblical types', *Journal of Supervision and Training in Ministry*, vol. 2, 73–81; Barry Estadt, John Compton and Melvin C Blanchette (eds) 1987, *The Art of Clinical Supervision*, New York: Paulist Press, pp. 66–82.

[5]   Matthew Lamb, 'The theory–praxis relationship in contemporary theology', *Catholic Theological Society of America Proceedings*, 31, 149–78.

[6]   Wood, *Vision and Discernment*, pp. 52–3.

It is interesting to note that the theological debate is explicit about the ways in which social and cultural factors may distort the Christian faith and theological enquiry, but very little attention is given to the institutional arrangements of power within a theological school. Neither is much attention paid to the consequences of the theological debate on a theological school's own social, economic and cultural location. My focus has been on the pain of change and resistance in the theological debate. Inherent in any resistance is the threat of the loss of power and authority.

Kelsey makes a somewhat depressing statement on resolving the theory–practice debate. He believes that the two [theory and practice] are incompatible:

> In either case, never suppose that you can synthesize the two types of excellent theological education. It may be that for historical reasons no ... theological education can abandon either type. All the same, the tensions between them are unavoidable. The best that can be hoped for is an unstable truce, constantly threatening to break down into educational incoherence. The underlying reason for this is that each type presupposes a different view of the nature of 'reason' and, indeed, a different view of 'human nature'. A decision to negotiate from within one of these two types and on its grounds is at the same time, however implicitly a decision to adopt its underlying assumptions about what it is to be human. One's 'appropriation' of aspects of the other type, then, is always a matter of abstracting it from its conceptual home in one kind of view of 'reason' and 'human nature' and grafting it onto an alien conceptual field. As a result, the seeds of conceptual confusion about the nature and purpose of theological education, if not seeds of outright incoherence, are as omnipresent as they appear to be historically unavoidable.[7]

Kelsey contends that the two methodologies cannot be synthesized and that the tensions are unavoidable; that the best that can be hoped for is an 'unstable truce'.

I believe that his position is an indictment of the message of hope found in the Gospel. It is no secret that *Schleiermachen* thought still dominates in many faculties. The classical theologians often express it in an attitude of superior knowledge, while some practical theologians say that theory alone is irrelevant to the needs of the church. It is difficult at times to ascertain whether members of faculty have deep ideological and methodological differences or are attempting to preserve their power and, therefore, resist change.

On the surface my proposal of a group model of theological reflection and the open-ended curriculum would suggest that Kelsey is correct in his assertion that it is impossible to 'synthesize the two types of excellent theological education'. From the faculty's point of view his view has validation, but from a student's point of view theological reflection as advocated in this book is both theological and holistic. Integration – or synthesization – does occur, albeit with many obstacles placed in the way of this process.

I have argued that theological reflection is a method of integration within the curriculum of UCTC. I have stated that pastoral supervision mediates as a vehicle for theological reflection. These claims have been illustrated by an integrated approach through the TRS in my theological institution. I have made a claim that

---

[7]   Kelsey, *Between Athens and Berlin*, p. 228.

the TRS meets many of the expectations of the report of the Task Group set up to review ministerial education within the UCA. I have been reasonably successful in both of these claims. However, I have fallen short of my claim that the TRS has the potential to be a catalyst for reform of the curriculum for the UCTC. Elsewhere, I have stated my reasons for this apparent failure.

Further, the open-ended curriculum developed by the core curriculum committee at UCTC to meet the expectations of the *Report of the Ministerial Education Commission* fell short of our expectations. The proposal was built around the strengths of the two different curriculum options in order to meet the objectives of the new core curriculum. It emphasized groundwork in theology, experience and developed a model for integration. It gave power to the students by providing a flexible course with relatively few requirements in the second part of the curriculum and an emphasis on choice to enable the students to pursue subjects that develop their individual gifts and ministry. Staff resisted this proposal.

The major strength of the TRS was that it developed a model and a method. While the Ministerial Education Commission's report and the proposal developed by the core curriculum committee developed models for theological education, they lacked a method. The Uniting Church report lacked theological depth and, while the core curriculum proposal did have a theological rationale, it lacked an educational rationale. A process or method was lacking in both proposals.

Why is theological field education on the edge of theological education?

In my introduction I asked the question: Why is TFE on the edge of the main body of theological education? TFE has made a tremendous contribution to an understanding of pastoral supervision and theological reflection that mainly begins with lived experience. This book validates that claim. However, there is a perception among many people that practical theology, especially pastoral theology and TFE, is devoid of a sound body of knowledge. This perception is reflected in my colleague who naively described an arm of practical theology as 'mere feeling'. But people's perceptions contain some truth. There is no doubt in my mind that pastoral care, pastoral supervision and theological reflection contain a sound body of knowledge. The contents of this book and a multitude of literature on the subjects pay testimony to this. It seems, however, that, it is still fashionable to describe such arms of practical theology as the bridge metaphor, practical skills and mere feeling descriptions in theological education circles.

So why is TFE (pastoral supervision and theological reflection) on the edge of the main body of theological education? There are four major reasons for this exclusion.

*Practical theology has been reduced to the role of the bridge in theological
education*

Historically, there have been at least three bridge metaphors that have distorted the
theory–praxis debate and certainly the place of practical theology in the theological
curriculum.[8] The fourth distortion arises from within TFE itself.

- The bridge metaphor begins with a strong affirmation and indicates a
  dominance of theology. If a bridge is to be built it is built from the study of
  theology as a whole. Then a particular field (practical theology) is nominated as
  the bridging unit. Such an approach fosters in each field the obligation to bridge
  theory and practice and, at the same time, justifies the existence of practical
  theology as the discipline that accomplishes the bridge.
- The bridge metaphor as a way of interpreting theory–praxis is the distancing of
  theology and practice in theological school. When this process model is at work
  it is not necessary for each field or course to be a moment of high relevance,
  meeting the student's existential needs or addressing world crisis problems.
  Here the student expects to be distanced not only from the immediate
  application, but also from that student's own specific biographical needs and
  interests at that time. A course or unit can be effective and important in the long
  term precisely because of its distance from the immediacies of autobiography
  and culture. Farley cites an example of this argument when he says:

> If Augustine's writings are approached only for the purposes of discovering their
> immediate applicability to the activities of ministry, the vision, unity, depth and
> distinctiveness of these writings may never be grasped. Augustine's potentially
> explosive impact is ironically neutralised by the attempt to construct a bridge to praxis.[9]

I have stated earlier that to interpret an event or an experience too soon can render
the meaning lost. Patton believes 'one must "bracket" all speculative and
constructive views of the event so that there can be disciplined "seeing" '.[10] I am
also critical of those whose only purpose in studying theology is in making
practical application. In doing so their approach fragments and can deny a deeper
understanding of their faith. Any stance that is taken to distance a theological
conversation between all the disciplines is to affirm the legitimacy of the
separation of theory and praxis.

- The bridge metaphor is preoccupied with technique, indicated by the way in
  which theory–practice is used as criteria for education. Thus, the bridging of
  theory to practice is talked about as something that either happens or does not

---

[8]   I am indebted to Edward Farley for information regarding the first three bridge
metaphors in the theory–praxis debate. Farley 1981, 'The reform of theological education as
a theological task' *Theological Education*, Spring, 93–117.

[9]   Ibid., 105.

[10]   Patton, *From Ministry to Theology*, p. 37.

happen. In a successful field course, it happens. When it does not happen, matters remain academic and the course is not successful. This suggests that there are things that can be done to make it happen, if only we can discover what they are. If the theological schools do more interdisciplinary teaching, restructure the faculty in a certain way, add certain types of courses, then the bridge will be accomplished. In this metaphor if you find the correct technique the bridge will be completed and crossed. From experience we know this simply does not work.

• The fourth bridge metaphor comes from within the discipline of TFE itself. In 1987 Lynn Rhodes addressed the membership of the Association for Theological Education. In part she said:

> We are 'bridge people', which as the poet [and novelist] Marge Piercy reminds us is a fine place to walk over, but very difficult to live on. We are the connectors between the academies and the churches; between those who think theory and practice can be separate entities and those who demand relevance out of everything we do ... we sometimes found ourselves on the boundaries of every group and institution, church and college 'where the action' is in the world. As chaotic, unfocused and diffused as that can be, I do believe it is also our strength; never having a place of stability, never quite legitimate.

I agree with my colleague that this bridge could be a dynamic place to be, but this book asserts it is the place where others have wanted us to be, and not where we want to be situated. Those present at this conference found Rhode's words inspirational. However, the bridge metaphor has become pervasive, gradually seeping into the veins of theological schools and continues to have influence, making it a serious distortion of the meaning of theological study.

A methodology that begins with experience is unusual in theological education

It is more common in theological education to begin forming one's theological stance with Scripture, systematic theology, church history or philosophy, but not experience. This book makes a claim that the formation of a theology can begin with experience and also makes a claim for the priority of experience in understanding God and the world.

The Whiteheads begin with ministerial experience that includes not only ministers, but also the wider community of faith. For them a ministerial style of theological reflection is a corporate task. This model identifies experience as a critical voice in the theological conversation. Of particular interest to them is the authority of experience, befriending the tradition and the missing voices and privileged experience that can distort the theological conversation. The Whiteheads also highlight the experience of 'the sense of the Faithful'.[11]

---

[11]   Whitehead, *Method in Ministry*, pp. 50–1.

The praxis model of theological reflection focuses on the cultural experience. This model places greater emphasis on cultural and social change, which includes political and economic systems and assumes that any articulation of faith cannot be politically or economically neutral. The model is committed to privileging marginal perspectives – primarily, the poor.

The transcendental model begins with the experience of the authentic self. I have elaborated in Chapters 2 and 3 my understanding of experience. In this book my understanding of experience does not emphasize the new, creative and positive events that we bring to theological reflection. While I do not rule out this understanding of experience I have based my understanding of experience not on experiences that we bring, but how open we are to new and often unexpected experiences that enter our lives and have the potential to change and transform us. My understanding of experience is shaped by the problematic, disruptive, crisis events in our lives. Further, it is my contention that it is out of these unexpected experiences – critical moments or convictional moments – that a spiritual truth can occur in our lives. I further assert that it is the spiritual component of this critical moment that provides a way for authentic practical theological reflection.

The key to this authentic theological reflection is the critical reflection on the experience. Without the critical reflection it is an experience only, one that is without a context or does not have meaning. Wood pays little attention to the importance of lived experience in theological education. However, in his discussion on the relationship between faith and critical enquiry he says: 'It is clear that theological understanding requires personal engagement.'[12] He says that because there are so many concepts used in Christian witness – creation, sin, grace, hope – these concepts can be instruments for self-understanding.[13] While he cautions against the temptation to exhaust the meaning of these concepts by their relevance to the illumination or transformation of selfhood, he believes that their meaning has 'a certain capacity to understand *oneself* by them …'[14] This is why theological enquiry and theological education might rightly be seen to involve something along the lines of "spiritual formation …".'[15] Wood seems to be advocating a unity of life and thought when he says: 'One may not properly criticize what one does not understand.'[16] While he gives credence to the importance of self-understanding with the association of concepts used in Christian witness and spiritual formation he does not explicitly address the issue of personal experience or the importance of developing a theology from experience.

The feminist model of theological reflection as envisaged by The Mudflower Collective obviously concentrates on women's experience, but with very specific connotations. They make it clear in their publication that women's experience is

---

[12]   Wood, *Vision and Discernment*, pp. 85.
[13]   Ibid., p. 86.
[14]   Ibid.
[15]   Ibid.
[16]   Ibid.

itself not one thing, but rather pluralized by race, ethnicity and class, and that theological schooling's inadequacy to provide genuine pluralism correlates with its reliance on universalizing.

The perception that Theological field education lacks theological depth

This perception continues to be present in theological circles and there is some truth in it. If we wish to use the identifying term 'theological' in our understanding of field education then we need to be more explicit in our expression of a theology that begins with experience. Kinast is a little critical of those who assert that experience has an inherent theological character. Those who do:

> tend to invoke as their rationale a theology of revelation or a theology of incarnational grace and redemption: those who assert that experience has an affinity to theology tend to look at parallels, common themes, similar issues and analogous insights between experience and theology.[17]

Kinast believes that advocates of either approach will need to develop their positions with more 'explicit theological arguments'.[18] He says that translation or representation of experience is needed for theological meaning to be recognized and affirmed: '[T]heological reflection relies on a critical awareness of one's experience.'[19]

In Chapter 2 I have developed an integrated approach towards my personal experience, a Biblical theology of ministry and the professional implications emerging from this theology of ministry. The integration comes about as a result of my praxis in my personal, Biblical, and professional life. In a different context, Colin Hunter[20] has used a phenomenological method of research designed to identify and describe student experiences of SFE. Hunter identified five metathemes or research findings:

- mutuality of learning
- intersubjective learning
- chosen vulnerability
- revelation as a path to a new understanding
- experience as a locus for learning

From these findings he not only developed a Biblical model for supervised TFE, but has also developed a contemporary theological foundation. His theology of supervision is based on the contemporary renewal of interest in Trinitarian theology and, particularly, in the work of feminist theologian Catherine Mowry La

---

17 Kinast, *What Are They Saying About Theological Reflection?*, pp. 65–6.
18 Ibid., p. 66.
19 Ibid.
20 Colin J. Hunter 2003, *"Supervised TFE: A Phenomenological Enquiry?"* DMin Studies, Melbourne: MCD, pp. 179-212.

Cugna. I believe Hunter's research will be affirmed and recognized in theological circles. We need more theological field educators who can critically assess experience and develop a theology that has depth and relevance.

A theology that begins with experience challenges the traditional sources of theology

Lucian Richard, a systematic theologian, says:

> The sources are the formative factors that determine the character of a given theology. In Christian theology, the fundamental source has always been revelation in such a wise that theology and theological education are directly related and affected by the understanding of the nature of revelation.[21]

Traditionally, the sources for an understanding of revelation have come from Scripture or a church tradition. The encounter between God and humanity takes place primarily by means of the history recorded in the Scriptures or by means of the church. While there has been recognition of other sources, such as women's experience and culture, in theological education they still retain their influence as secondary sources. There has been little or no place in traditional theology for personal experience and its impact in defining the nature of revelation. The reason put forward is that personal experience is understood as being subjective, superficial and arbitrary, an obstacle to objectivity.

This book not only makes a strong claim for the place of personal experience in defining revelation, but also makes the claim for the priority of experience in understanding revelation. It is my claim that a dynamic faith comes from within, not from an externally imposed authority. Further, in my experience, Scripture and tradition have enabled me to grasp more fully my own inner experience; they are not substitutes for my inner experience. In fact the three theological reflection models I have cited, together with Scripture and tradition, have not only illuminated my understanding of revelation, but have been important factors in the process of integration. The method in the three models of theological reflection highlights the conversation between ministry experience, cultural experience, and personal experience.

I can understand the fear within the tradition when it comes to a theology that understands revelation 'as the presence of God in history – in the events of everyday life, in social and economic structures, in situations of oppression'.[22] This understanding of revelation not only emphasizes the injustice of oppressive systems and structures as it relates to the poor and the oppressed in society, but its theological method can also reveal the oppression of structures in the life of the church. In my experience models and methods that unmask the oppression in

---

[21]   Richard, 'The existing malaise in the theologizing of field experience', 67–70. While this article was published in 1972 the situation that he describes in theological education and field education in relation to experience still largely exists today.

[22]   Bevans, *Models of Contextual Theology*, p. 68.

society and the church (for example, the SUMP and liberation theology) will also be on the edge of the tradition and the church because they are too threatening to the power structures and to an understanding of God's revelation.

Charles Wood's vision and discernment – some new understandings

Charles Wood's proposal of the concept of *Vision and Discernment* has merit, especially within my own institution and provides a way forward to resolving this theory-practice debate.

David Kelsey, in a scholarly manner, proposes Wood's model of theology as a 'new key' in the theological education debate.[23] I wish to acknowledge his seminal work and extend its importance to a context in which I am familiar. Wood's contribution contains not only a model, but also a method. It has a theological and educational rationale. It is concerned about process, presents an option that reduces the pain of the theory-praxis debate by presenting an alternative, advocates the strengths of theology and the practice of ministry and develops a process that engages the whole person. While I have outlined Wood's proposal in Chapter 1, I wish to highlight further points of attraction from his book which make a significant contribution to theological education and offer some hope towards ending the impasse of the theory–praxis debate with a new approach to institutional theological education.

A new understanding of the theory–activity debate

The overarching goal of theological education, according to Wood, is theological enquiry. Theology, he says, is 'a critical enquiry into the validity of Christian witness'.[24] For Wood theology is an activity, an activity that is constituted by a type of enquiry that engages the whole person. 'Theology is one component of the set of activities that comprise the ongoing praxis of Christian communities, for which "witness" is Wood's generic term.'[25] Wood is critical of the old concept of *habitus* that restrains its meaning to only a sense of 'disposition', that is, a yearning to be wise. Wood says: 'Being wise takes more than a yearning to be wise … a *capacity* for intelligent decision and action is also required.'[26] Therefore, the outcome of critical enquiry requires action. While Wood stresses the importance of theology for the practice of ministry he is insistent that the practice of Christian communities should also inform and influence theology. It is important to note that, while I am a teacher in a theological school, I am also a member of a Christian community who has a witness to bring to an understanding of theology. My transcendental model and method of theological

---

23   Kelsey, *Between Athens and Berlin*, pp. 199–220.
24   Ibid., p. 21.
25   Kelsey, *Between Athens and Berlin*, p.202
26   Wood, *Vision and Discernment*, 87.

reflection bear witness to this claim. What seems at first glance a personal and individual model is an extremely communal model.

It is my experience that when you begin with yourself, people have a point of identification and, while they might not completely share your world view, they are often put in touch with some deep-seated issues in their own lives. Still, beginning with myself involves more than a point of identification for others. It also derives from a strong vocational drive that is passionate about relationships between God and human beings in order that people may know the presence of God in their lives more fully. Further, the theological issues that are of great concern for myself and others are not off the top of my head, but are worked through the agony and passion of my own life and through my commitment to the lives of others.[27] These beliefs shape my personal life, my ministry and my relationship with God.

Wood is critical of any theology that divorces itself from the influence of the church. This criticism often surfaces in the claim by the church that theology is distant from real life or that the theology taught does not address the importance of professional issues or the practice of ministry. While this may be true or untrue the issue here is not the development of certain skills or practice, but the ability of theory and practice to inform each other in a reflective, reciprocal and respectful way. The issue of reciprocity between the various theological disciplines and the Christian communities will be addressed later.

Wood's most significant contribution to the theological education debate is in a new understanding of the relationship between theology and practice. He proposes that, instead of explaining the relation between theology and practice by using the terms 'theory' and 'practice', we think about the relationship between vision and discernment in enquiry and other types of action. Engaging in any action requires capacities for 'insight into particular things or situations in their particularity' (discernment)[28] and capacities for 'a general, synoptic understanding of some range of data or field of objects' (vision).[29] Each of these capacities also needs each other. Wood says:

> They require each other at a deeper level than that on which they struggle against each other; and the most complete realization of either comes not at the expense of the other but rather in conjunction with the other's own fuller realization.[30]

It is the capacity for critical discernment, not practice, that serves as a corrective to vision's vulnerability to idolatry and ideological distortion. '*Both* vision and discernment are informed by, and in turn inform, practice … at the same time, vision and discernment *together* – and not vision (or 'theory') alone – are

---

[27] McFague, *Speaking in Parables*, pp. 157–61. McFague has been influential in my understanding of autobiography and its use in my life.

[28] Wood, *Vision and Discernment*, p. 68.

[29] Ibid., p. 67

[30] Ibid., p. 75.

constitutive of theological reflection.'[31] In this understanding competition diminishes while the value of worth and reciprocity required in both capacities are highlighted. Further, the over–under understanding and the subjective–objective stance inherent in the theory–action positions disappears, as theology requires both the overview and the particular for it to be effective.

I would claim that my transcendental model and method for theological reflection incorporates both of these capacities. It encapsulates a vision for reaching out to new horizons envisaged in culture, the tradition and the personal experience of the person. However, this vision is corrected by the discernment required in the model. In my model the corrective is identified as the danger of self-deception. Vision and discernment are essential ingredients; both are required in my model of the authentic self.

In my own institution faculty members, in teaching their own theological discipline, incorporate the vision and discernment capacities of theology. However, it is in our various competing disciplines that the old theory–action paradigm is most active. Wood offers a new understanding of how the theological disciples might relate to each other.

A new understanding of the independence, dependence and interdependence of the theological disciplines

Wood believes that the new understandings' interests guide any enquiry. In particular, he says critical enquiry into the validity of Christian witness has three dimensions, each of which can be expressed in a question. The three leading questions are these.

1. *Is this piece of verbal or non-verbal witness genuinely Christian?*

Wood calls critical enquiry guided by this question 'historical theology'.[32] He includes critical enquiry into the Bible here, for what is at stake in historical theology 'is identification of the criteria by which to test the faithfulness of witness to Jesus Christ'.[33]
This question infers a conviction: Is the witness faithful to itself?

2. *Is this piece of witness truly Christian?*

Wood calls critical enquiry guided by this question 'philosophical theology'.[34]
Wood says: 'To bear witness is to represent something as the truth: to assert it, to commend it, to endorse it as worthy of acceptance.'[35]
This question is more emphatic: Is the witness truth?

---

[31] Ibid., pp. 72–3.
[32] Ibid., p. 42.
[33] Kelsey, *Between Athens and Berlin*, p. 205.
[34] Wood, *Vision and Discernment*, p. 45.
[35] Ibid., p. 39.

3. *Is this witness fittingly enacted? Is it appropriately related to its context?*[36]

> Wood calls critical enquiry guided by this question 'practical theology'.
> Practical theology is not narrowly concerned with church leadership: 'but rather
> with the enactment of Christian witness in its entirety – that is, with the entire
> life and activity of the church as the community of witness'.[37]

It is this third dimension of critical enquiry I wish to develop. Wood states some
important beliefs about the place of practical theology in relation to the other
dimensions of theology. He believes that each theological dimension is practical,;
for example, each enables better practice. However, he goes further and says that
each theological dimension is also theoretical – that is, each requires a body of
knowledge for it to be effective.[38] This statement alone makes the facile division of
theological education into the theoretical and the practical dubious, at least.

Wood makes a strong claim for the dependence of the three dimensions of
theology as each responds to the three questions vital for the Christian witness –
meaning, use and context. Of interest particular to me is his statement that, while
'one might pursue any one of these inquiries without an *interest* in the other two,
one may not pursue any of them without becoming involved in at least some
aspects of the other two'.[39]

I agree with his statement of dependence and independence of the three
theological dimensions. One can develop a theology from a different standpoint
and draw different conclusions without relying on the other theological disciplines.
For example, my theology begins with personal experience, while others' may
begin with Scripture, history, ethics or systematics. Wood would agree that as long
as the ingredients of vision and discernment are present in this single theological
enquiry the enterprise is valid. I warm to his concept of the independence of the
three theological dimensions, as beginning our theology at different points can
provide a variety of meanings and a different understanding of God and the world.
The uniqueness of practical theology is that the social sciences – psychology,
sociology, anthropology, history and their various offspring – inform it.[40] Practical
theology, due to its different angle of vision, provides another understanding of
God and the world. I also agree with Wood that the theological enquiry is not
complete without being involved with some aspects of the other theological
disciplines. While my theology begins with personal experience, and seeks insight
from the social sciences, it is given further depth from its conversation with
Scripture, which in turn results in a new understanding of professional practice.

The capacities of vision and discernment are ever present in the development of
my theology. While I advocate the possible new theological insight found in the
independence of the theological disciplines, my model and method of theological

---

[36] Ibid., p. 40.
[37] Ibid., p. 48.
[38] Ibid., p. 47.
[39] Ibid., p. 50.
[40] Ibid., p. 48.

reflection has been to stress the interdependence of the theological dimensions in my theological institution. In my institution there are six theological dimensions (philosophy, Biblical languages and literature, church history, systematic theology, moral theology and Christian ethics and practical theology) compared with Wood's three dimensions of theology. Wood includes two other theological dimensions: systematic theology and moral theology. The purpose of systematic theology is to integrate the three dimensions of theology in a comprehensive and constructive fashion.

The defining interest of moral theology is the validity of Christian witness concerning human conduct. Wood is concerned that these two theological dimensions are not seen as brokers between theory and practice, but as an enquiry are defined by an interest in the integration and unity of these three reciprocally interrelated dimensions of theological enquiry.[41] The task of systematic theology is to mediate between the past and the future. In fact, systematic theology has been the most influential of all the theological dimensions and has dominated contemporary theology.[42] To place systematic theology at the midpoint is to acknowledge that theological enquiry centres on the task of mediation between past and future, between what has been received and what is to be done with it.[43] In terms of integration systematic theology has been in a prime position to carry out this important responsibility. I believe that students should be immersed in theological dimensions that inform them of the Christian witness of the past – Scripture, church history and philosophy – but this must be done simultaneously in conversation with practical theology, not apart from it. These theological disciplines should inform one's deliberation of the shaping of that tradition for the future and that, according to Wood, is the responsibility of practical theology.

Unfortunately, systematic theology has not adequately lived up to its integrative possibilities. First, in reality, the flow of traffic among these disciplines is one-way. Systematic theology, though it may try to anticipate the needs of practical theology in the way it shapes the presentation of its material, can remain uninformed by practical theology. It is assumed that the questions of the authenticity and truth of Christian witness can be settled apart from and prior to a consideration of its relation to its context. In this structure systematic theology informs practical theology, but practical theology has no influence on systematic theology in the formation of an understanding of Christian witness. It is further assumed that practical theology's place in defining an understanding of Christian witness is basically one of application, that practical theology is concerned primarily with techniques for moving from the general to the specific, from theory to practice.

Some theologians who believe that offering effective pastoral care is akin to understanding the methodology and theory of the discipline take this stance. It is believed by many that systematic theology has fallen short in its effort of integration. There have been some who have advocated practical theology as being

---

41   Ibid., pp. 50, 54.
42   Ibid., pp. 62–3.
43   Ibid., p. 51.

responsible for the integration of theory and practice. Primarily, this claim has been focussed on the bridge metaphor, the responsibility of which is to integrate theory and practice. This concept has also failed due to the lack of reciprocity between the theological disciplines and the belief among many that practical theology lacks a body of knowledge and is only concerned with skills and leadership in the life of the church. I agree with Wood that practical theology is concerned about the fittingness and context of the validity of the Christian witness, but it is also more.

TFE is classified as a specialized discipline of practical theology, as are worship, liturgy, pastoral care, music, Christian education, spirituality, CPE and the SUMP. Each of these specialized disciplines of practical theology contains a body of knowledge. Each has the potential to incorporate the two capacities of vision and discernment and deepen the understanding of Christian witness. The most effective teaching in which I have been engaged has been a course entitled 'Pastoral Care and Ritual' that I co-taught with a colleague whose speciality was worship and mission. While we firmly believed in the independence of both disciplines we discovered through our teaching how both disciplines could be enriched through their interdependence. The capacities of vision and discernment had new meaning for each of us; this interdependence has not been fully realized with the other theological disciplines within my institution.

There are a number of reasons why this has not occurred, which may include the lack of opportunities, the lack of courage or vision to engage in such activities or, perhaps more troubling, the belief of some that practical theology has little to offer in the area of theory.

TFE continues not only to struggle for recognition as a discipline with the capacities for vision and discernment within the other theological disciplines, but also for equal standing among the specialized disciplines of practical theology. It is largely viewed as a subject that only teaches practical ministry skills. The models and methodologies for theological reflection and pastoral supervision enshrined in this book stress the importance of the interdependence of experience, the tradition and culture. Each model has a body of knowledge that enriches our understanding of the critical enquiry into Christian witness. Further, in these models there is more than one theological discipline or one point of interpretation that has responsibility for integration. The responsibility for integration is placed on the methodology of each model. Perhaps more important in this process of integration is the person's ability to reflect in order that the capacities of vision and discernment might be fully realized.

The reciprocity of faith and critical enquiry in making theological judgements

What does it mean to reflect or be reflective? Wood is correct when he says, 'being reflective, or being critical, is more like a "character trait" than like a skill'.[44] Wood firmly believes that being critical involves skills and abilities of all varieties, but it also requires what John Passmore 'calls "open capacities" in which complete

---

[44]   Ibid., p. 88.

mastery is out of the question because the enquiry continues to develop in ways which cannot always be anticipated and which call for imagination and inventiveness'.[45] Learning to exercise these capacities – theological judgement, discernment and envisioning – is a kind of personal formation. Of particular interest to me is Iris Murdoch's description of these open capacities, which she calls 'attention' remarks: 'It is the *task* to come to see the world as it is'.[46] It involves recognizing and overcoming 'the issue of self-aggrandizing and consoling wishes and dreams which prevents one from seeing what is outside one'.[47] This capacity requires openness and not a predetermined response. Wood says this kind of capacity 'demands patience, humility, and compassion.'[48] It seems to me that these capacities can be found in what is described as personal formation or spiritual formation. Wood believes there is no reason why critical enquiry and these 'open capacities' cannot work together to establish theological judgement. In fact, Wood believes 'there is good reason to do so: namely, to counteract the frequently resurgent false and dangerous characterization of faith and critical enquiry as warring forces, one of which must ultimately vanquish the other'.[49] I warm to Wood's emphasis on the importance of both faith and critical enquiry forming theological judgements. Unfortunately, many aspects of theological education: personal formation, spiritual formation, faith and critical enquiry, are still at war with each other. If only they could complement and inform, rather than fragmenting each other, then theological education could be more holistic. In the transcendental model for theological reflection, critical enquiry is focussed in self-deception, while spiritual formation is a precursor to further critical enquiry.

The educational aim of theological education is the capacity to make judgements

Theological reflection also has an educational role to play in the formation of a Christian witness. The aim of its educational value is to make sound theological judgements where judgement 'informs practice by equipping the practitioner not with ready-made deliberative judgements but rather with the capacity to make them'.[50] Further: 'It is not the mere possession of 'a theology' that is the measure of a theological education; it is rather one's ability to form, revise, and employ theological judgements that count. Vision and discernment are exhibited in practice'.[51]

Wood's vision for the educational aim of theological education is to help the student learn how to think rather than what to think. Theological colleges and seminaries have been criticized for their inability to make the student's work practically relevant. If the theological institution does not provide practical skills

---

[45]   Ibid.

[46]   Iris Murdoch 1971, *The Sovereignty of God*, New York: Schocken Books, p. 91.

[47]   Ibid., p. 59.

[48]   Wood, *Vision and Discernment*, p. 88.

[49]   Ibid., p. 89.

[50]   Ibid., p. 80.

[51]   Ibid., p. 82.

for ministry, then the criticism is valid. However, the motivation behind theological education is not seen in a preoccupation with the 'what', but with the need to explore the unknown. Theology is dead when the sole aim of the teacher is to impose or absolutize his or her own understanding of doctrine, Scripture or even church teachings onto the student. A dynamic theology and belief should in no way support dependency, passivity or acquiescence.[52] The task of the theologian is that of trying things on for size.

Theology is constantly tentative and experimental. I am aware that the emphasis on the how-to-think capacity can cause pain among conservative colleges and seminaries, even in more liberal colleges in relation to church doctrine. I am also aware that many in the Christian faith are more comfortable with the doctrine of absoluteness that leaves no room for ambiguity or even discovery. I cannot deny that some people live creative lives while subscribing to a doctrine of absoluteness. However, in my experience and in my long professional life as a pastor and educator, people get into difficulty when they are faced with a crisis that creates a dichotomy between what they believe and what they feel. The result is confusion that can lead to unresolvable pain. People who think (using their faith and critical enquiry capacities) and face the ambiguities that confront them emerge with a stronger faith and a theology that they can call their own, with conviction. This struggle leads to a dynamic faith. This is the prime role for theological education; my own theological institution carries out this role excellently.

The aim of the three theological reflection models – whose method invites personal discovery – is to assist people in how to think through personal, faith and cultural issues. The outcome not only calls for some immediate action, but the method also invites an ongoing discovery when circumstances change. I testify in my model of theological reflection to the importance of discovery of new meaning as my circumstance change. There is no denying the ongoing pain, but I can also claim my dynamic faith.

Recommendations for structural integration

Whatever the future of the theory–praxis debate there are a number of lessons to be drawn from Charles Wood's thesis and the effort to implement a TRS that places emphasis on a person's personal and faith experience and the introduction of an open-ended curriculum.

1. While the six-fold structure of theological education may not change in the immediate future the reframing of the structure by Wood is something to consider. Perhaps more importantly is the need for faculty to read his work. It is scholarly and understands the history and traditions of theological education; the important consideration is that Wood has a concrete vision for the future of theological education.

---

[52]   Hugh Kerr 1971, 'Seminarians and self-directed study', *Princeton Seminary Bulletin*, LXIV, 1, March, 69–77.

2. Wood offers an exciting possibility for reframing the theory–praxis debate in his understanding of vision and discernment. In his understanding there would be no such thing as theory and practice, subjectivity and objectivity, rather, there would be vision and discernment, which offers a coherent, holistic and unified understanding without the theological disciplines competing with each other. Respect and reciprocity would be the hallmarks of such a relationship.

3. The process of the framework for theological reflection and curriculum changes must be fully explained to faculty and students. This occurs through an educational process.

4. There needs to be more clarity in the meaning of the term 'experience'. Faculty not only need to be present, but their model of theological reflection also needs to be heard in the seminar.

5. Historically, systematic theology has been the integrating agent for theology and practice. Therefore, due to the equalization of the partners in the process of theological reflection it is important for systematic theology to be involved in the process of curriculum changes and understanding the concept of experience in theological reflection.

6. Less responsibility needs to be placed on a particular discipline to be responsible for integration. More responsibility needs to be given to the method and the individual to undertake the integration.

7. There is a need to confront the issue of resistance with both faculty and students. It is important to recognize that resistance often encapsulates a threat to a person's faith or position of power.

8. There is a need to challenge the need for students and faculty to collude. Outside influences often cut across the potential for learning.

9. Compromise is an important ingredient in this process. There is a fine line between compromise and prostituting a conviction.

10. A healthy respect for each theological discipline is required for the theological reflection process and new curriculum changes to occur.

Conclusion

This writing set out to demonstrate, first, that pastoral supervision and theological reflection are integrating factors and do in fact enable students to do theology themselves and, second, that this model and method has the potential to be a catalyst for reform of the curriculum within UCTC.

The evidence provided in the case studies in Chapter 4 and the student evaluations of the TRS lead me to support my contention that many students were able to do theology themselves, that is, they were able to develop, understand and practise their own model of theological reflection.

The TRS may in itself have fallen short of catalysing curriculum reform in the UCTC, but it has modelled a way of integrating theory and practice as envisioned in the UCA Ministerial Report. The seminar has achieved more than this, not the least of which has been the provision for students of another model for ministry and learning within theological education. Further, its inclusive and critical approach to the formation process has had a significant impact on a number of students. However, we need to give more attention to developing theological reflection models that are holistic and transportable. In my research previously referred to, many field educators are concerned that theological students are leaving the theological institution and entering a life of ministry, not with an integrated theology, but with a fragmented theology. Integration from experience to the personal, the pastoral, the cultural, the theological and faith issues is often hard work and requires insight and an ability to make connections; it is also risk taking. For theological reflection to be holistic and transportable there needs to be a connection between these levels of influence on our lives. When we can achieve this theological integration in our lives we know how empowering and transforming our faith and ministry can be. It is for this reason that the work of Charles Wood is so important. His thesis offers unity and diversity, dependence and interdependence, reciprocity and respect in theological education, but, most importantly, it offers an exciting new way of interpreting the theory–praxis issue for theological education. The capacities of vision and discernment offer a holistic approach to theological education.

At points in this book I have been critical of members of faculty and myself in the whole process of developing a new curriculum. This criticism is not meant to be personal, but is intended to highlight the many issues in developing a new curriculum. Indeed, I have a high personal and professional opinion of and respect for my colleagues. Since my retirement one of the opportunities I have missed has been the monthly faculty seminar. In these seminars my understanding of the meaning of critical enquiry was enhanced and the opportunity to weave the social sciences, faith, theology and spirituality into my papers was of profound importance for my growth and understanding. Many times faculty was my supervisor who allowed the process of spiritual development to occur, but at the same time brought to bear the importance of critical enquiry. If only we could have transferred that wonderful structure for learning into the life of the theological curriculum. It was in this seminar that spirituality, faith and critical enquiry celebrated each other's contribution in the development of Christian witness, rather than being competitors.

I have already documented the factors that have hindered this claim and I do not wish to recap them. While I do not wish to apportion blame it is my opinion that the lack of theological underpinning and methodology in the UCA Report has not been helpful in our discussions. It would have been more helpful had the taskforce elaborated on their sources and rationale for their model of ministerial education. The absence of this evidence has intensified the theory–practice dichotomy among faculty members.

These findings highlight the fact that one of the difficulties for theological colleges is their lack of understanding of the aims of TFE. Many faculties believe that TFE is concerned only with developing ministerial skills.

However, there is some encouragement. The UCA and other churches are beginning to reclaim and recognise the importance of pastoral supervision and theological reflection. Pastoral supervision is given prominence in the four phases of ministry education in the report. Further, a group of people with pastoral supervisory skills has been commissioned by the UCA Ministerial Education Commission to develop models of supervision for ministers within the UCA. From this commissioning there has developed the Train-the-Trainers program where selected ministers and lay people are being trained at a considered level of competence in supervision and theological reflection. The outcome of this training is to equip them to be trainers for people engaged in pastoral supervision. This is an important step for the ongoing formation of ministers as they engage in the ministry of the church and the world.

This has been an important journey for me. While it has been set in a particular context, I hope some of the passion I have felt in this journey has been infectious for all those people committed to the ministry of pastoral supervision and theological reflection. Sometimes anger and despondency have been part of this passion, but it is a journey I have not regretted and hopefully it will continue.

Appendix 1

The integration of personal experience, social sciences, spirituality, theology and pastoral care

In this book the search for integration is the key to my spirituality. When aspects of my life are in disharmony I struggle in my spiritual life. The following highlights the importance of the integration of experience in my life.

The author's experience

The important experiences were those that confronted him, surprised him and made him vulnerable.

Implications for this definition of experience

The emphasis on this type of experience is not on what we bring but how open we are to new and often unexpected experiences that enter our lives and have the potential to change and transform us.

Social science interpretation

For an experience to be an experience, according to philosopher H.G. Gadamer, it must run counter to our expectations.[1] Only through being surprised can we really acquire new experiences. However, these unexpected experiences can make us vulnerable.

Spirituality

These unexpected experiences or critical moments can result in a divine/human encounter where we grapple and endeavour to make sense of the place of God in our lives.

---

[1]   Gerald Bruns 1992, *Hermeneutics Ancient and Modern*, New Haven: Yale University Press, p. 155. Cited in Terry A. Veling 1996, *Living in the Margins*, New York: Crossroad, p. 41.

Biblical interpretation

These unexpected experiences, which can make us vulnerable, can be signs of God's grace in our lives. 'My grace is sufficient for you, for my power is made perfect in weakness'. [2 Cor. 12:9]

Theological interpretation

Theologian Bernard Lonergan believes God's grace is radical and is expressed as 'being in love'. He goes on to say the 'the gift of love occurs as something as a holy disruption into the routine flow of life'. To theologically experience and act on this radical grace of God means that there are consequences for all of one's life. To experience this love [this 'holy disruption'], according to Lonergan, brings us to the point where we sense the dismantling of our former horizons, only to be drawn into an unrestricted horizon illuminated by the love of God.[2]

Pastoral care interpretation

Personal experience, social sciences, Biblical sources and theology should inform pastoral care practice, as pastoral practice should inform the sources of interpretation.

Mutuality between vision and discernment creates a powerful pastoral care identity. It is the responsibility of pastoral care to integrate these themes not only in our lives but also for the person for whom we care. Hopefully, this will result in new life and hope.

The author's spirituality has been informed and formed by those important experiences that confronted, surprised him and made him vulnerable. The emphasis on this type of experience is not on what we bring but on how open we are to new and often unexpected experiences that enter our lives and which have the potential to change and transform us. These unexpected experiences can make us vulnerable but can also provide an awareness of the presence of God in our lives. In fact, these unexpected experiences with God are precursors for any theological interpretation.

---

[2]   Anthony J Kelly, CSSR and Francis J. Moloney SDB 2003, *Experiencing God in the Gospel of John*, New York: Paulist Press, pp. 5.

Appendix 2

Theological reflection – student handout for pastoral care seminar

The aim of the course is to

Introduce you to different models and methods for theological reflection on the experience of pastoral ministry with a view of critical appreciation of them. You will present a ministry and a life experience of your own on which to reflect. It is expected that you will develop your own model and method for theological reflection. The unit will be conducted on a seminar basis, with you sharing reading, presenting reports and case studies. Faculty members and other people in ministry will be invited to share their models and methods of theological reflection.

Prerequisites

The TRS on Pastoral Care is a second level course numbered DP203.15 and taught by the UFT at Parkville, Melbourne, Australia. You should have completed one year of theological studies. This unit assumes that you have completed an approved placement in Field Education and that you have the skill development, cultural and social awareness and theological awareness to complete this course. An interview with the unit leader is preferable in order to assess your readiness to undertake this unit. Consideration will be given to people who are not in a current Field Education placement, but who have had a significant Field Education experience. This unit is offered as a prerequisite for DP325.15 (Theology of Pastoral Care).

Class time

Three hours per week.

Assessment

One reading report of 1000 words critiquing a model for theological reflection (20%)

Two reports each of 750 words of theological reflection: one on a ministry and the other on a personal experience. (40%)

One 1500 word essay on your model and method of theological reflection. (40%)

Models and methods in theological reflection

The methods and models used in this Seminar may be unfamiliar to some of you and for this reason it is important to offer some explanatory information.

A *model* for theological reflection offers a way to structure the conversation between the partners in the conversation (e.g. tradition, culture and personal experience). Usually, models highlight the sources of information that are important to insight and decision-making. Patricia O'Connell Killen and John de Beer indicate the dynamic nature of these sources: 'Sources are aspects of experience ... even though we separate experience into aspects to make reflection possible the meaning of any particular event is revealed only when we attend to those aspects or sources and their mutual relationships ... sources for theology are constructs we put on experience to organise it.'[1] These sources are also points for differing interpretations of the experience. Different models use different ways of dividing the flow of experience, and employ different names for similar sources. For example, the Whiteheads name their sources as tradition, culture and personal and corporate experience, while Holland and Henriot name their sources as insertion (ministry experience), social analysis, theological reflection and pastoral planning.

The *method* describes the process, dynamic or movement of the reflection. It outlines the stages through which the conversation proceeds. Methods provide a framework for theological reflection. They are maps that can guide us. Mueller uses an everyday working tool to describe method when he says: '(a) method is a tool. Like a good multi-purpose screwdriver, a method improves upon what weak fingers and fragile fingernails cannot do. A method extends our abilities, improves upon our limitations, reminds us of forgotten procedures, and allows others to see how we arrived at our conclusions'.[2] The Whiteheads describe the processes of their method as attending, assertion and pastoral response, while for Holland and Henriot with their sources linking justice and faith, the process is facilitated by asking questions. Who makes the decisions? Who benefits from the decisions? Who bears the cost of the decisions? It is out of a response to questions such as these that theological reflection emerges.

As the Whiteheads indicate, leaving out one or another of these conversational partners may reduce the scope of enquiry, insight and action significantly. I will elaborate further on the Whitehead model later, but it seems important at this point to highlight the consequences of a theological reflection method which neglects some sources while highlighting others. They illustrate this issue with the following diagram.[3]

---

[1]   Killen O'Connell, J. and P. de Beer, *The Art of Theological Reflection*, New York: Crossroad, p. 5.
[2]   Mueller, *What Are They Saying About Theological Method?*, p. 1.
[3]   Whitehead and Whitehead, *Method in Ministry*, p. 83.

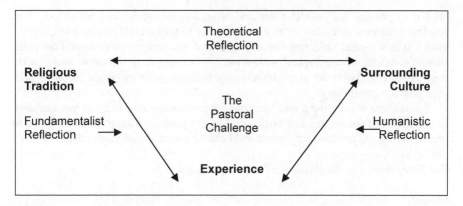

Fig. A2.1   The Whitehead model

The diagram indicates that focusing on person and tradition alone could result in a fundamentalist interpretation; on tradition and culture alone a purely theoretical interpretation; on culture and person alone an undifferentiated humanistic interpretation. If the experience of the person is omitted then it becomes an academic mode of theological reflection. If the experience of the person is not included there is no room for transformation or change. The Whiteheads in the above diagram highlight ways in which the mutuality is necessary for theological reflection to be effective.

You will receive further instruction on models and methods during the introduction session in the class.

The TRS is a holistic, integrative and interdisciplinary process

The TRS is a holistic, integrative and interdisciplinary process. It is holistic because it gives recognition and equal importance to the tradition, culture and your personal experience. This equalization of the different partners in theological reflection may be a problem for some who give precedence to one of the partners in the theological reflection process. It is integrative because of its desire to integrate the tradition, culture and personal experience. It is interdisciplinary in its desire to recognize and work with all theological disciplines, cultures and traditions.

Seminar leaders

Due to the nature of the TRS on Pastoral Care, at least one of the seminar leaders will have particular expertise in theological reflection and pastoral supervision. Pastoral supervision, due to its desire for integration and its ability to facilitate theological reflection, has an important place within the seminar processes. The Seminar has been co-led at different times by a New Testament scholar, spiritual director, and a feminist scholar. Each of these leaders has been committed to both inductive and deductive learning. From time to time, members of faculty will be invited to present and model their understanding of theological reflection. The Seminar leaders and invited faculty are there not to try and tell you how to do your model of theological reflection but to model and encourage you to search for your authentic model of theological reflection. For example, the leaders, along with your peers, may point out some incongruity between your espoused theology and your practice of ministry.

While there will be input and leadership from the Seminar Leaders you are also encouraged to take on this responsibility too, by your active participation in your presentations and the encouragement and critique you make of yourself and others.

The Three Stages of the theological reflection seminar

Stage 1

This presentation will be in the first hour of the Seminar. You will be required to select and write a critique of a model and method of theological reflection. In the first session of the unit you will be given the opportunity to select from a number of models contained in the *TRS Handbook*. This is not a review, but a critique. The point of the exercise is to engage the model and the method. It requires you to assess the model and method and then critique its strengths and weaknesses. Some of the questions you may ask in assessing the model of your choice may be the following:

- What is the beginning point of the model? Experience, tradition, culture or some other beginning point?
- How does this sit with your perceived model of theological reflection?
- Does the article enlighten your understanding of theological reflection?
  If yes – why? If no – why?
- Does it challenge your understanding of theological reflection?
  If yes – why? If no – why?

The following articles have been selected for the unit:

Robert L. Kinast 1993, 'If only you recognized God's gift – John's Gospel as an illustration of theological reflection', Grand Rapids: William Eerdmans, pp. 1–26.
Sallie McFague 1975, *Speaking in Parables*, Philadelphia: Fortress Press, pp. 66–89.
Kenneth Pohly 2001, *The Ministry of Supervision: Transforming the Rough Places,* Franklin, TN: Providence House Publishers, pp. 111–31.
Oliver Sacks 1986, *The Man Who Mistook His Wife for a Hat*, New York: Harper & Rowe, pp. 23–42.
John E. Paver 1994, 'The Influence of Memory on Ministry and Spirituality', *Ministry, Society and Theology*, 8/2, 52–67.
Dan O. Via 1990, *Self-Deception and Wholeness in Paul and Matthew*, Minneapolis: Fortress Press, pp. 1–18.

Charles M. Wood 1985, *Vision and Discernment: An orientation to theological study*, Atlanta: Scholars Press, pp. 57–77.

Joe Holland & Peter Henriot 1998, *Social Analysis: Linking faith and justice*, New York: Orbis Books, pp. 7–30, 102–5.

Gideon Goosen 2000, *Australian Theologies*, St. Paul's Publications, pp. 55–88.

James D. Whitehead 1987, 'The Practical Play of Theology', in Lewis S. Mudge and James Poling (eds), *Formation and Reflection*, Philadelphia: Fortress Press, pp. 36–54.

John Patton 1990, *From Ministry to Theology*, Nashville: Abingdon Press, pp. 11–48.

James N. Poling 1991, *The Abuse of Power: A theological problem*, Nashville, Abingdon Press, pp. 183–91.

Letty Russell 1993, *Church in the Round*, Louisville: Westminster/John Knox Press, pp. 20–45.

Report of the Ministerial Education Commission Task Group to Review Ministerial Education in the UCA, 1997. C22.4–C22.10.

The Rainbow Spirit Elders 1997, *Rainbow Spirit Theology*, Melbourne: HarperCollins, pp. 1–28.

The books mentioned are on reserve in the library. The *Theological Reflection Handbook*, which contains the articles from the selected books, will be available on the first day of the course. It is strongly recommended that you read the complete book from which the article has been selected.

Stage 2

This stage focuses upon a case study reflection report on a ministry experience and the presentation of a life experience.[4] These presentations will usually occur in the second and third hours.

The case study reflection on a pastoral ministry involves a written report on a ministry in which the student has been involved. Students are encouraged to include in verbatim form a part of the conversation they have had with a person. While some students comment on the difficulty of writing about a significant ministry experience so compactly, the method does provide a concrete text to anchor the interaction. This Case study report on the conversation enables the group and the supervisor to judge the actual quality of the ministry. The Case study report involves known and observed information about the person. For example, Who is this person and what did you know about him/her before this encounter? (Examples: age, gender, race, marital status, sibling rank, parents, children, religious beliefs, social concerns, political allegiance.) The observed information includes physical appearance, setting, and a description of the student's response to this information. Perhaps the key to the collation of this information is the effectual response by the student to this information. (Examples: Was the person interesting,

---

[4] For further information on the case study reflection in ministry see Jeffrey H. Mahan et al. (eds) 1993, *Shared Wisdom*, Nashville: Abingdon Press, pp. 115–39.

boring, attractive, repulsive, or enjoyable? Did this person make you anxious? Did you find yourself engaged, turned off, or withdrawing?). This information can be of assistance to the student, peers and the pastoral supervisor when assessing the quality of the pastoral ministry. It can also be an indicator of any incongruence which may occur between the student's claims and the theological reflection assessment.

Following the verbatim account of the pastoral conversation comes a reflective assessment of the pastoral conversation, and an assessment of the ministry leading to theological reflection on the ministry. It is the incorporation of all the above factors, which allow the student and the group to proceed to the theological reflection section of the case study reflection report. Questions asked in this section include:

• What theological issues emerged from the event and/or conversation?
• Where do you see the redeeming activity of God in this event?
• What biblical events seem parallel to your reported ministry?
• In what ways are the two similar?
• Can you identify the model of theological reflection used in this Case study?

Theological reflection is concerned with bridging the gap between theory and practice, but it also embraces matters of personhood, spirituality, and ministerial perspectives. It integrates this knowledge, but it also connects this knowledge with matters of wisdom and the heart too. Therefore, the Case study reflection structure is concerned with all parts of the person.

Crucial to the development of theological reflection is often the incongruence between the religious images or images of God and humanity that emerge from the pastoral conversation and those recorded in the student's theological reflection. While the focus is on the effectiveness of the pastoral care to the person, the Seminar also attends to issues for the student which may have been detrimental to or have enhanced his/her ministry. It is often revealed that the student's learned ministry is at odds with that of the one operative in a particular pastoral ministry. It is often within these tensions that the presence of the spirit of God is discovered.

The second part of Stage 2 is the presentation by you on a life experience. In this section the presentations have included a variety of forms – poetry, Scripture, autobiography, biography, art, film, liturgy, wedding, funeral, etc. The rationale behind this presentation is that it allows you to present something close to your heart, as you are encouraged to give free rein to your creativity and imagination. It also gives the message that God is present in ways other than ministry and supervision. This section is theological reflection because we are seeking to discover God's presence through clues to or signs of divine reality in human experience. God's word may be hidden among the details of nature and the experiences of men and women. As Karl Rahner describes it, God is the mystery and depth dimension of human experiences such as love, friendship, death, and hope.[5] Even loneliness, suffering, violence, or disappointment can be revelatory moments, opening us to the transcendent. You are not provided with an outline of expectations for this report of 750 words, as the topic can be expressed in the form of your choice.

Stage 3

Guidelines for final paper

1. This paper will describe your model and methodology of theological reflection. Diagrams can be used to illustrate your model. Creativity and imagination are encouraged.
2. You can consult the papers in the handbook, verbatim, and any information that might describe your model and methodology.
3. The model describes the conversational partners; the method is the process in which these partners engage each other.
4. Generally, in theological reflection, the conversational partners include the tradition, culture and experience or ministry of the person.
5. It may be helpful to identify the starting point of theology, that is, to query whether you begin your theological reflection with experience, theology or culture. The question of the starting point is significant. The point where theological reflectors begin influences where their theological reflections will lead them.
6. What is the purpose of theological reflection? Is its outcome to engage in some action or simply to deepen our understanding of God? Or something else? How would you define theological reflection?
7. Perhaps the best way to begin to engage your model and methodology is to think and feel how you go about reflection in your everyday life.

This stage is the culmination of the other two stages in assisting you to develop your own model for theological reflection. You have been exposed to many theoretical models of theological reflection, and you have made a life experience and ministry presentation to the seminar group. You are now expected to write a 1500-word essay on your own model and method for theological reflection. The essay is not presented to the class for feedback, but handed to the seminar leader for comments and an overall grade.

---

[5]   Lamoureux, 'An Integrated Approach', 145.

Core curriculum – objectives and options

Objectives

1. The development of a curriculum that prepares people effectively for the various ministries of the church within the framework developed by the Ministerial Education Commission of the UCA. Such a curriculum will need to:

   a) provide students with a sound grounding in the fundamentals of theology that ministry requires
   b) support and assist students to integrate their theological learning with all the other dimensions of their lives (personal, spiritual, emotional, pastoral, familial and communal)
   c) enable students to develop their particular skills and gifts.

2. A curriculum that will facilitate the provision of theological education for the wider church and community.
3. A curriculum that will facilitate students developing a capacity for life long learning and teaching.
4. A curriculum that will sustain the energy and enthusiasm of teaching staff.

Options

Two broad approaches to the curriculum appear open, each with their own advantages.

The discipline-centred model

Advantages

- it facilitates students continuing to higher levels of theological education which are structured on a discipline basis
- it is valuable in ensuring that students are introduced to the full range of theological disciplines required for ministry.

The interdisciplinary model

An interdisciplinary model in which courses are structured around themes (for example, creation, Christology, church.

Advantages

It facilitates the objective of an integrative theological education. There are two broad approaches to the structuring of student participation in the curriculum:
- a structured course with a high proportion of subjects being required with the aim to ensure students have a solid grounding in all areas of theology
- a flexible course with relatively few requirements and an emphasis on choice to enable students to pursue subjects that develop their individual gifts and ministry.

The proposal

The proposal presented was built around the strengths of the two curriculum options in order to meet the objectives of the new core curriculum. The framework for the course is the BTheol (with some suggested modifications), a field education program and the Uniting Church-specific theological formation program. There were, essentially, two halves to the curriculum, which reflected the two curriculum options.

1. Groundwork in theology

In order to meet the need for students to have a basic understanding in the fundamentals of theology that ministry requires, it is proposed that the first part of the course consist of a series of discipline-based introductory courses. These introductory courses would aim to provide students with an overview of the subject, an awareness of the key issues in the field and an alertness to the key issues of the relationship to other fields and knowledge of the resources available to pursue independent learning in the subject. Set within the framework of encouraging students to develop an integrative approach to theological study, the first year would consist of the more foundational disciplines of biblical studies, systematic theology, church history, pastoral theology and Christian education. In the first year there would also be a three-week presessional introductory course in pastoral care and counselling. There would be no field education placements in this first year to better enable students to focus on theological study. As students enter field placements in the second year, the first half of the second year would focus upon the more integrative subjects of liturgy and Christian ethics (and theological reflection in the second semester). It was recommended that these introductory courses could be offered for those in the wider church seeking further theological education.

The committee strongly believed that each subject should aim to develop in students a strong independent learning and teaching capacities. To support this objective the subject 'Introduction to Learning and Teaching in the Church and Community' is a pivotal element of the entire program. If students want to take biblical languages in the second semester of the first year, then they will need to take this subject in the second semester of the second year.

Table A3.1 Groundwork in theology

Pre-sessional (one of)				Introduction to Pastoral Care and Counselling
1st year 1st Semester	Introduction to Old Testament	Introduction to the Philosophy of Religion	Church History Survey Course	Biblical Languages
1st year 2nd Semester	Introduction to New Testament	Introduction to Systematic Theology	Church History Survey Course	Introduction to Learning and Teaching or Biblical Languages
2nd year 1st Semester	Field Education	Introduction to Christian Ethics	Introduction to Liturgy	Major 200a
2nd year 2nd Semester	Theological Reflection			Major 200b

To facilitate coordination between subjects and to ensure that basic issues are covered, the coordinator of each subject will provide a detailed outline of the curriculum, including objectives, rationale, methodology and a description of the content of the studies committee of the faculty.

2. Theological enrichment

The second half of the course would be very flexible, in terms of both course format and student choice. The central aims of this half of the course are to enable students to develop their particular gifts and to further the objective of theological integration. The BTheol requirement – that a student complete either two majors or one major and two sub majors – does restrict the flexibility of the second part of the program. In order to support courses being tailored to respond to an individual's particular gifts and sense of call, it is recommended that the regulations be amended to permit majors and sub majors to be undertaken in any field. It is also recommended that the regulations be amended to permit a double major within any one field. The offerings in the second half of the course would be interdisciplinary and disciplinary so the students could choose courses that would support their individual educational and ministerial development. Staff would be invited to develop courses that engaged their own interests and enthusiasm and according to their preferred approach to teaching.

The field education program

Integral to the groundwork and enrichment dimensions of the course is a substantial field education program. Beginning in the second year students will undertake two subjects of TFE in addition to taking part in the TRS.

Ministerial formation program

The faculty is developing an educational program, which occurs on Fridays, to form people specifically for ministry within the UCA.

Integration

This program focuses upon theological integration through academic, experiential and reflective opportunities. While theological integration is an important element in all courses, the subjects in the first semester of the second year (ethics, liturgy and theological reflection) will place a particular emphasis upon it. TFE and the ministerial formation program provide an experiential context for integration. The dean, formation advisers and community worship play a central and ongoing role in supporting the reflective dimension of this integration.

Requirements for distinctive ministries

The groundwork in the theology section of the course aims to provide the basic grounding necessary for all forms of ordained and specified ministry. Groundwork courses will introduce students to the distinctions made in different disciplines between distinct forms of ministry. The development of distinctive ministries is supported by students undertaking field placements with a person exercising that ministry for which they are preparing. The offerings in the enrichment of the program provide the opportunity for students to undertake studies that develop their particular sense of calling and gifts. The groundwork in the theology program is shaped in such a way that it meets the Ministerial Education Commission requirements for the preparation of youth ministry candidates.

Mission and ecumenism

Given the importance of mission and ecumenism these issues will be tackled throughout the curriculum. Groundwork courses will consider issues of mission as an integral part of the curriculum. They will also introduce students to the ecumenical dimensions of each field. In the theological enrichment program there will be the opportunity for staff to offer special studies in these fields.

Prerequisites for admission to the core program

The personal, spiritual and theological demands of the core program are such that students struggling to develop academic skills as well are seriously distracted from the enrichment the program offers. Such extra study places burdens on the student that should be avoided. To avoid these problems the prerequisites are either the Tertiary Education Requirement score (or its equivalent) sufficient to enable entry to the Bachelor of Arts or science course at the University of Melbourne or two years of tertiary study for a Bachelor's level qualification.[1]

---

[1]   John E. Paver, Rufus Black and Gwen Ince, 1999, 'Core Curriculum Proposal'. Unpublished document relating to the implementation of the UCA report at Uniting Church Theological Hall, Melbourne, Australia.

Bibliography

Ames, S & Fullerton, D 1989. 'Doing Theology in the Parish-Three Levels of Theological Reflection', unpublished paper presented to seminar held at Otira College, Melbourne.

Anderson, H 1984, 'Forming a Pastoral Habitus: A Rich Tapestry With Many Threads', *Journal of Supervision and Training in Ministry*, 15, 231–42.

Baillie, J 1939, *Our Knowledge of God.* New York: Charles Scribner & Sons.

Beisswenger, D 1974, 'Differentiating Modes of Supervision in Theological Field Education', *Theological Education* 11/1, 58–66.

—— 1996, Field Education and the Theological Education Debates', *Theological Education*, 33/1, 49–58.

Bergland, J W 1969, 'Field Education as the Locus for Theological Reflection', *Theological Education*, 5, Summer, 338–45.

Berryman, P 1987, *Liberation Theology*, Oak Park, Ill: Myer Stone.

Bevans. S B 1996, *Models of Contextual Theology*, New York: Orbis Books.

Boys, M C 1999, 'Engaged Pedagogy-Dialogue and Critical Reflection', *Teaching Theology and Religion*, 2, 129–36.

Bruns, G 1992, *Hermeneutics: Ancient and Modern*, New Haven: Yale University Press.

Buttitta, K 1995, 'Theological Reflection in Health Ministry: A Strategy for Parish Nurses', in

Campbell, A V 1990 'The Nature of Practical Theology', in Duncan B Forrester (ed.), *Theology and Practice*, London: Epworth Press, 10–20.

Carroll, J W 1991, *As One With Authority*, Louisville: Westminster John Knox Press.

Chalmers, J 1997, 'Deep Structures: Reforming Supervision on the Cusp of the New Millennium', unpublished paper presented at Australian and New Zealand Association for Theological Field Education Conference, Brisbane.

Childs, B H 1990, 'Experience-Enlightenment', in R Hunter (ed.), *Dictionary of Pastoral Care and Counseling*, Nashville: Abingdon Press, pp. 388–9.

Clebsch, W A & Jaekle, C R 1964, *Pastoral Care in Historical Perspective*, Englewood Cliffs, NJ: Prentice Hall.

Close, W J 1983, 'Pastoral Hermeneutics and Field Education.' *Key Resources*, IV, 172–86.

Duke, J O & Stone H 1988 *Christian Caring: Selections from Practical Theology*, Philadelphia: Fortress Press.

Egan, M 1987, 'The History of the Association for Theological Field Education and its Contribution to Theological Education in the United States', unpublished PhD, St Louis University.

Ekstein, R & Wallerstein, R S 1976, *Supervision and Social Work*, New York: Columbia University Press.

Estadt, B, Compton, J & Blanchette, M C 1987, *The Art of Clinical Supervision*, New York: Paulist Press.

Farley, E 1983 *Theologia: The Fragmentation and Unity of Theological Education*, Philadelphia: Fortress Press.

—— 1987, 'Interpreting Situations: An Enquiry into the nature of Practical Theology', in S L Mudge and J N Poling (eds), *Formation and Reflection: The Promise of Practical Theology*, Philadelphia: Fortress Press, 1987, 1–26.

—— 1988, *The Fragility of Knowledge: Theological Education in the Church & the University*, Philadelphia: Fortress Press.

Feilding, C R 1966, 'Education for Ministry', *Theological Education*, 3/1, Autumn, 1–172.

Fingarette, H 1977, *Self-Deception*, London: Routledge and Kegan Paul.

Foskett, J & Lyall D 1988, *Helping The Helpers*, London: SPCK, 1988.

Fullerton, D 1989, 'Three Levels-Theological Reflection Model', unpublished paper.

Gadamer, H-G 1989, *Truth and Method*, New York: Crossroad.

Graham, E L 1996, *Transforming Practice*, London: Mowbray.

Hiltner, S 1958, *Preface to Pastoral Theology*, Nashville: Abingdon Press.

Holifield, E B 1990, 'Anton Boisen', in R Hunter (ed.), *Dictionary of Pastoral Care and Counseling*, 104.

Holland, J & Henriot P 1983, *Social Analysis: Linking Faith and Justice*, New York: Orbis Books.

Holmes, U 1978, *The Priest in Community*, New York: Seabury.

Hough, J C & J B Cobb 1985, *Christian Identity and Theological Education*, Chico: Scholars Press.

Hunter, G I 1982, *Supervision and Education – Formation for Ministry*, Cambridge, Mass.: Episcopal Divinity School.

Hunter, R J (ed). 1990, *Dictionary of Pastoral Care And Counseling*, Nashville: Abingdon Press.

Ives, W 1979, 'Field Education and Ministerial Training in Australia: An analysis and a proposal', DMin, San Francisco.

Kelsey, D H 1993, *Between Athens and Berlin*, Grand Rapids, Michigan: William B Eerdmans Publishing.

Kelly, A J CSSR, & Francis J. Moloney, SDB, 2003, *Experiencing God in the Gospel of John*, New York: Paulist Press.

Kinast, R L 2000, *What Are They Saying About Theological Reflection?*, Mahwah, NJ: Paulist Press.

Klink, T 1969, 'Supervision from a Clinical/Pastoral Care Perspective', report of the proceedings of the Tenth Biennial Consultation on Field Education, Berkeley.

Lamoureux, P A 1999, 'An Integrated Approach to Theological Education', *Theological Education*, 36/1, 141–56.

Lee, D 2002, *Flesh and Glory: Symbolism, Gender and Theology in the Gospel of John,* New York: The Crossroad Publishing Company.

Lonergan, B 1972, *Method in Theology*, New York: Herder & Herder.

McCarty, D 1975, *Supervising Ministry Students*, Atlanta: Home Missions Board, Southern Baptist Convention.

McFague, S 1975, *Speaking in Parables*, Philadelphia: Fortress Press

Mahan, J H et al. (eds) 1993, *Shared Wisdom*, Nashville: Abingdon Press.

Mitchell, K R 1990, 'Ethical Issues in Supervision: Justice, Authority, Equality', *Journal of Supervision and Training in Ministry*, 12, 153–61.

Morgan, B 1999, 'What Are We Looking for in Theological Reflection?', *Ministry, Society and Theology*, 13/2, 6–21.

Mueller, W J & Kell B L 1972, *Supervising Counselors and Psychotherapists*, New York: Appleton-Century-Crofts.

Muller, J J 1984, *What Are They Saying About Theological Method?*, Mahwan, NJ: Paulist Press.

O'Connell K, de Beer P & de Beer J 1994, *The Art of Theological Reflection*, New York: Crossroad.

Oglesby, W 1980, *Biblical Themes for Pastoral Care*, Nashville: Abingdon.

Patton, J 1990, *From Ministry to Theology*, Nashville: Abingdon Press.

Paver, J E 1996, 'Formation and Transformation in Theological Reflection', *Ministry, Society and Theology*, 10/2, 93–102.

—— 1997, 'The Place of Supervision in Theological Education', unpublished paper, Austin Hospital, Melbourne.

—— 1999, 'The Birth of a Professional Association', *Ministry, Society and Theology*, 13/2, 76–89.

—— et al. 1999, 'Core Curriculum Proposal', unpublished document relating to the implementation of the *UCA Report* at the Uniting Church Theological Hall.

—— 2000, *Theological Seminar Handbook 2000*, selected articles from bibliography of TRS.

—— 2000, 'The Art of Theological Reflection', unpublished paper, Theological Hall Faculty.

—— 2002.'The impact of Transference and Countertransference on Ministry and Pastoral Supervision', Unpublished paper. In this paper I discuss a number of approaches to transference that includes a theological rationale.

Pembroke, N 2000, *The Art of Listening*, Grand Rapids, Michigan: William B Eerdmans Publishing.

Pohly, K 2001, *The Ministry of Supervision: Transforming the rough places*, Franklin, TN: Providence House Publishers.

Pyle, W T & Seals, M A, 1995, *Experiencing Ministry Supervision*, Nashville: Broadman and Holman.

Ramsay, N 1991, 'Pastoral Supervision: A theological resource for ministry, *Journal of Supervision and Training in Ministry*, 13, 190–205.

Rhodes, L 1991, 'Sexual Ethics: Power, role and authority in field education supervision', paper presented at the twenty-first Biennial ATFE Conference, Denver.

Richard, L 1972, 'The Existing Malaise in the Theologizing of Field Experience', *Theological Education*, Autumn, 67–70.

Rogers, C 1961, *On Becoming a Person: A therapist's view of psychotherapy*, Boston: Houghton Mifflin.

Rolheiser, R 1999, *The Holy Longing: A search for a Christian spirituality*, New York: Doubleday.

Schleiermacher, F 1889, *Brief Outline in the Study of Theology*, trans. W Farrer, Edinburgh: T & T Clark, 1889.

Schreiter, R J 1996, *Constructing Local Theologies*, Maryknoll, New York: Orbis Books.

Seabright, R 1984, 'A Model of Supervision for the Integration of Social Awareness and Ministry Functioning during a year of Internship in Lutheran Theological Education', unpublished DMin, Ministry Project for United Theological Seminary, Dayton.

Sheehan, M E 1984, 'Theological Reflection on Theory-Praxis Integration', *Pastoral Sciences*, 3.

Smith, C M1996, 'Preaching the Art of Resistance', in C Conzad Neuger (ed.), *The Arts of Ministry*, Louisville: Westminster John Knox Press.

Soelle, D 1990, *The Window of Vulnerability*, Minneapolis: Fortress Press.

Stengel, C A 1999, 'Pastoral Supervision in Theological Reflection: The role of the ministry reflection report and supervisory conversation in ministry'. DMin. United Theological Seminary, Dayton.

Stroup, G W 1981. *The Promise of Narrative Theology*, Student Christian Movement.

Support Document for the Interim Code of Ethics 1997, 'Being Professional and Honouring the Pastoral Relationship.' Uniting Church in Australia, 1–11.

The Holy Bible, 1989, *New Revised Standard Version*, New York: Oxford University Press.

The Mud Flower Collective 1985, *God's Fierce Whimsy*, New York: The Pilgrim Press.

Tracy, D 1970, *The Achievement of Bernard Lonergan*, New York: Herder & Herder.

—— 1987. *Plurality and Ambiguity: Hermeneutics, Religion, Hope*, London: SCM Press Ltd.

Veling, T A 1996, *Living in the Margins*, New York: Crossroad.

Via, D O 1990, *Self-Deception and Wholeness in Paul and Matthew*, Minneapolis: Fortress Press.

Van Den Blink, A J & Poling, J N 1991, 'Theology and Supervision', *Journal of Supervision and Training in Ministry*, 13, 257–73.

Uniting Church in Australia 1997, *Report of the Task Group to Review Ministerial Education in the Uniting Church in Australia*, Sydney.

'Theological Reflection on Pastoral Care' 1999, in *United Faculty of Theology Handbook*, Melbourne: United Faculty of Theology.

Wheeler, B G & Farley, E 1991, *Shifting Boundaries: Contextual approaches to the structure of theological education.* Louisville: Westminster John Knox Press.

Whitehead, J D 1987 'The Practical Play of Theology', in L S Mudge and J Poling (eds), *Formation and Reflection.* Philadelphia: Fortress Press, 36–54.

—— & Whitehead, E 1975, 'Educational Models in Field Education', *Theological Education* 11, 273–7.

—— 1980, *Method in Ministry: Theological reflection and Christian ministry*, Kansas City: Sheed & Ward, revised 1995, 112–22.

Williams, A 1999, 'Clinical Wisdom – A Major Goal of Supervision', *Psychology in Australia*, 6/1, 26–30.

Wink, W 1984, *Naming The Powers*, Philadelphia: Fortress Press.

—— 1986, *Unmasking The Powers*, Philadelphia: Fortress Press.

—— 1992, *Engaging The Powers*, Philadelphia: Fortress Press.

Wood, C M 2002, *Vision and Discernment: An orientation in theological study,* Eugene, Oregon: Wipf & Stock Publishers. Previously published by Scholars Press, 1985.

Ziegler, J H 1975, 'Editorial Introduction', *Theological Education*, 11, 262–3.

Index